THE MOCKINGBIRD IN THE GUM TREE

The Mockingbird in the Gum Tree

A Literary Gallimaufry

LOUIS D. RUBIN, JR.

Louisiana State University Press
Baton Rouge and London

Copyright © 1991 by Louis D. Rubin, Jr.
All rights reserved
Manufactured in the United States of America
First printing
00 99 98 97 96 95 94 93 92 91   5 4 3 2 1

Designer: Glynnis Phoebe
Typeface: Sabon
Typesetter: G&S Typesetters, Inc.
Printer and binder: Thomson-Shore, Inc.

Library of Congress Cataloging-in-Publication Data

Rubin, Louis Decimus, 1923–
    The mockingbird in the gum tree / Louis D. Rubin, Jr.
      p.   cm.
    Includes index.
    ISBN 0-8071-1680-7 (cloth)
    1. American literature—Southern States—History and criticism.
2. Southern States—Intellectual life.   3. Southern States in
literature.   I. Title.
PS261.R646   1991
810.9′975—dc20   90-27597
                                     CIP

For George and Susan Core
and for Lewis and Mimi Simpson

CONTENTS

PREFACE

The contents of this book constitute the latest installment in one person's continuing and compulsive effort to understand the American literary imagination, and in particular its Southern manifestations. Prepared for various occasions, the pieces bear the marks of their origins; some were originally shaped as public addresses, others as individual essays, as contributions to symposia, as forewords to books, as review essays, and so on. I saw no particular benefit to be gained by attempting to regularize them for this collection, that might compensate for the risk of distorting the rhetorical modes involved. Because of the occasional nature of these writings, there is a certain amount of repetition and overlap. A few quotations appear several times; arguments and points are sometimes repeated. Each use, however, seemed necessary in context, so I have let them stand as first written.

When I look back at the lengthy excursion I have been making into the realms of authorship and the social and historical dimensions of imaginative literature, what strikes me is the impurity of my approach. It has been catch-as-catch-can all the way. Especially for one whose doctorate, years ago, was taken in the Aesthetics of Literature (I couldn't stomach the pedantry of the Johns Hopkins English Department as then constituted), and whose dissertation was directed by Georges Poulet and read by George Boas and Leo

Spitzer, there is a singular deficiency in the concern shown for literary theory. Perhaps this is because my interest has always been so closely bound in with history, especially that of the American South.

I have never bought the argument that an unwillingness to read literature in terms of theory is itself an unexamined assertion of theory. I do not doubt that there are theoretical assumptions implicit in any attempt to think about literature (or anything else). But it seems to me that there is a considerable difference between approaching literature, or anything else, in terms of its relation to theory, and holding certain theoretical assumptions as one reads. One might just as logically argue that because all boats are designed to convey objects across an expanse of water, therefore aircraft carriers and cruise liners should alike be considered in terms of their structural design rather than their itineraries, cuisines, accommodations, personnel, and so forth. Doubtless the way the boat is built affects those latter considerations, but for someone engaged in planning a winter cruise it is of decidedly secondary importance.

If literature has any claim to be privileged discourse, it seems to me, it has something to do with its recalcitrance, its refusal to settle for categories, systematizing, abstraction as an adequate explanation or interpretation of our experience. It resists summary; it uses language to re-create experience, and in so doing it gives order to experience by arranging it so that the patterns can be recognized. But the order is not that of an outline; it is paraphrasable only in the sense that some of the patterns are capable of being identified and extracted from it for purposes of description. The patterns are not the experience itself; they are never more than interpretations of it.

What the literary critic does is to point out the existence of those patterns, and to relate them to what readers know about experience through their own immersion in it. In so doing, criticism helps the reader to recognize the commentary that the literary work is offering on human life in time; the critic helps make the experience of the poem or story available to others. The fact that no two persons can ever have exactly the same experience does not invalidate the procedure. For while no item of experience, no phenomenon, ever presents itself identically to two persons, there is enough about it that is shared to make communication (and civilization) possible. It is on that shared experience that literature is predicated—and what gives the literary work its peculiar usefulness, its unique reason for being, is that it communicates that shared experience not as abstraction but as particularity, with the patterns embodied in the details, just as in everyday life they are so embodied. Literature is thus *knowledge,* even wisdom—but not separated from what it is knowledge *of,* or wise *about.*

The notion, so fashionable today, that we can never know reality, but only language—or rather, that the language *is* the reality— seems to me to miss the point both of language and of literature. For the sticks, stones, and bones of the tangible, phenomenal world, however we may codify them for purposes of discussion, are *out there.* Language is our vehicle for identifying and making sense of *them.* That the identification can only be partial, approximate, does not invalidate it, for it is precisely in the transaction between the phenomena of our experience in and with the world, and our efforts to identify and understand them, that our imagination functions. And in just this way literature plays its part, for it goes at the matter on the assumption that the gap between the two is bridgeable through perceiving the sense *in* the phenomena, as patterns, rather than trying to deal with either the sense or the phenomena separately and apart from each other.

It is all very well to say that language is an agreed-upon symbolic code, and that the symbols, not what they symbolize, are what language permits us to confront. But the symbols themselves are efforts to reproduce the phenomena that they symbolize, and they do give us at least a partial access to the phenomena themselves. In kicking the large stone with his mighty foot, Samuel Johnson may not have refuted the idealism of Berkeley, but he did demonstrate the nature of the problem, for both he and Boswell saw him rebound from it. Manipulation in terms of the symbols alone could not produce the space probes, or *The Tempest*—or for that matter, Buchenwald and Dachau.

I enter into such quasi-metaphysical discourse because the literary pieces that follow are by intention *about* works of literature and the men and women who wrote them. As noted before, I have never taken kindly to the notion that the proper task of the critic is to deal with the act of critical perception itself, and not with the thing being perceived. Certainly the former—criticism of theories of criticism—is a legitimate critical activity, and one that happens to be particularly popular just now—but it is by no means the only critical mode. Indeed, it is a *secondary* mission only, performed with the object of strengthening the primary goal. I believe that the ultimate and by far the most important goal of literary criticism is to make the work being read—the story, the poem—more nearly available to readers, and that as such the critic and the critique are ancillary to the work. I believe it *can* be made more available, though never entirely so. Anyone who claims greater usefulness for criticism than that, and demands a status for the critic co-equal with that of the poet or novelist, whether in the name of "freedom" or anything else, is to my mind afflicted with delusions of professional (or perhaps professorial) grandeur.

The critical pieces that follow are intended as enabling acts; the test of their efficacy is the degree of success with which they aid readers to take advantage of what the literary imagination can tell them about their experience. I remain convinced that works of fiction and poetry *can* tell them a great deal about it, and in ways that would otherwise be unavailable to them.

To the *Sewanee Review* and to its editor, George Core, I am indebted for permission to reprint the following essays, review essays, and miscellaneous items: "Alfred Kazin's American Procession," XCIII (Spring, 1985); "Bernard DeVoto All Told," LXXXIII (Winter, 1975); "Mr. Epstein Doesn't Like It," XCIV (Winter, 1986); "R. P. W., 1905–1989," XCVIII (Spring, 1990), "The Mencken Mystery," XCIX (Summer, 1991); "The Notebooks of Desmond Goohooligan, edited by Leonidas O'Dell," LXXXIII (Fall, 1975); "Thomas Wolfe: Homage Renewed," XCVII (Spring, 1989); and "Tory Formalists, New York Intellectuals, and the New Historical Science of Criticism," LXXXVIII (Fall, 1980). "Thomas Wolfe: Homage Renewed" was written for delivery at an "Oktoberfest" held at the University of North Carolina in 1989 to commemorate two joyful occasions, the sixtieth anniversary of the publication of *Look Homeward, Angel,* and my retirement from the Department of English. I am grateful to Joseph Flora for arranging the event.

"Asa Bart's Way" was written as the "Foreword" to *Tournament,* by Shelby Foote (Birmingham, Ala.: Summa Publications, 1986).

"The High Sheriff of Yoknapatawpha County: A Study in the

Genius of Place" first appeared in *Faulkner and Popular Culture*, edited by Doreen Fowler and Ann J. Abadie (Jackson: University Press of Mississippi, 1990), and "The Dixie Special: William Faulkner and the Southern Literary Renascence" in *Faulkner and the Southern Renaissance*, edited by Doreen Fowler and Ann J. Abadie (Jackson: University Press of Mississippi, 1982). Both were written for delivery at the Faulkner and Yoknapatawpha Conferences of the University of Mississippi, and I am grateful to Evans Harrington and to the editors and publisher of both books for permission to reprint them here.

To the *Virginia Quarterly Review* and its editor, Staige Blackford, I am grateful for permission to reprint the essay "From Combray to Ithaca; or, The 'Southernness' of Southern Literature," which was first published in Volume LXVI (Winter, 1990). The essay was originally prepared for delivery at a National Endowment for the Humanities Institute on Southern Literature and the Southern Community, held at the University of North Carolina at Chapel Hill in 1989.

"*I'll Take My Stand*: The Literary Tradition" was written for delivery at Vanderbilt University in 1980 and appeared first in *A Band of Prophets: The Vanderbilt Agrarians After Fifty Years*, edited by William C. Havard and Walter Sullivan (Baton Rouge: Louisiana State University Press, 1982).

"James Henry Hammond, Slaveholder: 'Why God Let Us Lose the War'" was written as the "Foreword" to *Secret and Sacred: The Diary of James Henry Hammond, a Southern Slaveholder*, edited by Carol Bleser (New York: Oxford University Press, 1988) and is reprinted by permission of the Oxford University Press.

"The Mockingbird in the Gum Tree" was first published in the *Southern Review*, n.s., XIX (Autumn, 1983), and I am grateful to its editors, especially Lewis P. Simpson, for permission to reprint it here.

"Young Men in Search of a Vocation" was written for delivery at Virginia Commonwealth University, Richmond, Virginia, in 1990.

Chapel Hill, North Carolina   L. D. R.
March 1, 1991

PART I

THE GENIUS OF PLACE

THE MOCKINGBIRD IN THE GUM TREE
NOTES ON THE LANGUAGE OF AMERICAN LITERATURE

(1983)

Up from the darkest wood where Philomela sat,
Her fairy numbers issued. What then ailed me?
My ears are called capacious but they failed me.
Her classics registered a little flat!
I rose and venomously spat.

—John Crowe Ransom, "Philomela"

Literature is written in language, and American literature is written for the most part in American English. Though the language of literature, whether of poetry or prose, is not merely the ordinary language of everyday life, when it gets too far away from it the literature is likely to suffer, because the language begins to impede the writer from dealing with his own experience. To accomplish the latter objective is never easy, and when the very idiom being used is such as to separate the writer from the words with which his experience is normally viewed, then the job is made doubly difficult.

The early American writer, of course, inherited a literary language. He was English, or had been until recently. But from Jamestown Island on, the American experience was not precisely the same as the English experience, and thereafter increasingly diverged from it. And language—not only words as denotative signs, but the con-

3

notative assumptions, political, social, ethical, religious, geographical, economic, and so on, that go along with the signs and the grammatical structures—embodies social attitudes.

Melville faced the issue squarely in *Moby-Dick*. Writing a romance of whaling which began turning into an epic tale of the human quest for meaning in an ambiguous universe, he confronted the fact that in order to give his story the meaning it demanded, he would have to make a whaling-ship captain into a tragic hero. But American whaling-ship captains were not kings, princes, or great commanders, as tragic heroes had always been. How, therefore, might one write accurately about whaling-ship captains—which is to say, indifferently schooled, practical-minded, middle-class Americans—and yet imbue them with the dignity, language, and profundity of insight customarily ascribed to the tragic hero?

It was a problem in literary diction, which was also a problem in political theory. Melville, the Jacksonian Democrat, therefore found himself composing an invocation to the muse, after the manner of epic poetry, in which he set forth the problem and called for divine aid:

> If, then, to meanest mariners, and renegades and castaways, I shall hereafter ascribe high qualities, though dark; weave round them tragic graces; if even the most mournful, perchance the most abased, among them all, shall at times lift himself to the exalted mounts; if I shall touch that workman's arm with some ethereal light; if I shall spread a rainbow over his disastrous set of sun; then against all mortal critics bear me out in it, thou just Spirit of Equality, which has spread one royal mantle of humanity over all my kind! Bear me out in it, thou great democratic God!

The statement is at once a testament of political faith and of literary intention. Tragic dignity, he declares, has nothing to do with rank or caste; it is inherent in all men, and the literature of the nation founded upon the premise that all men are created equal ought by rights to make its ordinary citizens into the kind of tragic heroes such as hitherto have been drawn only from the ranks of those possessing elevated social status. He will, in defiance of the aristocratic precedents of English and European letters, ascribe high qualities to what had always before been treated as low life; he will "touch that workman's arm with some ethereal light" previously reserved for the arm that wielded the scepter and the sword rather than the pickax and the harpoon.

His actual solution to the problem, however, is rather less drastic. What he does is to make his tragic hero, Captain Ahab, into a Shakespearean king, and this involves having him think and quite often speak in the idiom of a Shakespearean king, though with some adjustments for prose style. Thus:

> "What is it, what nameless, inscrutable, unearthly thing is it; what cozzening, hidden lord and master, and cruel, remorseless emperor commands me; that against all natural lovings and longings, I so keep pushing, and crowding, and jamming myself on all the time; recklessly making me ready to do what in my own proper, natural heart, I durst not so much as dare? Is Ahab, Ahab? Is it I, God, or who, that lifts this arm? But if the great sun move not of himself; but is as an errand-boy in heaven; nor one single star can revolve, but by some invisible power; how then can this one small heart beat; this one small brain think thoughts; unless God does that beating, does that thinking, does that living, and not I. By heaven, man, we are turned round and round in this world, like yonder windlass, and Fate is the handspike."

5

There are actually two separate language conventions in *Moby-Dick,* and they do not usually join. One is that of the factual, sometimes whimsical prose narrator, who is also Ishmael as crewman aboard the *Pequod,* and who gives us a great deal of documentary description about the operations and activities of the ship, and reports what the crewmen and the mates have to say and do. The other is that of literary meanings, in which Ishmael steps up from his status as chronicler-crewman in order to deal with Ahab and the metaphysical problems common to Ahab and to himself as author—but not himself as crewman. It was Melville's inspiration to think to make this separation into a thematic principle, so that Captain Ahab's tragic isolation from the sublunary and practical concerns and interests of the crew is manifested in a stylistic separation. He thinks and speaks in the intensified, embellished literary diction of the tragic hero; the others mostly think and speak in vernacular prose.

The result is one of the great works of prose fiction; but all the same, it is not a true solution to the problem that Melville posed in his invocation to the democratic muse. It is significant that in order even to raise the problem itself, Melville must use both a device of classical epic poetry and a language far removed from and quite beyond the capacities of the ordinary American democrat whom Melville proposes to elevate to tragic literary dignity. "If, then, to meanest mariners"—in the year 1851, to such a Nantucket mariner, or more properly, seaman, the word *meanest* would certainly never have signified "low, common, ordinary." The point is that Melville can give his Nantucket mariner the tragic graces he wishes for his story to have only at the expense of his documentary identity *as a meanest mariner*. The language in which Captain Ahab, as a tragic hero, speaks and thinks, and in which Melville writes about him, cannot function as that of a meanest mariner. To make Captain Ahab, as a tragic protagonist, into something *greater than* an ordinary whaling-ship captain, he must also make him into something *other than* a whaling-ship captain. Whereas, truly to fulfill his democratic objective of weaving tragic graces around ordinary people, and achieving "that abounding dignity which has no robed investiture," he would have to permit Ahab to attain those heights *as* a Nantucket ship captain, using language appropriate to such a person, rather than a Shakespearean king commanding a whaling ship.

II

The problem, as I have sketched it, takes the form of a language relationship, but as almost always with matters involving literary style, considerably more is at stake, as Erich Auerbach demonstrated in his great study of literary stylistics and culture, *Mimesis*. What it centers on are the aesthetic and social assumptions that go along with a *high* and *low* style. Traditionally the high style, the language of educated men, has been that of the upper social classes.

Before the rise of prose fiction, it was principally the language of poetic discourse and was used to deal with values: the ethical, social, religious meanings of human experience. As such, the high style was not supposed to concern itself with mundane, ordinary matters. Dr. Johnson, for example, censures Shakespeare for the use of the words *dun* and *knife* in *Macbeth*. A Thane of Glamis might dispatch a king with a dagger—"Is this a dagger which I see before me?"—but not with a knife. In comedy, on the other hand, the use of the word *knife* would be entirely appropriate, for comedy does not essay the high style. Comedy, in Aristotle's definition, represents men as worse than they are, and deals with characters of a lower type. There would be no problem with depicting a meanest mariner comically, or even in having him attack someone with a knife. In short, serious matters—ideals, meanings—are for the high style only, and are appropriate only for those capable of speaking and thinking in it.

7

What, though, as Melville was aware, of the fitness of the high style in a society without, in theory at least, class, nobility, aristocracy? How does it function as a way of imaging middle-class experience? The problem, particularly as it affected American poetry, can be comically illustrated in a passage by the South Carolina poet Paul Hamilton Hayne. Hayne, who before the Civil War had been part of the Russell's Bookstore group in Charleston, South Carolina, together with William Gilmore Simms and Henry Timrod, lost almost everything in the war, and afterward established himself in a small cottage near Augusta, Georgia. From there he wrote to his old friend William Gilmore Simms, a writer of considerably greater antebellum reputation who had likewise suffered terribly from the ravages of the war, inviting him to pay a visit to his cottage. He describes the episode in a sketch written for a magazine named the *Southern Bivouac* some years afterward. His invitation took the form of a sonnet, the sestet of which went as follows:

> We'll roam through breezy dell, o'er hill-side walk;
> Speak of lost loves, of fortune's lustier morn;
> But, lest such themes should make us too forlorn
> (Wreathing our souls with their sad cypress twine),
> In thoughtful pauses of memorial talk
> We'll quaff a Mermaid measure of rare wine!

And then, since his sketch for the *Southern Bivouac* was anecdotal and journalistic, he continued in prose:

> Let me modestly confess that I am just a little proud of the concluding line of this poem. It is the most imaginative line I ever wrote. "Tell it not in Gath," my good reader, "whisper it not in the streets of Askalon," but the plain truth may as well be acknowledged, the "rare wine" was rather "middling" "Monongahela," and the "Mermaid measure" a pewter cup of modest dimensions, which had seen service.

8

Here we see exemplified the limitations of the high style for American literature. Because the magazine memoir is prose, and journalistic nonfiction at that, the author can verbalize his experience there with the words he would ordinarily use for that purpose. But when he writes a sonnet he moves into a much more literary, more stylized vocabulary. Sipping Pennsylvania whiskey out of pewter cups becomes quaffing a Mermaid measure of rare wine. Only in this way, Hayne feels, can the experience be made into poetry: which is to say, be heightened to literary significance. The function of the literary style is thus to purify the experience by purging it of its middle-class drossness, and thereby elevate it into literary respectability. The high style, rather than accomplishing the intensification of experience that is the essence of the language of poetry, is being used to refine it into something other than what it is.

The strategy, it seems to me, is characteristic of much nineteenth-century American poetry. One could compile, for example, almost an entire anthology of period poems about mockingbirds, all composed very self-consciously in the high style. The reason is not hard to discern. There were available in North America no nightingales, no literary birds of mythical song. The American poet therefore felt impelled to demonstrate that the mockingbird was his nightingale: that, in other words, he was equally a Poet as any Englishman. In order to do this he felt he had to elevate this common and not notably fabulous songbird into full literary status, through use of the high style to describe its mode of discourse. Thus Richard Henry Wilde of Georgia on the subject:

Wit, sophist, songster, Yorick of thy tribe,
Thou sportive satirist of Nature's school,
To thee the palm of scoffing we ascribe,
Arch-mocker and mad Abbot of Misrule!

The preeminent American poet of the century, of course, was Walt Whitman, and it is no coincidence that Whitman is generally an exception to the rule about the use of the high style for purposes of elevation. A major portion of Whitman's best verse is made up of the effort, often successful, to demonstrate the worthiness of middle-class American experience as the subject of poetry; "Song of Myself" in particular is a poem about what it means to be an American poet. Almost alone among his poetic contemporaries, however, he did not proceed to do so by trying to use the high style to elevate middle-class experience into the realm of traditional poetic meanings. He was quite willing to accept that experience on its own terms; he would never have felt it necessary to disguise a pewter cup as a Mermaid measure. For Whitman a mockingbird is not a "Yorick of thy tribe" and "sportive satirist of Nature's school," but "the musical shuttle," "the solitary guest from Alabama," "the lone singer wonderful," and so on. But Whitman's achievement with the vernacular language was a very special thing, and proved of little or no use to succeeding American poets for at least another fifty years, for the reason that it ran counter to what the American audience wanted poetry to be.

Nineteenth-century American prose fiction, fortunately, managed to a considerable degree to escape the fate of American poetry, in part because as a relatively new, essentially middle-class literary form, the novel did not face the demand that it serve in the role of exemplar of High Culture, and also in part because of its very nature. That is, it always had an important function of documenting experience, presenting it in its detailed specificity, and it was closely allied to nonfiction, to journalism, which had no literary and high-cultural status whatever. Thus even when in the form of the romance, with realistic social depiction at a minimum, its language had to be sufficiently practical—in Dante's term, *curial*—to deal with the documentation of the world.

In *The Scarlet Letter,* for example, Hawthorne writes a tale

9

of seventeenth-century Boston and prefaces it with a scene set in nineteenth-century Salem. The vernacular is appropriate to the custom-house episode, which is nonfiction, the high style to the story of Hester Prynne and the Rev. Arthur Dimmesdale, which is romance. We may say that for both Melville and Hawthorne, the price of the separation of styles was an incompleteness in their greatest novels; and that in each case a virtue was made of the incompleteness. Melville could not permit his protagonist to be a tragic hero while at the same time remaining an American whaling-ship captain; and he had to omit any consideration of sexuality. Hawthorne set his story of individual need versus social necessity in remote seventeenth-century Boston rather than in the tumult of the nineteenth-century New England in which he lived and worked, and knew so well. Though less so than much of his work, *The Scarlet Letter* suffers to an extent, through the absence of the kind of experience imaged only in the custom-house episode, from an attenuation of characterization and impoverishment of social milieu that at times comes all too close to the thinness of allegory.

10

III

"All modern American literature comes from one book by Mark Twain called *Huckleberry Finn*." Hemingway's famous obiter dictum concerning the wellsprings of American literature has received a great deal of attention ever since he said it. It has been suggested that in so saying, Hemingway was confusing the literature of America with the fiction of Ernest Hemingway. It is certainly true, however, that the theme of Clemens' novel, the quest for freedom from the corruption and artificialities of society, and its ultimate frustration, has been a major American literary motif. Yet the real significance of the remark has to do with language. It was Clemens who in effect discovered for the American writer the literary potentialities of the vernacular speech in which he commonly wrote and thought. When Huck Finn, who has never read Milton or Wordsworth and has no acquaintance whatever with the high style, debates with his conscience whether or not to go after Jim and set him free again, foresees the eternal punishment awaiting him if he steals another person's property, and then declares, "All right, then, I'll go to hell," the American vernacular has finally established itself as the vehicle for a literature that can deal with ultimate values and moral and ethical meanings even while remaining close enough to the everyday experience to be able to document and affirm it on its own terms. What Clemens, in his greatest work, thought of the high style can be seen if we compare the comic Shakespearean soliloquy of the Duke aboard the raft with Melville's intensive use of Shakespearean language for Captain Ahab's dialogue in *Moby-Dick*. What for Melville is the intensification of language to allow it to become an ultimate meditation upon the nature of human fate and free will is for Clemens a way of evading reality through travesty and burlesque.

Clemens was by no means hostile to the high style. On the contrary, it was because he admired it so much, *as a high style*—saw it in terms of its traditional social and cultural associations rather than from inside, as an extension and intensification of his own way of thinking and writing—that it proved so singularly unsuited to his own needs, and so compelled him to develop a vernacular style to write his best books. The process that culminated in Huck Finn's decision to go to hell and a little later to light out for the territories is exemplified in a passage from *Old Times on the Mississippi*, the account of the cub pilot's education published first under that title in England and then incorporated into *Life on the Mississippi*.

Old Times on the Mississippi is the account of the discovery of a vocation, ostensibly that of becoming a river pilot, but symbolically that of becoming a writer. Scholars have often wondered why it was that Clemens, who often referred to his days as an accredited Mississippi River pilot as the richest and happiest of his life, never wrote about them. After describing how he learned to be a pilot, he jumps forward twenty years and, in the second and lesser part of *Life on the Mississippi*, describes a return visit to the river long after he became a man of letters. The answer, I think, has something to do with the fact that the meanings he saw in his piloting experience were in actuality those of his writing experience. To write about piloting, as he viewed it, was to write about *knowing* something rather than about *doing* something. (The relationship between piloting and writing in Clemens' imagination can be seen in the dual meaning of the word *craft*.) The passage in question, which shows the tie-in, follows an incident in which the cub pilot is told by his master that eventually he will learn to distinguish a bluff reef

11

from a wind reef—an actual reef from the shapes that the wind makes on the water—but that it will be an instinctive rather than a conscious judgment (which is a pretty good description of Clemens' literary strategy):

> It turned out to be true. The face of the water, in time, became a wonderful book—a book that was a dead language to the uneducated passenger, but which told its mind to me without reserve, delivering its most cherished secrets as clearly as if it uttered them with a voice. And it was not a book to be read once and thrown aside, for it had a new story to tell every day. Throughout the long twelve hundred miles there was never a page that was void of interest, never one that you could leave unread without loss, never one that you would want to skip, thinking you could find higher enjoyment in some other thing. There never was so wonderful a book written by man; never one whose interest was so absorbing, so unflagging, so sparklingly renewed with every re-perusal. . . . In truth, the passenger who could not read this book saw nothing but all manner of pretty pictures in it, painted by the sun and shaded by the clouds, whereas to the trained eye these were not pictures at all, but the grimmest and most dead-earnest of reading matter.

12

Once he had "mastered the language" of the river and come to know every feature of the river "as familiarly as I knew the letters of the alphabet," Clemens tells us, he had made a valuable acquisition, but he had suffered a loss as well, one that could never again be restored to him. "All the grace, the beauty, the poetry, had gone out of the majestic river!" he declares, and recalls a sunset that he had witnessed while still new to steamboating:

> A broad expanse of the river was turned to blood; in the middle distance the red hue brightened into gold; through which a solitary log came floating, black and conspicuous; in one place a long, slanting mark lay sparkling upon the water; in another the surface was broken by boiling, tumbling rings, that were as many-tinted as an opal; where the ruddy flush was faintest, was a smooth spot that was covered with graceful circles and radiating lines, ever so delicately traced; the shore on our left was

densely wooded, and the sombre shadow that fell from this forest was broken in one place by a long ruffled trail that shone like silver; and high above the forest wall a clean-stemmed dead tree waved a single leafy bough that glowed like a flame in the unobstructed splendor that was flowing from the sun. There were graceful curves, reflected images, woody heights, soft distances; and over the whole scene, far and near, the dissolving lights drifted steadily, enriching it, every passing moment, with new marvels of coloring.

He goes on to say that he "stood like one bewitched" and "drank it in, in a speechless rapture." It is a rhetorical set piece, presented in standard travel-book style. However, he continues, a day came when he could no longer see the river in such terms. Once he had learned to read it with an eye toward navigation rather than speechless rapture, the comment he might have made about the scene previously witnessed would go like this:

> This sun means that we are going to have wind to-morrow; that floating log means that the river is rising, small thanks to it; that slanting mark on the water refers to a bluff reef which is going to kill somebody's steamboat one of these nights, if it keeps on stretching out like that; those tumbling "boils" show a dissolving bar and a changing channel there; the lines and circles in the slick water over yonder are a warning that that troublesome place is shoaling up dangerously; that silver streak in the shadow of the forest is the "break" from a new snag, and he has located himself in the very best place he could have found to fish for steamboats; that tall dead tree, with a single living branch, is not going to last long, and then how is a body ever going to get through this blind place at night without that friendly old landmark?
>
> No, the romance and beauty were all gone from the river. All the value any feature of it had for me now was the amount of usefulness it could furnish toward compassing the safe piloting of a steamboat.

Throughout the above, the descriptions of the river as seen by the passenger and the yet-uninitiated cub are composed in the high

13

style—the conventional literary evocation of the scenic sublime, common to travel literature and filled with rhapsodic abstraction. But when he turns to describing what the pilot sees, the language becomes quite concrete and personal in its vernacular detail and diction. The point that Clemens is ostensibly making is that the perception of "the grace, the beauty, the poetry" of the river is possible only to the observer who can approach it aesthetically, as scenery; to view it in terms of its use as a waterway, with a knowledge that penetrates below its opaque surface, is to spoil its aesthetic possibilities. The high style is for contemplative purposes; for anything having to do with transit upon the river, in active involvement with it, the vernacular is the proper vehicle. Moreover, as Henry Nash Smith notes, to know the river in any relationship other than of detached contemplation is to perceive that it can be dangerous, menacing, even sinister, an affair of snags, shoals, rising water, channels, and landmarks that do not remain suspended in time but change and take new forms, making continued navigation a demanding task.

It should be obvious, however, that if literary grace, beauty, and poetry are what is involved, the passage in which Clemens presents the pilot's view of the river is every bit as literary as that describing the river as a tourist might view it. It employs such literary devices as personification, litotes, hyperbole, rhetorical questions, alliteration, parallelism, periphrasis, balance, and numerous other stylistic devices for intensification and emphasis. Moreover, the sentences go a considerable distance toward characterizing the narrator, and develop not merely a factual but an emotional response to what is being described. Far from the "romance and beauty" having gone from the river after acquisition of that kind of knowledge, then, these are if anything far more available, both to the writer and his reader.

The nub of the matter, of course, is what Clemens means by "the grace, the beauty, the poetry" in this instance. He is equating these with the high style, and for him the high style consists of a static, attitudinized response to the surface characteristics of a conventionally Beautiful situation. This is hardly what the high style is in the hands of Melville, not to say William Shakespeare; but for Clemens it pretty much fulfills that role. To get down to the real

14

meanings of his experience, therefore, the job as he envisioned it was to develop the vernacular style so that it could enable him to tell what he knew and felt. Thus by choosing for the narrator of *Adventures of Huckleberry Finn* a youth with only a tangential relationship to genteel Culture, and setting out to view his experience through that youth's eyes, which is to say, through an enforced dependence upon uneducated speech, he was able to intensify the vernacular style to a point at which it could deal with meanings even while remaining faithful to the documentation of everyday American experience:

> Two or three days and nights went by; I reckon I might say **15** swum by, they slid along so quiet and smooth and lovely. Here is the way we put in the time. It was a monstrous big river down there—sometimes a mile and a half wide; we run nights, and laid up and hid day-times; soon as night was most gone, we stopped navigating and tied up—nearly always in the dead water under a tow-head; and then cut young cotton-woods and willows and hid the raft with them. Then we set out the lines. Next we slid into the river and had a swim, so as to freshen up and cool off; then we set down on the sandy bottom where the water was about knee deep, and watched the daylight come. Not a sound, anywheres—perfectly still—just like the whole world was alseep, only sometimes the bullfrogs a-cluttering, maybe.

It is very much a scenic, "literary" description, and scarcely the unmediated representation of the thoughts of a lightly educated rural Missouri youth. As Leo Marx notes, "of course no one ever really spoke such concentrated poetry, but the illusion that we are hearing the spoken word is an important part of the total illusion of reality. The words on the page carry our attention to life, not to art, and that after all is what most readers want." In short, the discovery of Huck Finn's voice, via a route leading through newspaper humor, travel writing, *Old Times on the Mississippi,* and *Tom Sawyer,* meant that Clemens had evolved a style that would permit future American novelists to portray the captain of a whaling ship in quest of the white whale without being forced to give up any of the character's authenticity as a whaling-ship captain. That Clemens himself did not follow up the implications of his discovery is not important.

IV

The two great American prose stylists of the twentieth century are Ernest Hemingway and William Faulkner. Hemingway's achievement with the vernacular was possible in large part because he believed so thoroughly in the need for what it could do so well: cut through complexity and abstraction to get down to the elemental truths of the senses. No one was ever better at evoking the immediacy of sensuous experience, but it was also his genius to be able to relate that physical sensation to emotional awareness. His descriptions are always closely tied in with states of mind. Here is a middle-aged man thinking back about his now-dead father:

> His father came back to him in the fall of the year, or in the early spring when there had been jacksnipe on the prairie, or when he saw shocks of corn, or when he saw a lake, of if he ever saw a horse and buggy, or when he saw, or heard, wild geese, or in a duck blind; remembering the time an eagle dropped through the whirling snow to strike a canvas-covered decoy, rising, his wings beating, the talons caught in the canvas. His father was with him, suddenly, in deserted orchards or in new-plowed fields, in thickets, on small hills, or when going through dead grass, whenever splitting wood or hauling water, by grist mills, cedar mills and dams and always with open fires. The towns he lived in were not towns his father knew. After he was fifteen he had shared nothing with his father.

There is always, in Hemingway's prose, a mental correlative for the physical activity being displayed; in this respect he fulfills Emerson's prescription that "nature is the opposite of the soul, answering it part for part. One is seal and one is print." Lurking behind what he sees and describes, present at all times, is a sense of psychological tension, a nervous apprehensiveness, held in check by the will, which fastens its attention upon the world being communicated through the senses so as to avoid giving in to inner helplessness and despair. "Well, you better not think about it," a man says to Nick Adams in a short story, and it is just this thought—not a philosophy so much as an instinct—that lies, seldom voiced but always implicit, behind what Hemingway's characters observe and feel. It can be relaxed into a kind of wary armistice by wine and very occasionally by good fellowship, but it drops from sight only when attention is focused so completely upon an action—hunting, fishing, making love, fighting—that there is, literally, no time left for thinking about it.

The limitations of the Hemingway style become apparent only when it does become necessary, or advantageous, to "think about it." For the whole point of the vernacular style, as developed by Hemingway, is that it is designed to reveal what is undeniably and physically real, rather than what is merely thought to be real. Used for other than comic purposes, it not only cannot discriminate among ideas and values, but it asserts that such discriminations are without meaning. Thus when Hemingway attempts, for example, to discuss artistic matters, he is restricted to something like the following, from *Across the River and into the Trees:*

> It was a beautiful portrait; neither cold, nor snobbish, nor stylized, nor modern. It was the way you would want your girl painted if Tintoretto were still around and, if he were not around, you settled for Velasquez. It was not the way either of them painted. It was simply a splendid portrait painted, as they sometimes are, in our time.
>
> "It's wonderful," the Colonel said. "It is truly lovely."

In the prose of Hemingway you do not think about it; you say it is "truly lovely" and thus avoid falsifying the wholeness of the experience through fragmenting it into its component parts. But can the experience of viewing a portrait worthy of comparison with a Tintoretto or a Velasquez be adequately comprehended through being described only as "simply a splendid portrait"? If not, if the experience is such that if you do not analyze it you will fail to apprehend its meaning, then a vernacular style that is designed to

17

avoid linkings and relationships cannot embody it. Hemingway can tell us how his characters go about fishing or hunting or escaping from the carabinieri, and we can understand why they feel as they do about such activities. But he cannot tell us why Colonel Cantwell admires the artistic technique that produced his lady friend's portrait; he can only say that it is "truly lovely," with the implication that anyone desiring to go beyond that assertion, to give to paintings and works of literature and ideas in general the same kind of complex scrutiny that elsewhere Hemingway gives to trout-fishing and selecting wines and blowing up bridges in Spain, is wasting his time.

18   With adjustment for its adaptation by individual authors, it seems to me, this is the crucial limitation of the vernacular style. Admirably fitted to prevent the falsification of experience through abstract theorizing, over-refinement, cultural stereotyping, squeamishness, and the like, it cannot adequately reproduce the nuances of personality or discriminate among ideas. Its very virtues work against its ability to delineate mental complexity.

This is why the other major American prose stylist of our century, William Faulkner, was unwilling to abandon the high style, despite a formidable talent for utilizing the vernacular. Faulkner declined to settle for immediacy of evocative impact at the expense of complication. He entertained no such abiding distrust of the ability of language to formulate and categorize ideas; his characters do not say the equivalent of "you better not think about it." Where Hemingway identified the real with the elementary senses, Faulkner feared falsification of reality through over-simplification, and sought to force the full complexity of a time and place into his language. To delineate that complexity he was willing to risk imprecision, obfuscation, even vagueness.

Many of his viewpoint characters are not highly educated, verbally sophisticated folk. In order to make the rhetorical and connotative possibilities of the high style available to them, without at the same time being forced to turn them into something other than what they are, he uses several techniques. One way is to speak directly to us as authorial narrator, describing an event in language appropriate to it, then showing its effect upon vernacular characters not themselves possessed of the ability to verbalize it in such fashion. Another is to proceed on the quite plausible assumption that the complexity of the vernacular character's thoughts and emotions very much exceeds his ability to verbalize them, and therefore to interpret what such a person thinks and feels in language that he could not himself employ. Still a third method is to filter the events and characterization of a story through the mind, and therefore the language, of a narrator who can utilize the full resources of the high style to interpret the vernacular experience of others. Thus Quentin Compson in *Absalom, Absalom!* offers us his remembered interpretation of what Thomas Sutpen's experience means, even though Sutpen himself often did not perceive such meaning.

In all such transactions, Faulkner runs the risk of encountering the same difficulties that hampered the nineteenth-century writers in their employment of the high style upon vernacular experience. (We can see the dilemma at its most obvious in James Fenimore Cooper.) The relationship between the narrator, the locus of the high style that can intensify the events of the story and give meaning, and the vernacular characters to whom the events happen, must not be one of cultural condescension. The story must be capable of moving casually and effortlessly back and forth between high style and low, without a crippling incongruity, and the distance between the narrative voice and the vernacular characters must not involve superior rectitude or wisdom, but only one of greater interpretative capacity. Faulkner's technique, his ability to blend the high style and the vernacular without damage to either, is nowhere better exhibited than in an episode from *The Hamlet,* in which several of the male inhabitants of Frenchman's Bend are on a porch mulling over the arrival of Flem Snopes from Texas with a corral of wild Texas ponies:

> They sat on the steps, their backs against the veranda posts, or on the railing itself. Only Ratliff and Quick sat in chairs, so that to them the others were black silhouettes against the dreaming lambence of the moonlight beyond the veranda. The pear tree across the road opposite was now in full and frosty bloom, the twigs and branches springing not outward from the limbs but standing motionless and perpendicular above the horizontal boughs like the separate and upstreaming hair of a drowned woman sleeping upon the uttermost floor of the windless and tideless sea.

19

For a little while they discuss the horses.

> The three speakers had not moved. They did not move now, yet there seemed to gather about the three silhouettes something stubborn, convinced, and passive, like children who have been chidden. A bird, a shadow, fleet and dark and swift, curved across the moonlight, upward into the pear tree and began to sing; a mockingbird.
>
> "First one I've noticed this year," Freeman said.
>
> "You can hear them along Whiteleaf every night," the first man said. "I heard one in February. In that snow. Singing in a gum."
>
> "Gum is the first tree to put out," the third said. "That was why. It made it feel like singing, fixing to put out that way. That was why it taken a gum."
>
> "Gum first to put out?" Quick said. "What about willow?"
>
> "Willow aint a tree," Freeman said. "It's a weed."

As Cleanth Brooks has noted, at such a moment the men are not unmoved by the beauty of what they see and hear. In response they deal with it not in terms of the aesthetic experience as such, but on a more available level. Faulkner does not condescend to them or caricature them, but neither does he restrict his depiction of the scene to their own ability to verbalize it. He makes unstinted use of the high style when appropriate for purposes of intensification, even while keeping the dialogue, and the emotional involvement, squarely within the vernacular experience.

Faulkner can thus endow his own version of a meanest mariner, someone like Thomas Sutpen of *Absalom, Absalom!,* with the dignity and meaning of a tragic hero, while letting him remain a crudely ambitious parvenu of dubious ancestry and little education. The full rhetorical intensification of the high style is available, but without any surrender whatever of the ability to document the experience being described. The mockingbird can sing in the gum tree without the necessity of being rudely forced into the vocabulary and habits of a nightingale in order to be properly musical. American literary English is now fully able to say what it thinks.

FROM COMBRAY TO ITHACA
OR, THE "SOUTHERNNESS" OF SOUTHERN LITERATURE

(1990)

Everybody—well, almost everybody—is willing to concede that there is such a thing as Southern literature, by which is meant that which, when present in a work of imaginative writing, links that work with the particular region of the United States known as the South. Moreover it does this not merely geographically or historically, but in the sense that the imaginative dimensions of the work, the versions of human experience that it images, take the shape that they do because of the relationship.

We make this assumption, and we have ample reason to make it, but when it comes down to identifying what the element or elements that make the work of literature "Southern" are, we are by no means certain. Not only do the answers vary widely, but our responses tend to become involved with all manner of political, social, cultural, and even theological allegiances, and too often what ought to be a matter of descriptive analysis becomes an assertion of value.

I have spent a considerable amount of time during the past four decades or so attempting to skirt the issue of exactly what the "Southern" quality in Southern literature might be. Phrased like that, the particular question can be counted upon to make me want to draw back. In recent years I have even taken to announcing that

21

the one question I will not attempt to answer is, "What is 'Southern' in Southern literature?"

I suppose that the reason for my reluctance on such occasions is that the person who asks the question thinks that it can be answered in a few sentences, in the way that one might respond to a question such as "What is the infield fly rule?" or "What is botulism?" Anyone who has done much thinking about Southern literature knows that it is not a simple question at all, but one that involves much complexity, and any attempt to rattle off a quick response is almost certain to be superficial, or programmatic, or both. The "Southernness" in Southern literature might be said to be like the "sex" in sex appeal—we know it's there, and we know how to respond to it, but frequently there is no explaining why it works the way it does or precisely how it achieves its effect.

Even so, it is this question that I propose to tackle now. I want to look into this business of the "Southernness" of Southern literature. I do not propose to come up with an answer, or at least not in the sense of formulating any kind of simple, categorical definition. For upon reflection it seems to me that attempting to deal with the matter that way is precisely where we may go wrong. To do so presupposes that the "Southernness" of Southern literature is an ingredient, a quantity, whose presence in a work of literature contributes a material substance to that work—when in fact it is no such thing at all. Instead, to make use of a metaphor that has been used on at least several other literary occasions, it is no quantitative ingredient but a catalyst, whose presence causes a reaction, a change, in the components of the work without itself being affected.

In other words, a work of Southern literature, say a novel, is *Southern* not because it contains certain ingredients, whether those elements be language, subject matter, plot, characterization, or ideas, but because some or all of those elements have been made to take on attributes in relationship to one another that might not otherwise exist in just that way. So what I should like to be able to do is to try to identify certain aspects of what I think may be involved in the relationship.

At the outset I should point out that this inquiry will be just that: an inquiry, in which I set out to explore the problem. The strategy is inductive—I am not trying to prove a predetermined point, but to find out what I think. The method I propose to follow will not be merely to examine certain Southern novels, searching for what is unique (or at any rate characteristic). Instead, I am going to begin by looking at the initial episode of a novel that not only was *not* written by a Southern author, but is also not remotely concerned with the South, with a view toward asking what might have been done differently had the novel been Southern in its origins. Now obviously, dealing in terms of what *isn't* but *might* have been, rather than what *is* present in a literary work, can be a chancy, tenuous business. Yet it seems to me that approaching the subject obliquely, even negatively, in this way might turn up some interesting things.

23

I want to begin with the first important scene in one of the greatest of all twentieth-century novels, Marcel Proust's *A la Recherche du temps perdu*. It occurs in the first volume, *Du Côté de chez Swann*, or *Swann's Way*. The opening pages, "Overture," are related by a first-person adult narrator, who later in the novel identifies himself as Marcel, and who recalls an episode during his childhood, when he and his family are staying in the little garrison town of Combray, not too far from Paris. A family friend, Charles Swann, is expected for dinner. We are told that as far as the narrator's family is concerned, Swann, the son of a stockbroker, is, like them, of a fixed social caste. Not only have they no idea that he frequents the aristocratic salons of the fashionable Faubourg Saint-Germain, but so strong is the sense of fixed, hereditary social place in their lives that if they *had* known of Swann's highly fashionable identity away from Combray, they would have considered it improper, even degrading behavior. Any such violation of the strictly drawn lines of caste would be as unacceptable as is the wife Swann has recently married, whose reputation as a courtesan has made it impossible for the narrator's family, for all their longtime friendship with Swann, to receive her or even to acknowledge her existence.

The young Marcel is allowed to stay out in the garden with the family only until a certain hour. Swann arrives, and there is some humorous badinage involving Marcel's grandfather and great-aunts, who refuse to allow Swann and the grandfather to enjoy an anecdote Swann tells the grandfather about something he has read in the *Mémoires* of Saint-Simon, the point of which is to show

Saint-Simon's exquisite hauteur and sense of aristocratic status. Even before the narrator's prescribed time for being sent away to bed arrives, however, his father intervenes and orders him to leave, refusing even to let him give his mother the goodnight kiss that is so important to him.

Thus excluded and made to go upstairs to his bedroom, the young Marcel feels an agonizing sense of deprivation from his mother. He even writes a note begging her to come up to him for a moment, which the family's elderly maid, Françoise, is given to take to her. His mother declines to answer, so he determines, even at the risk of certain disgrace, to stay up until Swann has departed and wait for her. When the dinner party concludes and the parents come upstairs, his father, instead of becoming irate as expected, tells his mother to stay in his room with him that night and comfort him, since he is so upset. So the child's mother, her efforts to instill in him the willpower he needs to keep from giving in to his weakness having been thwarted, comforts him and reads to him from a novel by George Sand. From that time on in his life, we are told, his unhappiness would no longer be considered a fault for which he must be punished, but a nervous condition, an involuntary illness to be accepted. The episode concludes as the narrator tells us that his agony was soothed as his mother read to him, even though he realized that it would repeat itself the following evening. It is followed by the famous "madeleine" episode in which the adult Marcel achieves a momentary access to lost time—his childhood—that he will learn to follow up only at the close of the novel, and which will allow him to re-create the story we have been reading.

II

Very well. Let us try to imagine how this childhood episode might have been handled if it had appeared in a novel by an author of the American South rather than a Frenchman. Certain elements leap out at us immediately. Of course it would be difficult to imagine any Southern author with whose work I happen to be familiar predicating a childhood scene on so self-centered and positively neurotic an emotional sensibility, though perhaps if Truman Capote had written *Look Homeward, Angel* it might have been possible. However, we can readily imagine the family dinner, with the presence of great-aunts and grandparents and the like—surely those great-aunts of Marcel's are no more eccentric than those of the Fairchild family in Eudora Welty's *Delta Wedding*. Proust's description of the rigid caste system, whereby the family cannot conceive of Charles Swann, a stockbroker's son, moving in fashionable society, would have to be qualified somewhat if the scene were laid anywhere in the South except perhaps the Vieux Carré, and even there it is probably too ironclad, because the South at its most squirearchical was never so compartmentalized as that.

The interest of the grandfather and of Swann in the Duc de Saint-Simon's memoir, with its excess of aristocratic arrogance, might strike one as being a little too intellectual in taste for Southern society, but we can imagine a similar conversation taking place about something less cerebral than a book—say football, or five-card stud, or politics, or even local history. As for the business of the family's refusal to acknowledge Swann's déclassé marriage and his wife and child, that again is rather too extreme—unless miscegenation were involved, which might make it believable, although in that case not merely Swann's wife but Swann himself would have been unwelcome at the family meal. The old family servant, Françoise, would have fit in handily, of course, though she would have been black.

25

For these reasons, then, some of the details of the episode in Proust would not have been "right" for a Southern novel. Yet the role of the family, the dinner ritual, and, most of all, the sense of provincial and small-town self-sufficiency, the belief that the forms and attitudes of middle-class Combray are eternal and unchanging, would certainly have their counterpart in Southern fiction. There would also be the same sense of an underlying impermanence, the feeling that the presence of the greater world outside the town limits must eventually break in on Combray and that change is in the offing. (Again one thinks of *Delta Wedding,* and perhaps of Allen Tate's *The Fathers*.) In short, there is very little in the behavior, interests, and motivations of Proust's people that, if in somewhat less extreme manifestation, would render implausible their translation into Southern social and psychological terms. Yet we would never mistake Combray for Morgana, Mississippi.

III

Now let me reverse my strategy. This time I should like to take up an episode from Southern fiction, and to speculate on what in it might have been presented differently if it had been written by someone other than a Southern writer. The novel I have in mind is Walker Percy's *The Last Gentleman,* and the episode is that in which Will Barrett, who is living in New York City and has been watching for two women he had seen on a bench in Central Park, discovers one of them about to board the same subway train he is taking. When she gets off the subway at Washington Heights, he does so, too. He follows her into a hospital building, and finds himself on the tenth floor. The woman goes into a room, and at once an elderly man emerges and comes up to him. At first the man assumes that Will is a member of the medical staff. They fall into conversation, and Will deduces from the man's accent that he is from north Alabama. "Birmingham? Gadsden?" he asks. "Halfway between," the man says. Then:

> "Don't I know you? Aren't you—" snapping his finger.
> "Will Barrett. Williston Bibb Barrett."
> "Over in—" He shook his hand toward the southwest.
> "Ithaca. In the Mississippi Delta."
> "You're Ed Barrett's boy."
> "Yes sir."
> "Lawyer Barrett. Went to Congress from Mississippi in nineteen and forty." Now it was his time to do the amazing. "Trained pointers, won at Grand Junction in—"
> "That was my uncle, Fannin Barrett," murmured the engineer.
> "Fannin Barrett," cried the other, confirming it. "I lived in Vicksburg in nineteen and forty-six and hunted with him over in Louisiana."

The upshot is that the man, who is named Chandler Vaught, takes Will into the room where his youngest son Jamie is hospitalized, and introduces him to other members of his family including his wife, his daughter Kitty, and his divorced daughter-in-law

Rita. There is conversation all around, and when Barrett departs it is with a cordial invitation to come back the next day, which he will assuredly do.

What is fascinating in the episode are the social deductions that Will Barrett is able to make, merely from listening and observing as Chandler Vaught and his family speak. He is able to pick up the fact that Vaught didn't know his father nearly as well as he pretended, that he had probably been a political opponent of his father, and that his social origins were markedly more plebeian than those of his wife. The Vaughts were, Will deduced, a "Yankee sort of Southerners, the cheerful, prosperous go-getters one comes across in the upper South, in Knoxville maybe, or Bristol." Entirely on the basis of a brief conversation, Will Barrett can tell what kind of people the Vaughts are; where they are from; the fact that Mrs. Vaught had "married down," as they say; that Vaught's political allegiances are, or were, with the "redneck" or rural white faction that had opposed the upper-class political interests represented by his own family (and by the Percy family as well); and that both Vaught and his wife have themselves identified his assured social status and are much impressed with it.

I have tried to imagine that scene taking place in a novel by a Midwestern or an East Coast author, but without much success. That is, it would not be difficult to conceive of a young man striking up an acquaintance with a family in a hospital room, and even discovering that they are from the same geographical area as himself. But the kind of precise social gradations and cultural nuances, the awareness of relative status and even of political allegiances, would have no counterpart. Even a status-conscious novelist such as Scott Fitzgerald, who could contrast Jay Gatsby's parvenu origins with those of the inherited wealth of Tom and Daisy Buchanan, would scarcely have sought to encapsulate such material in a scene of that kind.

But in Marcel Proust's fiction one might well imagine it happening—because, like Walker Percy, the French novelist was fascinated by and attuned to the nuances of diction, the ever-so-slight yet telling marks of status, the interactions of manners and conversational styles that exist in firmly defined social situations. In Proust's work the class distinctions would no doubt have been more striking and

27

even exaggerated, because the chasm between the bourgeois society of the Swanns and the Verdurins and the hereditary aristocracy of the Faubourg Saint-Germain was deeper.

The delineation of class comes naturally both to Proust and Percy. Moreover its manifestations are not developed primarily along economic lines, as they would have been had an author like Theodore Dreiser or even Scott Fitzgerald been doing the chronicling. It is true that it is wealth that presumably enabled Chandler Vaught to "marry up" and that will ultimately, in *Remembrance of Things Past*, make possible the union of the Prince de Guermantes and the widowed Madame Verdurin. But the consciousness of possession of money and the things that money can buy is not the principal ingredient that establishes, for Percy or for Proust, either the terms of discourse or the behavior of the fictional characters. If, as in every society, money and possessions play their part, and if money is ultimately the solvent, the means by which the passage from one social class to another is negotiated, nevertheless neither Walker Percy nor Marcel Proust presents his characters' motivations as being predominantly financial. (Neither, of course, is Jay Gatsby's motivation at bottom financial, but Fitzgerald's point is that the American society he portrays has been so corrupted by wealth that money has become the symbol of its aspirations; as Gatsby tells Nick Carraway, Daisy Buchanan's voice sounds like money.)

It seems to me that Percy's and Proust's fiction both presuppose not only the existence, but the central importance of a community relationship, and one that is so powerful that it can override any other considerations. What Will Barrett perceives in his encounter with the Vaught family at the hospital in New York could have meaning to him only if those involved live in a community that is sufficiently tangible and ongoing that the status, origins, and relationships of those within it can possess genuine significance. Their identity and actions are defined to a considerable extent by the terms of their membership within the community. It has got to *matter* that Will Barrett's social status is so assured that Chandler Vaught and his wife are eager to pursue his acquaintance. It is also essential to the story that Will and Chandler Vaught be drawn to one another *because* both are members of a community, no matter

28

that their roles within it are different. Everything that will take place thereafter in *The Last Gentleman* will be possible only because these two men discover that they speak a common social language, if with different accents. The fact that this identity will ultimately prove insufficient for Will Barrett's needs, so that he will leave it again and the story will conclude in the desert Southwest, does not lessen its importance. For it is the presuppositions of the community as to *role* that account for Barrett's unsatisfied and unfulfilled expectations.

Now if we will look again at the episode in Proust's great novel, much the same dynamics are at work. Charles Swann likewise has a role to play; he is the son of a stockbroker, a family friend, and he both expects and is expected to come by for dinner, to bring a gift (wine or fresh fruits from his garden), in general to fulfill the assumptions of the narrator's parents, grandparents, and great-aunts. That he has not been content to remain within the appointed boundaries of his role, and while continuing to fulfill it has also expanded his activities to include the playing of another role in fashionable society, is of no importance to the Combray community, which is concerned only with his performance of his accustomed and allotted part. But in choosing to marry outside the permitted boundaries of his social position, and taking for a wife a woman of unacceptable standards, he has to that extent failed to play his community role, and the community therefore declines to recognize the existence of that wife and the child she has given him.

Insofar as Charles Swann is concerned, then, there is a clash between his appointed place in the Combray community and his own private desires and needs, and he has chosen to disregard the former. The decreed role has to that extent been insufficient to permit Swann to define his identity within and through it. Yet he is by no means willing to abandon it entirely—at least not yet. Still, this early depiction of Charles Swann at Combray is anticipatory of what will be happening throughout the first several volumes of *Remembrance of Things Past*, for as we shall see, Swann will also prove willing to diminish his glittering position in the Faubourg because of his desire for his future wife and the pleasures of bourgeois domesticity and fatherhood, and later, when the Dreyfus case shakes the foundations of French society, he will be unwilling to suppress the fact that

29

he is a Jew, and so will jeopardize his status within the Faubourg even more.

There is another potential conflict between community role and individual need present in the family dinner scene at Combray. Although at this stage it seems no more than a matter of childhood self-centeredness, the narrator's insistence upon waiting up to see his mother in defiance of what is considered proper and manly will have its ramifications. The child's mother and grandmother, who wish to develop his powers of self-discipline and help him to overcome his weakness and need, do so out of their love for him and because they want to prepare him for his future role as a mature citizen. But the narrator will not accede in their wishes—and it is precisely this powerful individuality on his part, which here has the appearance of no more than childhood weakness, that will eventually cause him to decline to accept the validity of any such identity within society, and lead him to the discovery of his vocation as artist.

Walker Percy's Will Barrett, like the majority of other protagonists of Southern fiction, isn't destined to become an artist—although like Leopold Bloom in Joyce's *Ulysses* he does seem to have a touch of the artist about him. But that he is motivated and even driven by a powerful sense of role is obvious. The Southern community set out a part for him to play—the stoic aristocrat, the "last gentleman"—and he can't play it, because the time and place for such a role to encompass his needs, to afford him the identity he requires, have supposedly passed by.

This notion of roles becoming outdated is basic to the way that Percy sees the modern South. We need only remember that brief but marvelous scene which takes place outside the family residence in Ithaca at night, after Will, having briefly returned, remembers his father's suicide—a suicide motivated by the seeming erosion of aristocratic community and role. A young black man comes walking along in the darkness of the water oaks, whistling. Will sees the black man before being seen, and he thinks that in times past "it had been his, the Negro's, business, until now, to see him first." But no longer:

> They looked at each other. There was nothing to say. Their fathers would have had much to say: "In the end, Sam, it comes

down to a question of character." "Yes suh, Lawyer Barrett, you right about that. Like I was saying to my wife only this evening—" But the sons had nothing to say. The engineer looked at the other as the half second wore on. You may be in a fix and I know that but what you don't know and won't believe and must find out for yourself is that I'm in a fix too and you got to get where I am before you even know what I'm talking about and that is why there is nothing to say now. Meanwhile I wish you well.

IV

31

It seems safe to say, therefore, that to the extent that Proust's novel and Walker Percy's are representative of their communities, one of the features of human life in both is a very tangible sense of the individual as being assigned a social role within a palpable and defined social organism. I choose the word *role* rather than *purpose* or *function*, since to speak of a role is to imply the presence of a cast and audience, and not just a solitary individual's doings.

Just as we have seen with Proust's novel, it is precisely in the discrepancy between role and purpose—between what the individual is expected to do and be and what the individual might wish to do or be—that we have the tension that can make a work of fiction memorable. Suffice it to say that the expected role of an individual within a community can become more clearly defined and even more rigidly prescribed in direct ratio to the extent to which that community's presence is of greater and more pervasive importance in the lives of the human beings who constitute it.

Now if we think of the existence of this community role, and what it means, in twentieth-century Southern fiction, its importance will be evident. Isn't it obvious that it is the motif of the expected but absent community role in *The Last Gentleman* that provides a context for Percy's theological concerns? There are untold numbers of works of fiction that center on a young man's search for purpose and belief; but what gives Percy's version of that oft-explored story its particular quality is the context in which it takes place, the decaying (as he sees it) set of community expectations involved in the role that Will Barrett now finds all but meaningless.

The same concept of role, and usually its supposed erosion as well, exists in most Southern fiction. Let me choose only a couple of examples. Consider the instance of Thomas Sutpen in William Faulkner's *Absalom, Absalom!* Sutpen's purpose in coming into the Mississippi territory of the early nineteenth century is so powerfully and rigidly defined as to constitute a veritable Design. He wishes to be a planter—to own a plantation and to establish a dynasty: Sutpen's Hundred (in direct imitation of the Virginia dynasties he has encountered as a child). He would establish the House of Sutpen, so to speak, in order to perpetuate his presence within the community beyond his own death. But so ignorant is he of the community responsibility involved in such an ambition that he is constantly at loggerheads with the people he lives among. Sutpen covets the status of a gentleman-planter, an aristocrat, without the community role it entails, the external trappings without the inward obligations and responsibilities; in Cleanth Brooks's words, he approaches the community tradition "as an assortment of things to be possessed, not a manner of living that embodies certain values and determines men's conduct." And it is his utter self-centeredness, his sweeping disregard for the needs of others, that both enables him to come so far in his quest and also makes his ultimate failure inevitable.

The significance of the story of Thomas Sutpen is by no means confined to one of individual need versus community role. Indeed, what gives that story so much of its scope and magnificence, and makes it so profoundly tragic, is the universality of Sutpen's quest, which is ultimately that of a human being intent upon giving his life a meaning that will outlast and confute human mortality itself. It is no accident that when he dies, it is at the hands of a bearded old man wielding a rusty scythe. But surely the way in which that quest is embodied within a community situation, so that Sutpen's effort at fulfilling his chosen identity assumes the tangible shape of a conflict between private will and community role, gives Faulkner's great novel so much of its richness of texture and singularity of reference.

We need only compare *Absalom, Absalom!* with another remarkable novel about an ambitious parvenu who fails, Fitzgerald's *The Great Gatsby,* to see at once how the availability of the time, place, and setting of the Southern community enabled Faulkner to

32

sharpen and dramatize the social and moral significance of an ethical problem common to both novels: that of the individual impelled to pursue his own ideal of fulfillment at the cost of using means that are corruptible. There is that about showing a man beheaded by a poor white in the guise of Father Time which having a distraught auto mechanic pot somebody with a bullet while he lounges on a float in a suburban swimming pool cannot quite equal.

Or consider another example: Eudora Welty's *The Optimist's Daughter*. In this novel about a middle-aged woman returning home to a Mississippi city for the funeral of her father, it is not merely that Laurel McKelva Hand must confront the nature of loss and the survival of human love in time. That problem would be implicit in any such situation. But in Miss Welty's novel the past, the conflict between personal fulfillment and the continuity of identity that a family situation can afford, can take the form and definition that are possible when such things are embodied in a confrontation of roles. To be the daughter of Judge and Mrs. Clinton McKelva of Mount Salus, to live where one's identity is embodied in rituals and institutions, involves a prescribed and conspicuous community role, against and within which the nature of one's personal needs and wishes may be delineated and the costs identified and understood. Thus the drama of the protagonist's exploration of what her parents and her memories mean for her can be dramatized and tested in a rich, vivid, and resonant social texture. Human identity in time becomes human involvement in a place—a specific, concrete, tangible locus of emotional states.

Now all novels are set in a place; as the saying goes, everybody's got to be somewhere. But what makes the oft-remarked Sense of Place in Southern fiction so important is the vividness, the ferocity even, with which it implies social and community attitudes. This is because the writer's own experience of a place has involved those attitudes so pervasively that for the writer to evoke the place is to confront the community's values. It isn't, therefore, the depiction of place as such that gives Southern literature its particular nature; could any novel, for example, evoke a physical place much more vividly than Hemingway's *The Sun Also Rises,* or than *Ulysses?* Rather, it is what the particularities of Ithaca, Morgana, Mount Salus, Yoknapatawpha, Altamont, Burden's Landing, and other

33

such fictional communities whose lineaments are drawn from their authors' experience, are made to mean for the characters, what the patterns of their daily life do to the way the characters act, think, feel, and imagine, that lead us to identify the fiction as Southern.

And that is my point. For just as the complex nature of Southern life cannot be compressed within a single definition or category, so its literature, which takes its image and idiom from the Southern experience of its authors, resists any kind of quantitative lining up of descriptive categories like so many ducks in a row. What makes literature a unique form of knowledge is its complex ordering of human experience into images; and what the novelists take from the experience that they shape into images is the complexity, the relationships, the totality.

What I have sought to show with Proust is that certain characteristics that we are wont to single out as uniquely or peculiarly "Southern" are equally present, and important, in a novel by a Frenchman who so far as I know never saluted a Confederate flag, damned a Yankee, or enjoyed a sip of bourbon-and-branch in his life. No one, having read ten pages into *Swann's Way,* would doubt that he was writing about France and Frenchmen, and not Americans or Englishmen or anyone else. And, just as Proust's France is not Gide's or Stendhal's or Flaubert's, yet France is identifiably rooted in the books of all of them, so Faulkner's and Welty's and Percy's Souths—and those of Ernest Gaines and Flannery O'Connor and William Styron and Kaye Gibbons and of all the other Southern writers as well—are each different and yet unmistakably Southern communities all.

So that is why I feel compelled to keep insisting that the Southern literary imagination as we have known it in our century is not simply a matter of the presence within works of fiction of particular elements such as place, language, a sense of evil, an historical consciousness, an attitude toward nature or God or tradition or the like. As we have seen, and as is quite obvious, other bodies of literature share those characteristics. Can we demand a more palpable historical sense than that in Irish fiction? A greater sense of evil than in, say, the work of Dostoyevsky or of Thomas Mann? Could any fiction ever written image agrarian experience more thoroughly and pervasively than Thomas Hardy's? Surely the nature of provincial life could not be given greater vividness than in Chekhov. For that matter, isn't it difficult to imagine a particular place and culture being evoked more formidably than the island of Manhattan is in Salinger's *The Catcher in the Rye,* or than the city of Chicago at the turn of the century is in *Sister Carrie?* And so on.

All of those elements, and more besides, are present to a greater or lesser degree in *all* good fiction. What makes us recognize and identify certain works of fiction as Southern is the particular and special ways in which such elements are arranged, the characteristic shapes that they assume in respect to one another, the manner in which they cause people to behave and writers to choose metaphors. And these special ways, particular forms, traits of behavior, and resources of language come out of the Southern community experience, a community that, however much it may differ from place to place and individual to individual, so shapes the imaginative response of its literary people that when they write their stories and poems they do so, to a markedly recognizable degree, as *Southern* authors.

What is "Southern" about Southern literature? Nothing more or less than the Southern community itself—as a whole, as an image, as a convergence. Add the Southern community as catalyst to a writer's imagination, and in one way or another almost everything in the writer's fiction is affected, rearranged, changed. The degree to which this is so varies from writer to writer, just as the vividness with which the human experience is imaged will depend upon the richness of the writer's imagination and the skill with which the writer can embody it in language. But one would have to add that, if we are to judge from the books that have been made available to us in our time, the South has had something to do with the availability of that richness and the nature and presence of that gift of tongue.

THE DIXIE SPECIAL
WILLIAM FAULKNER AND THE SOUTHERN LITERARY RENASCENCE

(1982)

> "Because he's the head bear. He's the man."
> —William Faulkner, "The Bear"

On the grounds of the capitol of Ohio in Columbus is a large statue in which that Midwestern state is represented, in classical garb upon a granite pedestal, as Cornelia, mother of the Gracchi, holding forth her hands and declaring, "These are my jewels!" The jewels, depicted in bronze statuary below, are Ulysses S. Grant, Philip Sheridan, James A. Garfield, W. T. Sherman, Edwin M. Stanton, Salmon P. Chase, and Rutherford B. Hayes. Unfortunately William McKinley, Mark Hanna, and Warren G. Harding came along too late to make the cluster.

I wish to propose, to anyone who has political influence, that a similar statue be erected on the capitol grounds in Jackson. Let the State of Mississippi be Cornelia. Let the gems in her tiara be William Faulkner, Eudora Welty, Richard Wright, Elizabeth Spencer, Shelby Foote, Tennessee Williams, and the late Major Frederick Sullens. (Major Sullens' replica should have its eyes averted from the others.) I leave it to the State Fine Arts Commission to decide whether the Roman motif should be carried out in all details. I cannot quite imagine William Faulkner clad in a toga, though I daresay it would seem no more incongruous upon him than the riding habit in the famous Cofield photograph. One thing is certain, however: in any such cluster Faulkner should be placed in the center, with the others grouped around him.

The Southern Literary Renascence, as it is called, is now some sixty years old. It was the literary product and image of the belated and violent confrontation of the Southern states with modern, secular, industrial civilization. A closely bound community, threadbare, traditional, agricultural, religiously orthodox, with a somewhat flexible system of class and a very rigid, inflexible caste system, infused with a powerful mythology and a commonly shared history of pride and defeat, rejoined the American Union. The reunion had been long in coming. Slavery, the defeat of the war, Reconstruction, and then decades of social, political, and economic trauma had held off the impact of the industrial revolution and its technological, urban-centered society. When finally the change did begin to come to the Southern community, the social and moral drama of its advent, the dislocation of sensibility, was uncommonly intense.

Because the Southern community had always had a pervasive, if hitherto mostly ineffectual, literary tradition, and had for generations, in pulpit, hustings, editorial sanctum, and front porch, been given to defining itself in and through language, it was only to be expected that it would be in literature, through stories, novels, poems, that the transaction would be articulated. In short order the Southern literary imagination shook off its blinders of local color and apologia. As Allen Tate noted, with the war of 1917–1918 the young Southerners of his generation looked around them and began realizing, for the first time, that the Yankees were not to blame for everything that was unsatisfactory about Southern experience. From rhetoric—the defense of the community from fixed, preestablished premises, the quarrel with others—the literary South moved into dialectic—the quarrel with oneself, the effort to define oneself in relation to the community.[1] *Who am I in time and place? What is my history?*

1. See Tate's essays "A Southern Mode of the Imagination," in Allen Tate, *Essays of Four Decades* (Chicago: Swallow Press, 1959), 577–92, and "Faulkner's *Sanctuary* and the Southern Myth," in Tate, *Memories and Opinions, 1926–1974* (Chicago: Swallow Press, 1975), 144–54.

The ideological headquarters for this investigative activity was Nashville, Tennessee. There, in and about Vanderbilt University, the question was articulated topically and programmatically. The publishing headquarters, alas, was New York City, which posed certain difficulties for the writers, and still does. The artistic headquarters was clearly Mississippi, though there were numerous additional branch offices from Texas to Virginia. The Renascence is still going on.

Why did so many of the very best writers of the Southern Literary Renascence come out of Mississippi? In part, perhaps, because of all the Southern states it was the most rural, the most threadbare and quixotic, the least removed from the conditions of a frontier. The two largest cities in Mississippi, it used to be said, were Memphis and New Orleans. In Mississippi the suddenness of social and cultural change was most violent, the contrasts it offered most dramatic. "Mad Ireland hurt you into poetry," the poet Auden wrote of William Butler Yeats; one might also say the same for the sole owner and proprietor of Yoknapatawpha County.

39

But all this sounds rather more like sociology than literary analysis, and one feels uncomfortable making such generalizations. One might justly feel uncomfortable, indeed, talking about an entity known as "Southern Literature," instead of about the works of this particular writer or that. Yet what can one do? If there were only Faulkner, or only Eudora Welty—or only Thomas Wolfe, or the Nashville Fugitives, or whoever—the matter could be ascribed simply to the workings of chance and the unaccountability of the incidence of genius. But there are so many of them, and all at the same time and in the same place. The economically deprived, culturally remote states of the onetime Confederacy, with a modest-sized population, a high illiteracy rate, and a substandard economy, produced, during the years when President Roosevelt called the South the nation's Number One economic problem, a disproportionate number of widely talented writers. Faulkner was the most distinguished of a galaxy of accomplished literary artists.

The resemblances, the common subjects, themes, attitudes toward human nature and history shared by most of the writers of the Southern Renascence have long since been documented, and I have nothing very new to add to that now. Suffice it to say that the adjectives "modern" and "Southern" modify the noun "literature" not merely geographically and temporally but artistically and culturally, in terms of history, politics, language, and even religion. However the lineaments of Yoknapatawpha County may differ from those of Altamont in Old Catawba, or from Morgana 150 miles or so to the south, or from Burden's Landing down on the Gulf Coast, however individual the imaginations of every one of the modern Southern writers, they are united by shared concerns and common attitudes that make their work, whether in verse or prose, identifiable culturally and geographically. "The South," a young Canadian remarks to a young Mississippian in a Faulkner novel. "The South. Jesus. No wonder you folks all outlive yourselves by years and years and years." And again, "What is it? something you live and breathe in like air?" [2] Whatever it is, or was, it provided the Southern Renascence with a recognizable and distinctive literary flavor, one unlike that of any other notable body of American writing.

Leslie Fiedler wrote that the "mythopoetic genius" of Faulkner has largely been responsible for the fact "that the South has remained through the last three decades our preferred literary arena of terror"; the regional confrontation with racial difference is also responsible for that, he says.[3] Yet even without Faulkner's work the output of the literary South in the twentieth century would have been considered quite remarkable indeed. Nor is it merely Fiedler's particular obsession—gothic terror, the angularities of violence and pain—that is its hallmark. The rituals of community experience, the complexities of social involvement, the celebration of idiosyncrasy: these have also characterized a body of literature that has been unmistakably identifiable as growing out of a place and time.

Of course there can be little doubt that Faulkner is the giant of the Renascence—as Sam Fathers would put it, he is the Head Bear. A younger contemporary, Flannery O'Connor, was always ready to reply to the almost inevitable question of how she felt, as a Southern author, about working in the shadow of Faulkner, that nobody likes to get caught on the tracks when the Dixie Special comes

2. William Faulkner, *Absalom, Absalom!* (New York: Random House, 1936), 377, 361.

3. Leslie A. Fiedler, *Love and Death in the American Novel* (New York: Criterion Books, 1960), 448.

through. As for Faulkner himself, he appeared to take little interest in the work of most of his Southern contemporaries. Allen Tate wrote that "it is a part of Mr. Faulkner's legend about himself that he did appear, like the sons of Cadmus, full grown, out of the unlettered soil of his native state, Mississippi. But we are under no obligation to take his word for it. Two other modern writers of prose-fiction, Mr. Stark Young and Miss Eudora Welty, quite as gifted as Mr. Faulkner, if somewhat below him in magnitude and power, are also natives of that backward state, where fewer people can read than in any other state in the union."[4] I would say that Tate was right about Miss Welty, who to my mind is nearest to Faulkner's stature among all their contemporaries, and that about Stark Young he was betrayed by his own weakness for authentic plantation ancestry into elevating a talented local colorist into the company of two great writers. No matter; the point is that as one of the better modern Southern authors, William Faulkner was not unique but exemplary: *primus inter pares.*

41

Faulkner's attitude toward his identity as a Southern writer was rather ambivalent. At times he readily accepted the identification, at other times he sought to deny it. We need pay little heed to his remarks of the latter sort. They were made mostly in interviews, and depending upon his mood at the time, how much he had had to drink, and his feeling toward the interviewer, Faulkner was prone to say almost anything, however outrageous, during the course of an interview. He is also not the only good Southern author of his day who felt compelled at times to deny the regional literary identification; they seem to fear that to be labeled in such fashion would rob them of some of their universality and make them into genteel local colorists who purvey the quaint surfaces of regional life. Joel Chandler Harris and Harry Stillwell Edwards were Southern writers; therefore, to be a Southern writer is to write like Joel Chandler Harris and Harry Stillwell Edwards—so the equation goes. Faulkner knew better, however, as when he told the youth of Japan in 1955 that "I believe it is war and disaster which remind man most that he needs a record of his endurance and toughness. I think that is why after our own disaster there rose in my country, the South, a re-

4. Tate, "Southern Mode of the Imagination," 577.

surgence of good writing, writing of a good enough quality that people in other lands began to talk of a 'regional' Southern literature until even I, a countryman, have become one of the first names in our literature which the Japanese people want to talk to and listen to."[5]

A characteristic aspect of Faulkner's public personality was his dislike of being taken for an intellectual, a mere littérateur. It is this that accounts in large part for his notable reluctance to associate with other literary people or to admit to an interest in his fellow Southern authors. Joseph Blotner, in his splendid biography, tells about the occasion in 1931 when Ellen Glasgow and Professor Southall Wilson of the University of Virginia organized a conference of Southern writers. Faulkner was one of thirty-four authors invited to take part. He was obviously flattered at being asked to come to the University of Virginia, but he was also uneasy with the idea of being involved in such overt literary doings. In his letter of acceptance he replied that "you have seen a country wagon come into town, with a hound dog under the wagon. It stops on the Square and the folks get out, but that hound never gets very far from that wagon. He might be cajoled or scared out for a short distance, but first thing you know he has scuttled back under the wagon; maybe he growls at you a little. Well, that's me."[6] He showed up well fortified for the literary occasion and spent much of his time thereafter replenishing his armor. At the opening session, as Ellen Glasgow offered a series of authoritative pronouncements about "The Southern Writer and His Public," Faulkner would raise his head slightly and murmur, "I agree, I agree." Obiously he wasn't very comfortable at being part of an intellectual and social event involving so many formidable men and women of letters. He also graciously informed a newspaper reporter that Southern writers of the day were only pioneers, and nothing "of any real value" was likely to emerge from the South for at least twenty-five years.[7]

5. William Faulkner, "To the Youth of Japan," in *Essays, Speeches, and Public Letters by William Faulkner,* ed. James B. Meriwether (New York: Random House, 1965), 83.

6. Joseph Blotner, *Faulkner: A Biography* (2 vols.; New York: Random House, 1974), I, 706.

7. See *ibid.,* I, 707–16, for Blotner's description of the conference at Char-

The image of the hound dog, ostensibly so modest and self-deprecatory, is really nothing of the sort. What Faulkner was suggesting to James Southall Wilson, and what he was doing when from time to time he described himself as just a plain old countryman, was that he was no intellectual with lean brow and hollow eye, given to unseasonable meditativeness, who went about attending literary teas and discoursing learnedly about the artist in the modern world; he was the real thing, a natural-born storyteller, of the earth earthy, with nothing of the highbrow about him. If this fails fully to explain how *The Sound and the Fury* got written, never mind. The same stance, somewhat more skillfully camouflaged, is characteristic of almost all the Southern writers of his time (and, indeed, of many other American writers). It has been very important to the Southern writer of Faulkner's generation to insist that, for all his literary interests, he is still a working member of the general middle-class community. One must not be set apart from the hurly-burly of the practical, everyday, non-literary world. Ideas and the intellect are to be kept in their place.

43

Intellectually and temperamentally, a distrust of abstract ideas has been a long-standing characteristic of Southern life. Perhaps in part it goes back to the time when the South was forced to defend the massive and complex reality of the Southern community, defaced as it was with the presence of human slavery, against the single-minded ideological assault of Abolitionist reformers. Whatever the origins, the Southern sensibility has long been marked by a suspicion of intellectual formulations, and the fear that too great a reliance upon theory will falsify the complexity of real life. Is it merely coincidence that the one important school of literary criticism that the Southerners have developed should be based upon the assumption that ideas alone will not do, that theories will of themselves never suffice to explain the poem?

Faulkner, of course, was no theorist. But the same distrust of the pure idea is very much a part of his aesthetic. His very style itself, with the long sentences, the liberal deployment of adjectives, the pa-

___

lottesville. Dorothy Scura gives an account of the conference in "Glasgow and the Southern Renaissance," in *Ellen Glasgow: Centennial Essays,* ed. M. Thomas Inge (Charlottesville: University Press of Virginia, 1976), 46–61.

rentheses, and the parentheses within parentheses, proceeds from the conviction that reality can be represented only when presented in its full complexity, leaving out nothing that is important. His admiration for Thomas Wolfe, he said on several occasions, was for that novelist's attempt, however impossible of fulfillment, to put all experience on the head of a pin.

In any event, the suspicion of theory as leading to oversimplification is something that the Southern writers of Faulkner's generation came by naturally. There is more to it than this, however; it is not only a philosophical attitude that is involved, but a psychological need. For the writers of the Southern Renascence were not merely dubious about too much cerebration; they were also zealous to avoid giving the *appearance* of being intellectuals. As I have already suggested, when Faulkner informs a reporter that he is no intellectual but only a countryman who writes stories, he does so because he feels uncomfortable at being thought of as an intellectual. To assume such a role, or to appear to be assuming it, would be to concede that one is no longer a working member of the general middle-class community.

Thus when Faulkner was informed by a Swedish newspaper correspondent that he had been awarded the Nobel Prize, his response was typical. Having expressed his gratitude, he said that he would be unable to come and accept the prize in person: "It's too far away. I am a farmer down here and I can't get away," he said.[8] (Later he changed his mind about not going.) Not long after the award was announced he went on the annual hunting trip to the Delta with his friends, and though he said nothing about it, one of his companions read about the prize in a newspaper someone had brought along. That evening it was Faulkner's turn to help wash the dishes, and Uncle Ike Roberts spoke up:

> "Bill," he said, "what would you do if that Swede ambassador came down here and handed you that money right now?"
>
> With scarcely a pause, Faulkner answered, "I'd tell him just to put it on that table over there and grab a dryin' rag and help," he said, to the delight of his companions.[9]

8. Blotner, *Faulkner*, II, 1338.
9. *Ibid.*, 1347.

44

He had passed the test. He was, in other words, still one of the boys.

Elsewhere I have suggested that an important part of the dynamics lying behind the art of William Faulkner is the creative tension between his ardent desire to write and be a writer, and the feeling, in the small Southern community in which he grew up as oldest son of one of the leading families, that there was something undignified and even unmanly in pursuing such an occupation rather than being a red-blooded, stalwart man of affairs.[10] Throughout his best work there is not just a division but a dichotomy between the man of sensibility and the man of action: Horace Benbow and Bayard Sartoris in *Flags in the Dust*, Quentin Compson and Dalton Ames in *The Sound and the Fury*, Quentin and Thomas Sutpen in *Absalom, Abasalom!*, Darl and Jewel Bundren in *As I Lay Dying*, and so on.[11]

This kind of division, which Faulkner felt so strongly during his childhood and early manhood, is by no means peculiar to the South, as witness what was possible to another young man growing up in Oak Park, Illinois, at about the time. But it is certainly characteristic of the South, because the South was small-town, middle-class, with a long military heritage, given to outdoor pursuits, with little place within the doings of the community for the cultural and intellectual sophistication whereby artistic inclinations on the part of a young man might be understood. Writing poetry or fiction, taking them seriously: that sort of thing was for women. Any young male who did so, and who had the sensibility to do so, must perforce be less than properly masculine: sicklied o'er with the pale cast of thought, so to speak (or perhaps, since literary and intellectual inclinations usually went along with heresy on racial issues, with the thought of pale caste). This is why Quentin Compson is made so to despise himself for his inability, as protector of the honor of the family females, to stand up to Dalton Ames; he faints dead away. And why he is both fascinated and horrified at the story of the ruthless, unfeeling, entirely masculine Thomas Sutpen. For though Quentin is not overtly a poet or a novelist, he is very obviously Faulkner's

45

10. Louis D. Rubin, Jr., "William Faulkner: The Discovery of a Man's Vocation," in *Faulkner: Fifty Years After "The Marble Faun,"* ed. George H. Wolfe (University: University of Alabama Press, 1976), 43–68.

11. For an excellent discussion of this, see Daniel V. Gribbin, "Men of Thought, Men of Action in Faulkner's Novels" (Ph.D. dissertation, University of North Carolina at Chapel Hill, 1973).

young man of sensibility, with the emotional resources of the artist. And this is clearly related to Faulkner's anti-intellectual, country-boy pose. No Quentin Compson he!

I have observed very much the same kind of assumption in the work, and the lives, of almost every one of the modern Southerners, from Cabell and Will Percy on to Wolfe, Tate, Caldwell, Warren, and on up through Walker Percy, Shelby Foote, James Agee, and James Dickey (and in a diminished mode, I do not except myself, either). All seem impelled to demonstrate their masculinity. The element of overkill in Cabell's repeated insistence upon his amatory propensities while young and unmarried is all too obvious. Tate's amusing insistence upon challenging his literary foes to duels was well known. Warren's use of four-letter words for his redneck characters seems highly self-conscious. Wolfe continually depicts his youthful autobiographical protagonists as ridiculed by a crass, unfeeling commercial community because of their artistic leanings. Dickey's novel *Deliverance* is full of it: the ultimate atrocity is to be forced by a redneck to engage in sodomy. And so on.

What I am getting at is that, along with all the other Southern authors of his time, Faulkner's relationship with the rank and file of the Southern community from childhood on was of profound significance, involving powerful tensions and ambiguities. It is not the situation commonly portrayed as that of the writer in modern industrial society—that of the alienated artist. There are elements of alienation, but also strong emotional and intellectual ties to the community. When Faulkner insists that he is no literary man but merely a plain dirt farmer, when he tells James Southall Wilson that he is like the old hound dog who is out of place and uneasy at being in town, he is protesting against an identity that his artistic talents and achievements have tended to force upon him: that of someone who is no longer part of the community. He is denying any such alienation.

And rightly so. For despite the obvious fact that the people who read and valued his fiction were mostly not his fellow townsfolk at all, but outsiders who lived in big cities and taught in universities and were sophisticated moderns, nevertheless he wrote the fiction about the community, as a way of giving form and order to his experience as part of the community.

The more that I read and think about the work of the Southern writers, the more convinced I am that it is virtually impossible to overstate the importance of the relationship with the Southern community. The writers of the Southern Renascence grew up in a closely knit community. The terms of membership were not merely economic but social, political, historical, cultural. It was not the cosmopolitan society of the urban metropolis, but a small-town and small-city community, mostly middle-class, without vast extremes of wealth and station. The Faulkners may have been the local squirearchy, but the boys went to public school with the children of rich and poor, played with them, grew up with them. Though William Faulkner's nascent literary interests set him apart in certain respects from his fellow townsfolk, and though for a time in his very young manhood he made a point of appearing to be different in a small town, he shared, and continued to share, numerous interests and attitudes with his neighbors. Any change in condition or situation, any adult role that tended to remove him too far from his membership in the community made him uncomfortable, because a great deal of what he considered as real and important in his experience was bound in with the life of the community.

47

Thus the gestures that he made from time to time in the way of emphasizing his community identity constituted a means of assuring not only others but himself as well that he was still a part of the community. It was a way of remaining in close touch with much of what he continued to believe was in important ways *reality*. To do otherwise would be to deny vital aspects of his own identity. He was an artist, and he was a Mississippian; and they were not, so far as he was concerned, mutually irreconcilable roles. Moreover, to be the artist he *had* to remain a Mississippian, for otherwise his contact with reality would be imperiled. His best fiction was an exploration of the sometimes tortured relationship.

This is true not only of Faulkner but of every one of the writers of the modern South, without regard for whether or not they actually lived and worked in their home communities or even in the South at all. It was there that their imagination had its origins and its links with actuality. The late Robert Penn Warren, for example, lived in Connecticut for more than three decades, yet he remarked that if he were to write a story about a Connecticut farmer, "I wouldn't know where to begin. But writing a story about such a family, rich or poor, grand or miserable, in the South, I wouldn't have any hesitation. It would be as natural as breathing to me. I'd know what they did, I'd know what they ate, I'd know what they'd say."[12] What is striking about the comment is the assumption that the story he would write would perforce be about a farmer or a farming family: when he thinks about writing fiction he thinks in terms of the Southern community of his boyhood and youth. For the Southern novelist of Warren's generation, there is where the stuff of fiction is to be found: in the middle-class, non-specialized community experience that he knew before he became an adult writer and man of letters. His fiction is a way of reasserting that identity, not as nostalgia but through the passionate examination of its meanings.

It is true that the very fact that the books are written is emblematic of the writer's distancing from the community. For one thing, the nature of writing poetry and fiction is such that no one would want to do it who was completely and creatively satisfied with the everyday actualities of his experience. For another, the intense exploration of the underlying dimensions of community experience within himself, the insistence upon discerning patterns and meanings, could only come as the result of a perspective, a removal far enough away in time and space to make possible their recognition. But that distancing did not customarily produce, for the men and women of the Southern Renascence, precisely the maimed artist described in Edmund Wilson's wound-and-bow theory of the writer. The Southerners did not flee the community, whether geographically or inwardly, to live in a place of solipsistic pain and isolation. Far from it; emotionally and intellectually they stayed within the thick of things and sought to understand their time and place in the unique way that literature does: through the passionate rendition of the detailed specificities of that time and place.

The difference between Faulkner's generation of Southern writers—that of the Renascence—and those of an earlier day lay in just

12. "The South: Distance and Change. A Conversation with Robert Penn Warren, William Styron, and Louis D. Rubin, Jr.," in *The American South: Portrait of a Culture*, ed. Louis D. Rubin, Jr. (Baton Rouge: Louisiana State University Press, 1980), 305–306.

that combination of passionate involvement together with aesthetic and moral distancing. In Tate's formulation, the moderns did not view themselves as rhetoricians, charged with the promulgation and defense of Southern ideals. Here is Tate's description of the Southern literary situation before the coming of the modernists:

> The South was Uncle Sam's Other Province. This social situation produced a sentimental literature of Narcissism, in which the South tried to define itself by looking into a glass behind its back: not inward. It was thus not a literature of introspection, but a literature of romantic illusion; and its mode was what I have called elsewhere the Rhetorical Mode.
>
> . . . rhetoric in the Reconstruction South was a good way of quarreling with the Yankees, who were to blame for everything. The quarrel raged with some cunning and versatility, for it elicited a good deal of fiction in which the Southern gentleman was a Chevalier Bayard *redivivus,* the Poor White a picturesque buffoon who spoke a quaint dialect, and the Negro Rousseau's Natural Man spoiled by having been deprived of the benefits of slavery.[13]

49

The local-color writer was very much involved in the mythic delineation of what he already knew and felt about the community—about the experience of being a Southerner. I do not want to characterize the transaction as merely a patriotic rehearsal of Southern virtues; certainly it was undertaken lovingly and fervently, and it was not always uncritical. A writer such as Joel Chandler Harris, for example, not in his animal tales but his novels, sought to remedy what he saw as flaws in his community by appealing to its better instincts, thereby showing his fellow Southerners what could be while at the same time presenting to outside readers a depiction of Southern life that was both flattering and appealing. But just as it was only in the animal stories that Harris could look at *human* nature as it was, rather than as it ought to be, and describe, albeit as comedy, his own experience without making use of blinders or tinted glasses, so the fiction and poetry of the pre-1917–1918 South was for the

13. Tate, "Faulkner's *Sanctuary* and the Southern Myth," 146.

most part a celebration of pleasant surfaces, one which has not outlived its occasion.

By contrast the writer of Faulkner's generation, rather than adumbrating what he already knew about his community, engaged in an intense exploration of himself as a member of that community, writing about what he knew and felt about his community not to edify or encourage others but to understand himself. Faulkner describes the relationship vividly in the never-used introduction of a proposed new edition of *The Sound and the Fury*. The Southerner, he says, writes not about his environment but about himself. He has "figuratively speaking, taken the artist in him in one hand and his milieu in the other and thrust the one into the other like a clawing and spitting cat into a croker sack. And he writes. . . . That cold intellect which can write with calm and complete detachment and gusto of its contemporary scene is not among us." [14]

50

It is scarcely surprising that a literary art created in such a spirit would offend Southern partisans of the old school with its depiction of some of the less edifying traits of human nature as manifested in the Southern community. No wonder the late Major Sullens of the Jackson *Daily News* was outraged when a committee of Swedish academicians inexplicably decided to award the Nobel Prize to William Faulkner. The Major did not want literary explorations of the human heart in conflict with itself undertaken in Mississippi; he wanted a defense and reinforcement of contemporary Southern social and racial arrangements. And of course Faulkner was not alone in receiving such treatment. When Thomas Wolfe published *Look Homeward, Angel*, for example, his former classmate Jonathan Daniels declared in the Raleigh *News and Observer* that "here is a young man, hurt by something that he loved, turning in his sensitive fury and spitting on that thing. In *Look Homeward, Angel*, North Carolina and the South are spat upon." [15] And so on.

The onslaught also came from the other end of the spectrum sometimes—from Southern reformers who could not understand the kind of literary imagination that seeks to explore inwardly in-

14. Blotner, *Faulkner*, I, 811.

15. Daniels quoted in Elizabeth Nowell, *Thomas Wolfe: A Biography* (Garden City, N.Y.: Doubleday and Co., 1960), 151.

stead of taking to the pulpit to preach, as witness Lillian Smith's frequent slaps at Faulkner because he wouldn't produce well-intentioned, easily digested propaganda for racial justice such as her own *Strange Fruit*.

No doubt the speculation and theorizing on just why an outpouring of important literature in the South appeared when it did and in the forms it took will go on for some time to come. We are, after all, still arguing about just what was involved, culturally, historically, economically, theologically, in the American Renaissance (to use the customary spelling for that event) of the 1840s and 1850s. Such interpretations are always bound in with the needs, interests, and fashions of the age doing the interpreting, and these are constantly changing. The tendency for dealing with the phenomenon of modern Southern literature in recent years has been to turn from social history and to adopt the methods and the terms of psychoanalysis, with much talk of incest, doubling, repetition, father figures, and the like. I rather admire some of it—psychoanalysis is something I find fascinating—but I confess that I am too much bound in with the historical ordering itself to be able to do much with so conceptualized an approach to what for me is still very much contemporary literature—which may be where the trouble lies. Moreover, psychoanalysis, especially when conducted by English scholars rather than by trained psychoanalysts, can be a rather glib affair sometimes. The basic assumption ususally is that the writer is the neurotic patient, and the novel or poem that patient's daydream. The more imaginative the dream, the more neurotic the dreamer: thus a writer such as Faulkner becomes the South's all-time champion neurotic. What the assumption leaves out is that great art is distinguished by its powers of control and synthesis, of making the disparate and disjointed experience of life into that which is unified and whole: by its shaping form. This is precisely what the neurotic person is *unable* to do. Thus the analogy of writer with patient and work of art with the patient's dream-work is not enough; for if that is the kind of relationship involved, then the writer is also the psychoanalyst interpreting the dream, giving it coherence and pattern. Art is not merely neurosis; it is *wisdom*.

When, therefore, I encounter some of the Jungian, Freudian, and Lacanian readings of Southern literature, I tend to adopt the ap-

51

proach of Quentin Compson—in the historical, though not the geographical, sense. In *Absalom, Absalom!* Quentin keeps correcting the historical details of the Canadian Shreve McCannon's freely imaginative patterning, and finally he tells him that "you can't understand it. You would have to be born there."[16] I find myself in agreement.

No doubt the book that will offer a proper understanding of the relationship of Faulkner and his contemporaries to the South of the early decades of the twentieth century will ultimately emerge, but it would appear that the time is not yet. Yet in one very real sense, I think that William Faulkner himself may already have written that book for us. Each time I read *Absalom, Absalom!* I am more taken with the notion that, whatever his other concerns may have been in it, Faulkner was also writing about the Southern writer of his generation, and that this, in part at least, is what Quentin Compson is doing in that novel.

Faulkner was not an "autobiographical" novelist as the term is commonly used, but it has always seemed to me that Quentin occupied a special place in his imagination, one that went beyond the immediate demands of the stories in which he figures. In his own way Quentin is Faulkner's artist-figure, Southern-style, by which I mean that it is Quentin who most of all possesses the sensibility and the moral and psychological insight necessary to discern and pronounce the meanings of what happens.

Clearly this is why Faulkner resurrected him from his watery fate in *The Sound and the Fury* midway in the process of writing *Absalom, Absalom!* To his editor in New York he wrote that he had decided to use Quentin "because it is just before he is to commit suicide because of his sister [in *The Sound and the Fury*], and I use his bitterness which he has projected on the South in the form of hatred of it and its people to get more out of the story than a historical novel would be. To keep the hoop skirts and plug hats out, you might say."[17] But if that was his intention it changed almost at once, for there seems little bitterness in Quentin's telling of the story. He is

16. Faulkner, *Absalom, Absalom!*, 361.
17. William Faulkner to Harrison Smith, n.d. (probably February, 1934), in Joseph Blotner, ed., *Selected Letters of William Faulkner* (New York: Random House, 1977), 79.

first bored, then fascinated, then appalled, and finally almost overwhelmed, but he is neither cynical nor bitter.

It seems likely that in venturing to write a novel about what goes on in *Absalom, Absalom!*, Faulkner himself felt that simply to do so involved an act of bitterness toward the community, so that he wanted Quentin for his persona. He was, after all, proposing to portray the Old South, the Lost Cause, the institution of antebellum slavery, the planter aristocracy and the like, in ways that were quite unlike, and highly subversive of, the Southern mythos. This was not going to be a treatment of the community's history along the order of *So Red the Rose* (1934), by his fellow Mississippian Stark Young; the evil in Faulkner's novel was not going to be composed entirely of what was imported from outside by the Yankees. It was one thing, perhaps, to write about unpleasant goings-on in the contemporary South, and another to expose the presence of warts and excrescences on the sacred Confederate tradition. The 1930s, after all, were years when Confederate reunions were still being held, when Southern legislators could furiously assail the United States Post Office Department for daring to portray the visage of General William Tecumseh Sherman upon a stamp to be sold in Southern post offices, and the United Daughters of the Confederacy met regularly. The extent to which the treatment of race and racism in *Absalom, Absalom!* was heretical when it appeared is not often remembered today.

The bitterness that was being projected, therefore, and that needed Quentin Compson for its spokesman, consisted of looking at the legend of the Old South critically, and of daring to do so in print, in public. So Faulkner chose Quentin Compson, because Quentin embodied that aspect of his own imagination that could look at slavery, racism, noblesse oblige, the Confederate cause, the ambition of a poor white to become a planter, the class structure, openly and honestly. Yet at the same time it was not going to be an exposé, a naturalistic depiction of man at his least common denominator. He wanted the kind of sensibility that could recognize the heroism as well as the ruthlessness and callousness of a Thomas Sutpen, identify the pathos and agony of those caught in the toils of history, recoil at the violations of humanity, comprehend the historical plight of a Henry Sutpen.

We can get an idea of the process that led to Quentin's being chosen to tell the story if we look at the two short stories from which

53

the novel evolved: "Evangeline," written in 1931 and published for the first time in Joseph Blotner's edition of the *Uncollected Stories,* and "Wash," written somewhat later and first published in *Harper's* in 1934.[18] "Evangeline" is built around the story of Charles Bon and Henry and Judith Sutpen; it is told by a newspaperman and an architect-painter. It has little or nothing of the resonance of *Absalom, Absalom!* Thomas Sutpen is barely involved at all. Henry acts to slay Bon entirely out of his fear of miscegenation. "Wash" involves Thomas Sutpen's fathering of a child upon Wash Jones's granddaughter. The lowly Wash Jones's outrage at being used and then betrayed by the lordly Confederate colonel is what gives the story its direction and meaning. Unlike "Evangeline," it is told by an omniscient author.

54

To develop the story of Charles Bon and Henry and Judith Sutpen so that its full emotional and moral dimensions could be realized, however, Faulkner needed a narrator capable of exploring those dimensions and of articulating his findings. Moreover, he should be someone familiar with the local terrain and with a strong emotional stake in the history of the community over the generations. An outsider in search of a newspaper feature would hardly do. Otherwise the symbolic meanings of the racial theme for the history of the community and its people could not be developed; it would remain a melodramatic horror story about miscegenation. And to unite that theme with one involving the catastrophic impact of a stong-willed, ruthless man of lowly origins, ambitious to establish a plantation dynasty, upon the lives and fortunes of those who came into his orbit, the narrator must be someone who was very decidedly unlike that man, in no way selfish or ruthless or insensitive, but if anything hypersensitive to cruelty. What more appropriate choice for that narrator than Quentin Compson, bookish, of poetic temperament, vulnerable, of the fifth generation of a once distinguished family now fallen upon evil days, whose own ineffectiveness and inability to act boldly and decisively could contrast so

18. See Joseph Blotner, ed., *Uncollected Stories of William Faulkner* (New York: Random House, 1979), 583–609, 709n. "Wash" is included in *The Faulkner Reader: Selections from the Work of William Faulkner* (New York: Random House, 1954), 603–14.

strikingly with the arrogant, unthinking assertion of will that characterized the behavior of the story's central figure? A well-intentioned but weak young aristocrat to relate and to speculate upon the meaning of the story of a powerful, self-centered, supremely self-confident plebeian striving for status: what better way to articulate the meaning of the story of Thomas Sutpen and his descendants?

But again, there is more to it than that. There would also be needed a voice—and a way of seeing—that was clearly modern and a bit cynical and hardboiled, to protect against the almost unbearable intensity of some of the material and for purposes of narrative counterpoint. The newspaperman had furnished that voice in "Evangeline," in order to save that story from becoming too melodramatic even to be believable. Now, whatever the Quentin of *The Sound and the Fury* was, he was not hardboiled and cynical (melancholy, even when verging upon hopelessness, is not the same as cynicism).

What Faulkner did, therefore, was to divide Quentin's sensibility into two viewpoints, two ways of thinking and feeling. Sitting in the office of Miss Rosa Coldfield's home and listening to her telling her story, he became two Quentins—or rather, he identified *within himself* two different modes of response to his own experience:

> Then hearing would reconcile and he would seem to listen to two separate Quentins now—the Quentin Compson preparing for Harvard in the South, the deep South dead since 1865 and peopled with garrulous outraged baffled ghosts, listening, having to listen, to one of the ghosts who had refused to lie still even longer than most had, telling him about old ghost-times; and the Quentin Compson who was still too young to deserve yet to be a ghost, but nevertheless having to be one for all that, since he was born and bred in the deep South the same as she was—the two separate Quentins now talking to one another in the long silence of notpeople, in notlanguage.[19]

At the outset, therefore, as Quentin begins to tell his story, he becomes in effect the Southern writer, deeply involved in his material

19. Faulkner, *Absalom, Absalom!*, 9.

by virtue of his membership in the community, yet sufficiently detached from it to view it objectively both as a story and in terms of its moral and historical meanings. He is the citizen who shares the pieties, loyalties, and concerns of the historical time and place, and he is the modern who distances himself from the rhetorical responses and unexamined assumptions in order to explore and understand his own relationship to them. Obviously Faulkner recognized what he had arrived at, for the very next thing that Quentin hears Miss Rosa Coldfield saying makes the precise connection: "'Because you are going away to attend the college at Harvard they tell me,' Miss Coldfield said. 'So I don't imagine you will ever come back here and settle down as a country lawyer in a little town like Jefferson, since Northern people have already seen to it that there is little left in the South for a young man. So maybe you will enter the literary profession as so many Southern gentlemen and gentlewomen too are doing now and maybe some day you will remember this and write about it.'"[20]

56

Surely Lewis P. Simpson is correct when he declares of Faulkner that "once he looked through Quentin's eyes at Sam Fathers distanced in the mythic twilight [in the story entitled "A Justice"] and moved with Quentin's mind toward the day when he would pass from the ahistorical childhood vision of the old people into the knowledge of modernity, Faulkner discovered in Quentin the first profound portrayal of his own imagination—a fiction yet a symbol of a deep inner reality, a powerful apprehension of modern existence."[21] In being made to confront not merely the past but its impact upon and meaning for the present, Quentin is the Southern writer of Faulkner's generation. In Thadious Davis' words, "Quentin's major activity is imagining a world as real as his twentieth-century one." His division into the two Quentins, Professor Davis declares, "symbolizes the unresolved tensions of his existence as Southerner."[22]

20. Ibid., 9–10.
21. Lewis P. Simpson, "Faulkner and the Legend of the Artist," in *Faulkner: Fifty Years After "The Marble Faun,"* ed. Wolfe, 96–97.
22. Thadious M. Davis, "'Be Sutpen's Hundred!': Imaginative Projection of Landscape in *Absalom, Absalom!," Southern Literary Journal,* XIII (Spring, 1981) 7, 8.

As he moves toward his perception of the full implications of what Thomas Sutpen and his quest for dynasty mean, he becomes so deeply involved in the tale that someone else is needed to ask the questions and to collaborate with the answers. So Shreve McCannon comes into the narrative. Yet it is still, ultimately, Quentin's vision; it is the young Southerner who will someday enter the literary profession who hears what Shreve and himself are formulating, just as earlier on he recognized the modern and the ghost Quentins registering the significance of what Miss Rosa Coldfield's voice was saying. Throughout the narrative everything dissolves into Quentin's perceptions; even the language that the historical participants speak keeps turning into the language of Quentin's consciousness.   57

How fitting it is, then, that at the very end, Faulkner has Shreve McCannon ask Quentin the question he does: "Why do you hate the South?" It is not only a question that a disinterested outsider might ask, but also one that the Southern community itself would propose, in its puzzlement as to why this young man, of good family, brought up with all the proper schooling in the Southern mythos, should nevertheless insist upon telling a story so critical of that mythos. To which Quentin replies, quickly, at once, immediately, "I dont hate it":

> "I dont hate it," he said. *I dont hate it* he thought, panting in the cold air, the iron New England dark; *I dont. I dont! I dont hate it! I dont hate it!*[23]

As indeed he does not. What he hates is the injustice, the cruelty, the smugness, not because he is an outsider, and detached from it, but because he is *not*. It is *his* community, *his* country, and in denouncing its flaws and its sins he is simultaneously revealing the intensity of his affection, his love for it. As Faulkner himself wrote of his relationship to his native state: "Loving all of it even while he had to hate some of it because he knows now that you don't love because: you love despite; not for the virtues, but despite the faults."[24]

---

23. Faulkner, *Absalom, Absalom!*, 378.

24. William Faulkner, "Mississippi," in *Essays, Speeches, and Public Letters,* ed. Meriwether, 42–43.

The love-hate relationship—hating because one loves, loving despite the faults—between Quentin Compson and Yoknapatawpha County comes deeply out of William Faulkner's situation, and it mirrors that of the modern Southern writer and the South. It is personal, inward, and it is given public literary form out of the need of the men and women of Faulkner's literary generation to understand themselves. Language art was for them a way of knowing. A writer *tells* in order to *know*. And what the writer knows is discovered from within. Perhaps another Mississippi writer has expressed it best. She is ostensibly writing about photographs: "We come to terms as well as we can with our lifelong exposure to the world, and we use whatever devices we may need to survive. But eventually, of course, our knowledge depends upon the living relationship between what we see going on and ourselves. If exposure is essential, still more so is the reflection."[25]

58

I want to close this discussion of Faulkner and the Southern Literary Renascence by making one other point, which I think needs to be made nowadays as much as ever.

Quentin Compson is Faulkner's premier artist-figure, perhaps, but he is not the only one. Another is Isaac McCaslin in *Go Down, Moses*. In "The Bear," as is well known, Ike McCaslin decides, on the basis of what he has learned about man, nature, and God from Sam Fathers, to decline his patrimony because only in that way can he end his complicity in the racial evil that made it possible. In the same episode, when asked by his cousin McCaslin Edmonds why he had failed to take a shot at the bear named Old Ben when he was very close to him, Ike hesitates, and McCaslin provides the answer by reading some lines from Keats's "Ode on a Grecian Urn":

> 'She cannot fade, though thou hast not thy bliss,' McCaslin said:
> 'Forever wilt thou love, and she be fair.'
> 'He's talking about a girl,' he said.
> 'He had to talk about something,' McCaslin said. Then he said, 'He was talking about truth. Truth is one. It doesn't change.

25. Eudora Welty, "One Time, One Place," in Welty, *The Eye of the Story: Selected Essays and Reviews* (New York: Random House, 1977), 354.

It covers all things which touch the heart—honor and pride and pity and justice and courage and love. Do you see now?[26]

The dubious wisdom of Ike McCaslin's renunciation of his patrimony has been noted by numerous commentators, even as McCaslin Edmonds himself doubted it, and Lucas Beauchamp as well. In declining to own property tainted by his grandfather's inhumanity, Ike gains the personal comfort of a clean conscience in exchange for the ability to rectify future injustice, as we learn in the story entitled "Delta Autumn." He also gives up his hope for a family and posterity, for his wife will have none of a husband who declines to insure the material welfare of his family within the community which she and any offspring will inhabit. Ike McCaslin's decision may be seen as personally admirable, and in motivation even heroic in its way, but it is also a retreat from involvement in the world, an abnegation of responsibility, and a refusal to take such part as he might in any continuing effort for human betterment in a flawed time and place.

Not very much attention has been paid to the relationship between Ike's decision to give up his patrimony and his disinclination to shoot the bear, together with McCaslin's explanation for it, even though the two episodes appear almost side by side in the fourth section of "The Bear." Ike doesn't want Old Ben to die because he doesn't want the wilderness that the huge bear symbolizes to disappear. He wants the thrill of the chase without the finality of the kill. He wants, in short, immunity from all time and change. And this, as McCaslin Edmonds quite rightly indicates by quoting from Keats's poem, is possible only in art, not in life. The only way to arrest action in time and fix it so that it is impervious to change is to convert it into artistic form, whether in ceramics like the urn or in language, as Keats did in his poem and Faulkner also did in his story about the running and baying of Old Ben: "It fell just once. For an instant they almost resembled a piece of statuary: the clinging dog, the bear, the man astride its back, working and probing the buried

59

26. William Faulkner, "The Bear," in Faulkner, *Go Down, Moses* (New York: Random House, 1942), 297.

blade. Then they went down."[27] In sensibility and in wish Ike is not the hunter, but the artist. But a bear hunt is a human action in time, not a work of art. Ike may wish the chase to go on forever, but Sam Fathers knows better, and so do all those who have come to hunt the bear, and who are actively engaged in an event in time, not in an act of aesthetic contemplation. And if art is ultimately moral—"He was talking about truth"—then Isaac McCaslin's attempt to abdicate future responsibility for his patrimony, to get free of participation in history, is doomed to failure because of the fatal confusion, within Ike's sensibility, of what is possible to art and to life. The ideal exoneration from history for which he yearns can never be accomplished in life, through action, because it requires what is by definition *non*-life: freedom from involvement in time. Just as by its very nature the annual running of the bear cannot continue forever, so the escape from complicity in evil, past, present, and future, the attainment of a perfection of motive and action, is beyond the capacities even of a man named Isaac McCaslin.

The point is that Ike may be confused about what is possible in life and in art, but Faulkner is not confused. The sight of bear, man, and dog locked in the embrace of the kill *almost* resembles a statue for the young Ike McCaslin; it is not a statue. But to us, as readers of the episode, it *is* free of time and change, for we are not participating in a hunt but viewing a work of literary art.

I go into this because it is becoming fashionable to criticize William Faulkner, in common with many of his fellow Southern writers of the 1920s, 1930s, and 1940s, for the supposed failure of his fiction to take a properly activist role in the struggle for racial equality in the South. Some very sophisticated and intelligent critics have made this charge, and among them must be numbered Richard King in his stimulating and informative study *A Southern Renaissance* (1980). King doesn't fault Faulkner's intentions, but he sees his actual performance as leaving much to be desired. Discussing Isaac McCaslin's renunciation of his property, King declares that Ike "lacks a way of translating this new mythos" of racial justice "into a collective historical tradition to replace that of his grandfather, that is, the South's." Identifying Ike's views with Faulkner's,

27. *Ibid.*, 241.

he concludes that "it was the tragic fact of Faulkner's (and Ike's) world that historical consciousness and refusal to participate in the skein of injustice did not of itself lead to or suggest a way of translating moral gesture into political action." [28]

What King is doing, I am afraid, is to make precisely the same kind of error that Isaac McCaslin made, and which Faulkner portrayed him as making. In demanding that Faulkner's presentation of his community's heritage of racial injustice "lead to or suggest a way of translating moral gesture into political action," he is asking that literature become, in effect, the agency of action. But the novelist's responsibility to truth is through and in art; and the morality, racial or otherwise, of a work of fiction must lie not in a prescription for action but in its exploration, in language, of the human experience it recreates. To paraphrase something that Faulkner told Malcolm Cowley about *Absalom, Absalom!*, "I think [Isaac], not Faulkner, is the correct yardstick here. I am writing the story, but he not I was brooding over a situation." [29] Ike McCaslin's solution to the laying down of the racial burden, by way of renunciation, may have been personal and private, achieved at the price of its translation into future action, but William Faulkner's solution was artistic and public, and therefore capable of being read and having its meanings understood by others.

61

For literature *is* "moral gesture," not "political action"—a way of seeing and knowing in language. Faulkner's responsibility to truth, his commitment to action, was to the act of seeing, and thus making it possible for us to see. As Eudora Welty put it, "What is written in the South from now on is going to be taken into account by Faulkner's work; I mean the remark literally. Once Faulkner had written, we could never unknow what he told us and showed us. And his work will do the same thing tomorrow. We inherit from him, while we can get fresh and firsthand news of ourselves from his work at any time." [30]

28. Richard H. King, *A Southern Renaissance: The Cultural Awakening of the American South, 1930–1955* (New York: Oxford University Press, 1980), 139.

29. Faulkner quoted in Malcolm Cowley, *The Faulkner-Cowley File: Letters and Memories, 1944–1962* (New York, Viking Press, 1966), 15.

30. Eudora Welty, "Must the Novelist Crusade?" in Welty, *Eye of the Story*, 158.

King declares that "aside from Lillian Smith and W. J. Cash, it would be difficult to find a Southern writer, sociologist, or historian of Faulkner's era who so clearly identified and critiqued the essential foundations of the Southern tradition."[31] But if Faulkner "identified and critiqued" Southern racial injustice, he did so in a crucially different way than the authors of *Strange Fruit* and *The Mind of the South* did: he made it into a magnificent work of art. In Miss Welty's words, "the novelist works neither to correct nor to condone, not at all to comfort, but to make what's told alive."[32] That is why Miss Smith's *Strange Fruit* is all but forgotten as a work of art, and survives only for its value as an already-outdated document in American social history, along with *The Clansman* and *Freedom Road*. But *Absalom, Absalom!* and *Go Down, Moses* speak to us as clearly nowadays as on the day they were first published. They remain more powerful, wiser, more effective indictments of racial inhumanity *because* they are achieved works of literary art.

It is the accomplishment of William Faulkner and his fellow novelists and poets of the modern South to have given us an enduring set of artistic images of their time and place. Writing about themselves as human beings, they wrote about themselves as Southerners. Writing about men and women alive in history, they wrote about the community of people they knew and the history they shared with them. Because they wrote in order to know, we can know what they wrote. What we choose to make of it is none of their concern any longer. But we will ignore it at our own risk. In Flannery O'Connor's terms, nobody wants to get caught on the tracks when the Dixie Special comes through.

31. King, *Southern Renaissance*, 139.
32. Welty, "Must the Novelist Crusade?" 152.

THE HIGH SHERIFF OF YOKNAPATAWPHA COUNTY
A STUDY IN THE GENIUS OF PLACE

(1990)

Critics of literature have never been especially comfortable with the term *genius*—and for good reason. Too often it is used as a substitute for the kind of rigorous reading of works of fiction and poetry that can enable us to recognize and understand the dynamics of those works. There is the tendency, when a literary artist is described as having "genius," to stop right there and simply marvel at what has been written, as if all bets were thereby cancelled and any effort at intelligent examination of what is actually going on in a story or poem would be irrelevant.

Yet what other term can better describe the literary phenomenon that was William Faulkner?

From his early years onward, William Faulkner was convinced that his was not merely talent but genius. He happened to be quite right, but many years were to pass before anybody else, except perhaps his friend Phil Stone, was ready to concede that he was what he purported to be. Thus, in order to enforce upon his family and fellow townsfolk the notion that he was unique and special—and perhaps to reassure himself as well—he adopted a variety of disguises and poses, some of which later became a source of embarrassment to him. As is well known, the citizenry of Oxford took to calling him "Count No-Count" because of what they considered his uppity ways and his affectation of being superior to the ordinary customs and pursuits of his community, with so little in the way of worldly achievement to justify it. When fiction began appearing under his name in the *Saturday Evening Post,* which was the nation's most prestigious mass-circulation magazine, those Oxfordians who did much reading at last saw evidence that something might be said for William Faulkner's lofty estimate of himself after all. But my guess is that it was not until the movie of *Intruder in the Dust* actually began to be filmed in Oxford by MGM, and Hollywood actors, cameramen, and technicians showed up on the Square, that it finally became evident to the rank and file of his fellow citizenry that, as they would probably have put it, Bill Faulkner had a right to think he was something special.

64

My dictionary—the Merriam-Webster *New International,* Second Edition, 1952—offers several definitions for *genius.* The word is derived from the Latin, "tutelar deity or genius of a person or place, taste, talent, genius," from "*genere, gignare,* to beget, bring forth." In Roman religious usage, a genius was the "attendant godling or spirit of a person or place; tutelar deity. Primarily, the genius is the protecting companion, almost the fortune, of the man with whom it is born and dies." Another definition of the word is "extraordinary mental superiority; esp. unusual power of invention or origination of any kind; as, a man of *genius.*" This latter usage is illustrated with a quotation from James Russell Lowell: "Talent is that power which is in a man's power; *genius* is that in whose power a man is." The description of this particular way of defining the word concludes, "Also, a man endowed with transcendent ability; as, Milton was a rare *genius.*"

It is obvious, from such description, that there is an association of the word with the supernatural, which by definition would make it beyond human explanation and understanding. Lowell's distinction between genius and talent, with the suggestion that a man's genius controls him, whereas a man's talent is under his control, verges on this notion, for a power that can dictate the behavior of someone beyond his capacity to do anything whatever about it must surely come from outside—though whether from above or below is another matter. Another way to put it might be to say that a man possesses talent, but is possessed by genius, in the same way that we used to believe that people could be possessed by demons, spirits, and the like.

Presumably this notion is related to the Greek myth of the nine Muses, originally nymphs or mountain goddesses fathered by Zeus, and later domesticated on Mount Helicon, where they presided over the fine arts. The Christian writer Boethius denounced them as lascivious and immoral creatures who took possession of men's souls and diverted them from the exercise of reason. Moreover, the idea that a genius is "endowed with transcendent ability" suggests a quality of an extrahuman kind, or as Immanuel Kant would have it, something that is *a priori*—a given condition or boundary of human experience, so therefore beyond analysis. In theology, God is prior to and above the universe, existing apart from what is mortal and material.

65

Nowadays we are not so ready to view such problems theologically. We tend to regard someone not as possessed, but as driven—by unconscious compulsions that are seemingly irrational. The kind of power that Lowell described as possessing a man is seen as the result of psychological forces, and behavior that is uncontrollable is believed to be the product of mental illness—insanity, psychosis, madness. Such compulsion is no longer thought of as lunacy—that is, affected by the baleful influence of the moon—but as caused either by one's own psychological endowment or else by external, environmental factors: family, community, occupation, politics, and so on. And from Plato onward, there is a formidable tradition of viewing literary creativity as a species of insanity, whether temporary or permanent. "The lunatic, the lover, and the poet," Shakespeare deposed, thereby grouping three examples of persons whose behavior defied rational explanation.

In Faulkner's later years, when his literary performance had fallen off somewhat—though second-rate Faulkner was still better fiction than most writers' best—he must have looked back to the period from 1929 through the late 1930s, when he was writing most of his finest work, with a feeling almost of awe. Indeed he said as much to a young friend, Joan Williams, in 1953: "And now I realize for the first time what an amazing gift I had: uneducated in every formal sense, without even very literate, let alone literary, companions, yet to have made the thing I made. I dont know where it came from. I dont know why God or gods or whoever it was, selected me to be the vessel. Believe me, this is not humility, false modesty: it is simply amazement. I wonder if you have ever had that thought about the work and the country man whom you know as Bill Faulkner— what little connection there seems to be between them."[1]

I find the terms Faulkner used fascinating: "why God or gods or whoever it was, selected me to be the vessel." He makes an almost total separation between his everyday self and the person who wrote the books. It is as if he subscribed to the "tutelary deity" notions of the Romans, and believed that the literary creativity that had brought the novels into existence had been the work of a kind of separate being that had taken possession of him and had guided his imagination. This is what the Greeks meant in their notion of a "muse"—an inspiring goddess of art. There is also the image of being selected to bear the sacred message as if it were wine in a goblet, as when in Acts 9 : 15 God informs Ananias that the hitherto-hostile Saul of Tarsus is His chosen vessel for promulgating His doctrines.

It was at about this time, too, in 1953, that Faulkner wrote the piece about his friendship with Sherwood Anderson back in the mid-1920s, with its striking conclusion. Meeting Anderson in New York after several years' estrangement, he said, "again was that moment when he appeared taller, bigger than anything he ever wrote. Then I remembered *Winesburg, Ohio* and *The Triumph of the Egg* and some of the pieces in *Horses and Men,* and I knew that I had seen, was looking at, a giant in an earth populated to a great—too great—extent by pygmies, even if he did make but the two or perhaps three gestures commensurate with gianthood."[2]

The implication is that even though Anderson produced comparatively little work that was of major stature, what distinguished him from the rank and file of journeymen writers was the presence within him of the same kind of "amazing gift" that Faulkner himself possessed, and that made both of them, because of the nature of

1. William Faulkner to Joan Williams, n.d. (probably April 29, 1934), in Joseph Blotner, *Faulkner: A Biography* (2 vols.; New York: Random House, 1974), II, 1457.
2. William Faulkner, "A Note on Sherwood Anderson," in *Essays, Speeches, and Public Letters by William Faulkner,* ed. James B. Meriwether (New York: Random House, 1965), 10.

their imaginations, giants among ordinary mortals in their ability to create works of art out of language.

Faulkner also declared that as an artist Anderson had neither the "power and rush" of Melville, nor the "lusty humor for living" of Mark Twain. Nor did he exhibit "that heavy-handed disregard for nuances" of Theodore Dreiser. What Anderson had was "that fumbling for exactitude, the exact word and phrase within the limited scope of a vocabulary controlled and even repressed by what was in him almost a fetish of simplicity, to milk them both dry, to seek always to penetrate to thought's uttermost end." Disregarding for now the suggestions there for what Faulkner thought about the nature of his own particular artistic gift, we might note that what is implied is that Anderson's genius compelled him to strive for a clarity and simplicity of utterance beyond that of popular discourse. Anderson came to his art, Faulkner said, with a "humility and an almost religious, almost abject faith and patience and willingness to surrender, relinquish himself to and into it." Here again is the notion that true genius takes possession of its bearer, causing him to give his life over to his art with a dedication, a consecration even, beyond that of normal human experience. Just as Faulkner spoke of himself as having been "selected" to be the "vessel" whereby his stories were created, so Sherwood Anderson is one "whom the vocation of art elected and chose to be faithful to it." [3] It is something like the youthful narrator of James Joyce's story "Araby," who sees himself as bearing his chalice safely through a swarm of foes, even though at that juncture he is not yet the "priest of eternal imagination" that he will later proclaim himself in *A Portrait of the Artist as a Young Man* after rejecting the Jesuit ministry for the vocation of artist. [4]

67

II

When Faulkner, writing to Joan Williams, distinguished between "the country man whom you know as Bill Faulkner" and the author

3. *Ibid.*, 5, 7, 9.
4. James Joyce, "Araby," in Joyce, *Dubliners* (New York: Modern Library, n.d.), 6; James Joyce, *A Portrait of the Artist as a Young Man: Text, Criticism, and Notes,* ed. Chester G. Anderson (New York: Viking, 1968), 221.

who had created his novels, he implied that he did not understand the source of the "amazing gift" that made the fiction possible. He stressed the fact that the milieu in which he had grown up had not been "literary," and that his formal schooling had not been of a kind that is customarily undergone by literary people. Yet he was careful to make such reference only to his *formal* education—for he grew up in a Southern university town and his acquaintance included persons of considerable learning, notably Phil Stone, who came back home from Yale to practice law in Oxford, Mississippi, loaded with books of poetry and filled with enthusiasm for what was being written and talked about in contemporary literary circles. His friendship with Stone, which the latter described accurately as a tutelage, as well as with the author and dramatic critic Stark Young, was scarcely the customary intellectual fare for a small Southern community.

Such involvement with contemporary literature and ideas certainly had the effect of helping to confirm the young Faulkner's distance from the everyday concerns of his family and community. But before writing off Faulkner's artistic inclinations as alien to the everyday life of early modern Mississippi, it is well to keep in mind that the literary history of the twentieth-century South is made up to an inordinate degree of writers who likewise grew to maturity in Faulkner's own native state before, during, and after his time—including not only Stark Young but also William Alexander Percy, Maxwell Bodenheim, James Street, Eudora Welty, Hubert Creekmore, Tennessee Williams, Richard Wright, Elizabeth Spencer, Shelby Foote, Walker Percy, Ellen Douglas, and so on into our own day. Moreover, Faulkner was not without an example of the literary life to emulate in his own family—his great-grandfather William C. Falkner, who between railroad building, politicking, war, and several blood feuds wrote and published books of fiction and nonfiction, including at least one novel, *The White Rose of Memphis*, that was widely popular in its day.

It will be recalled that the classical origins of the word *genius* involved a close association with a particular locale; the tutelary deity might inhabit either a person or a place. The literary imagination of William Faulkner was deeply anchored in what he liked to call his little postage-stamp's worth of Mississippi soil. His fellow Mississippian Eudora Welty has written eloquently about the essential role of place in fiction—one of the lesser deities, she calls it, that preside over literary creativity. And surely, observing that distinguished array of Mississippi authors, anyone would have to conclude that the locale must have been involved in the literary situation that evoked the writings of Faulkner, Welty, and the others.

The similarity between the Southern circumstance in the early decades of this century and that of Ireland toward the close of the previous century has been remarked by Cleanth Brooks, who in comparing Faulkner and William Butler Yeats notes the importance, in the social and political background of both writers, of a provincial society, a strong folk element, a powerful religious presence, a rural and small-town environment with a certain level of violence and a stress upon manners, a heritage of defeat in war, economic stagnation, a colonial economy, a pantheon of heroes and a palpable mythology, and in both writers and their cultures the confrontation of all these elements with the oncoming modern urban-industrial juggernaut of nineteenth- and twentieth-century Western society.[5]

In a comment, cited earlier, from an introduction prepared for a hoped-for reissue of *The Sound and the Fury* in 1933 but not published during his lifetime, Faulkner had some pronouncements to make about the artist in the South. Unlike the situation in New York or Chicago, he declared, there was no place for art in Southern life. In the sense of being any kind of live, imaginative entity, the South, he said, died with the Civil War; what has been happening in the region since then is the work of outsiders trying to remake it in the image of the Midwest. The would-be Southern writer must choose between being an artist and being a man—between, that is, either living through and in his art, or else functioning as part of the community; and if he chooses art, which has no existence in Southern life, he must give it existence within himself: "It is his breath, blood, flesh, all." Thus the Southern writer is writing about himself, "not about his environment: who has, figuratively speaking, taken the artist in him with one hand his milieu in the other and thrust the

5. Cleanth Brooks, "Faulkner and W. B. Yeats," in *William Faulkner: Toward Yoknapatawpha and Beyond* (New Haven: Yale University Press, 1978), 329–44.

one into the other like a clawing and spitting cat into a croker sack. And he writes."[6]

Faulkner sees the Southern writer as electing either of two alternatives. One is to write "a savage indictment of the contemporary scene"—I assume he had in mind Thomas Wolfe, T. S. Stribling, or Erskine Caldwell, all three of whom were widely read just then. The other is to withdraw "into a makebelieve region of swords and magnolias and mockingbirds which perhaps never existed anywhere"—along the lines, perhaps, of Stark Young, who wrote a very popular novel entitled *Swords and Roses,* or any of a number of lesser chroniclers of plantation glories before the War.[7]

70

Both courses of action, Faulkner declared, were sentimental, and were manifestations "of violent partisanship, in which the writer unconsciously writes into every line and phrase his violent despairs and rages and frustrations or his violent prophesies of still more violent hopes." Neither alternative is the product of detachment and calm objectivity: "I do not believe there lives the Southern writer who can say without lying that writing is any fun to him. Perhaps we do not want it to be."[8]

As Faulkner saw it, then, the Southern writer may use his art in order to attack his community, or else as a means of escaping from it. Both responses appear to involve the element of compulsion; the fiction is written in response to the felt presence of the community. To write is to enter into a kind of dialectical relationship, in which the writer's status as a member of the Southern community forces him into violent struggle with his status as artist. In his Nobel Prize address Faulkner used almost the same image to describe what writers do; he referred to "the problems of the human heart in conflict with itself which alone can make good writing because only that is worth writing about, worth the agony and the sweat."[9]

So the force of the "tutelary deity" that possessed Faulkner and made him its chosen vessel for creating fiction would appear to have taken the form of a quality inherent in his community situation, and

6. William Faulkner, "An Introduction to *The Sound and the Fury,*" ed. James B. Meriwether, *Mississippi Quarterly,* XXVI (Summer, 1973), 411.

7. *Ibid.,* 412.

8. *Ibid.*

9. "Address upon Receiving the Nobel Prize for Literature," in *Essays, Speeches, and Public Letters,* ed. Meriwether, 119.

that propelled him into conflict with that aspect of his own identity involving his role as a citizen of his community. "*I dont hate it!*," as Quentin Compson furiously insists to himself at the close of *Absalom, Absalom!*[10] And the Faulkner who wrote an essay on the state of Mississippi for *Holiday* magazine some years after composing that novel spoke of himself as "loving all of it even while he had to hate some of it because he knows now that you dont love because: you love despite; not for the virtues, but despite the faults."[11] To be a Southern writer, therefore, is to be caught up in a love-hate relationship with the Southern community of which the writer is a citizen, and be driven to create works of literary art in reponse to the ways of that community.

71

Most people who inhabit a community, of course, do not write novels about it. And just as obviously, most of those who *do* write novels can scarcely be described as being possessed by anything having to do with genius, whether tutelary or otherwise. The genius would seem to manifest itself in the *quality* of the response. At first glance Faulkner might seem to be suggesting, in his comments on the Southern writer's relationship to the Southern community, that it is the intensity of the quarrel that accounts for the success of the art, or lack of it. If so, that formulation can hardly stand up to much examination, for surely the degree of violence characterizing any such love-hate relationship that an individual might have with the community cannot of itself ensure artistic achievement, even if the individual happens to be a writer. Clearly it is not the intensity of the conflict itself, but the intensity with which the conflict is recreated through being given shape in language, that accounts for the literary achievement. The ability to make the "sound and fury" signify something, one might say, the degree to which the writer can give form and meaning "in every line and phrase" to "his violent despairs and rages and frustrations or his violent prophesies of still more violent hopes," is what matters from an artistic standpoint. It is there, we may say, that the "genius" comes in: in the ability to make sense of the intense literary response to the time and place, as these interact with and against the personality of the writer.

10. William Faulkner, *Absalom, Absalom!* (New York: Random House, 1936), 378.

11. William Faulkner, "Mississippi," in *Essays, Speeches, and Public Letters*, ed. Meriwether, 42–43.

But let us make it clear what is involved, or rather what is *not* involved, when we talk about a novelist making "sense" of his experience. It used to be that we looked principally to philosophers and clergymen for such things as "sense" and "meaning"; nowadays we look to physical scientists and occasionally to social scientists. To the extent that one can predict the mutations of the stock market, analyze and enunciate the causes of physical or mental distress, diagnose and repair an automobile engine, prescribe the proper course of action to be followed during a football game or a military campaign, or fathom and make use of the needs of the electorate, one is said to possess knowledge, and to be wise, at least within one's own area of expertise. Plato's ideal was the philosopher-king, who governed because he was wisest as well as kingliest. We equate "sense" and "meaning" with abstract truth; the wise person is one who can discern and enunciate the universal principles, whether of matter or of the mind, that lie behind the surface particulars and individual instances.

Now, what room is there for a novelist or a poet in that concept of what wisdom is? As noted earlier, there is a long tradition, extending at least as far back as Plato, of the poet being thought mad, and his art the product of inspired raving. (There were no novelists around at the time, but I believe that Plato would gladly have included them in his indictment if he had only known about them.) Of course we have all heard the equivalent of Emily Dickinson's "much madness is divinest sense." Is this how we should consider an author like Faulkner as being involved in the wisdom business? Do we assume that the truths of "the human heart in conflict with itself" came to him through a kind of godlike frenzy?

On the relatively few occasions when Faulkner indulged himself in any kind of commentary on current events, he did not demonstrate extraordinary insight or startling sagacity. His public statements are not exceptional either in their content or their phraseology. They are for the most part sensible, appropriate, but not in their own right unusual or compelling. Nor was he what is called a "philosophical novelist," which is to say, a novelist such as Proust or Conrad or Walker Percy, the documentation of whose fictional world, as Robert Penn Warren (no slouch with an idea himself) wrote of Conrad, strives constantly to rise to the status of commentary on that world, and "for whom images always fall into a dialectical configuration, for whom the urgency of experience, no matter how vividly and strongly experience may enchant, is the urgency to know the meaning of experience." [12]

The ideas implicit in Faulkner's fiction can be gotten at through a process of induction, but there is almost never the sense that the fiction has been shaped importantly to assert or even to illustrate the ideas. Moreover, if we do isolate and identify such ideas, they will tend to seem fairly elemental and even obvious, in the line of truisms about human nature. In his Nobel Prize acceptance speech Faulkner spoke of the need for the novelist to allow "no room in his workshop for anything but the old verities and truths of the heart, the old universal truths lacking which any story is ephemeral and doomed—love and honor and pity and pride and compassion and sacrifice." [13] That is not exactly a call for the novelist to become involved in the intricacies and subtleties of philosophical inquiry.

73

Faulkner considered himself to be, first and last, a storyteller, a maker of tales. He did not even like to think of himself as an intellectual, and was notably uncomfortable in the company of other writers. His comment about the French as being too prone to allow ideas to take precedence over life itself is indicative of his attitude toward excessive intellectual formulation. To an extent this stance represented a kind of defensive posture, of course; *he* wasn't an intellectual, but a countryman, a farmer— just a plain old Mississippi boy who happened to write *The Sound and the Fury*. The reasons for this stance have been discussed elsewhere, and have to do with precisely that Southern community identity that he said he found so antithetical to the role of artist, so that being a Southern writer figuratively involved the equivalent of thrusting a snarling cat into a croker sack. Suffice it to say that it was important to the way that Faulkner thought about himself that he not appear to be cut off from the everyday customs and attitudes of the people of Oxford, Mississippi.

He was a writer of fiction who thought about his craft in terms of plots, dialogue, scenes. He published numerous stories in that quintessentially middle-class popular magazine of his day, the *Saturday*

---

12. Robert Penn Warren, "The Great Mirage: Conrad and *Nostromo*," in Warren, *Selected Essays* (New York: Random House, 1958), 58.

13. Faulkner, "Address upon Receiving the Nobel Prize," 120.

Evening Post. He enjoyed reading detective stories, and wrote some of his own in order to make money. For some years he supported himself and his family by working on movie scripts in Hollywood; the noted director Howard Hawks said that he was especially good as a troubleshooter who could take a key scene that wasn't working and make it work. [14] He was apparently a much better screenwriter than someone like Scott Fitzgerald—in large part, one assumes, because he approached the writing of film scripts solely as a skilled craftsman plying a trade. Where Fitzgerald was obsessed with achieving success and artistic renown in Hollywood, Faulkner was putting in time in order to earn enough money to go home to Mississippi and write fiction. That he made some use of certain cinematic devices in writing his novels, particularly for purposes of comedy, is quite obvious; but it is also obvious that he placed very little stock in the cinema as an art form. There is no indication whatever that when writing for the movies Faulkner was ever caught in the kind of struggle between the demands of the Southern milieu and those of art that he described as the habitual condition of the Southern writer. If any "agony and sweat" were involved, any "violent despairs and rages and frustrations," there is no record of it. Such conflict took place within him only during the writing of his prose fiction.

III

In his never-used introduction to *The Sound and the Fury,* Faulkner said an odd thing. Having declared, as we have seen, that the Southern writer's response to his milieu is either a savage indictment or an escape into a make-believe romantic region, he went on to comment that he himself had tried both approaches, and that when he read *The Sound and the Fury* again, five years after he had written it in 1929, he began to see that in writing that novel, "I seem to have tried both of the courses. I have tried to escape and I have tried to indict." Writing that novel "was the turning point: in this book I did both at one time." [15]

14. Blotner, *Faulkner,* II, 1125.
15. Faulkner, "Introduction to *The Sound and the Fury,*" 412.

We cannot be sure exactly what he meant by this, and he offered no real explanation. We can readily identify the presence within the book of an indictment of the contemporary scene: the decline of the once-proud Compson family; the ineffectuality of the alcoholic father and the vanity and selfishness of the neurasthenic mother; the debased evil of Jason, the "first sane Compson since before Culloden," as Faulkner ironically described him in the 1940s;[16] and above all else, the weakness of Quentin. There is no place in twentieth-century Yoknapatawpha County for anyone of Quentin's sensibility; and the qualities that might in an earlier and less decadent day have been allied with a determined fortitude and the ability to act effectively and decisively upon his beliefs and ideals, have in Quentin's time become hypersensitivity, an overdelicate fastidiousness, and despair. In the helpless vulnerability of the idiot-victim Benjy, the degradation of the Compsons is exemplified.

75

Where, however, is the other kind of response to the contemporary scene, the escape from it into a romantic South that never was? He goes on in the unpublished preface to say that in creating Candace Compson he was, without realizing it, "trying to manufacture the sister which I did not have the daughter which I was to lose."[17] In the love that Caddy gave to her brothers and the integrity with which she confronted her family situation, presumably she represented what was lacking in the author's life.

Yet if that is what Faulkner meant by the statement that in writing *The Sound and the Fury* he had "tried to escape" from what actually was, it is a curious business, because in the novel itself Caddy can hardly be said to have provided Quentin with very much sisterly solace. The story centers on the *loss* of Caddy and what she meant for Quentin and Benjy, in what Faulkner went on to refer to as "the dark, harsh flowing of time sweeping her to where she could not return to comfort [Quentin]," and that must "sweep her into dishonor and shame too."[18]

Did Faulkner mean, therefore, that in getting into the writing of *The Sound and the Fury* both the indictment of the contemporary

16. William Faulkner, "Appendix: Compson," in Faulkner, *The Sound and the Fury and As I Lay Dying* (New York: Modern Library, n.d.), 16.
17. *Ibid.*, 414.
18. *Ibid.*, 413.

Southern scene and the escape from it, he had enabled himself to move beyond the need to do either, so that in that novel and henceforth he would no longer be dominated by the compulsion to respond to his milieu in the way that he said the Southern writer always had to do? And that writing *The Sound and the Fury* constituted the "turning point" in his career because from that time onward he could at last write his fiction in terms of making it artistically satisfying, shaping and developing it as a master craftsman does, rather than merely using it as a means of expressing his personal despair, anger, and frustration or his wish to escape?

If that *is* what he had in mind, as seems likely, then it might be well to ask this question: What does *The Sound and the Fury* offer that none of the first three novels—not even that *Flags in the Dust* in which he discovered his fictional country of Yoknapatawpha County—provides? What was it about *The Sound and the Fury* that makes it the first novel in which William Faulkner's tutelary genius of place or whatever manifests itself so strikingly?

Faulkner spoke of the writing of his fourth completed novel as a time of delight. Composing the Benjy section, he declared, provided "that ecstasy, that eager and joyous faith and anticipation of surprise which the yet unmarred sheets beneath my hand held inviolate and unfailing." [19] Clearly the remark directly contradicts the statement, made earlier in the same never-published introduction, that "I do not believe there lives the Southern writer who can say without lying that writing is any fun to him." He began writing *The Sound and the Fury,* he says, after he had gone several years without finding a publisher for *Flags in the Dust,* and after his published novels had failed to earn him much in the way of royalties: "One day it suddenly seemed to me as if a door had clapped silently and forever to [*sic*] between me and all publishers' addresses and booklists and I said to myself, Now I can write. Now I can just write." [20]

Whether this was literally true or not—like more than one person of great literary talent, Faulkner did not always confine his imaginative writing to his novels and stories—there is undoubtedly an appropriateness to the statement, in that with this novel the au-

19. *Ibid.,* 414.
20. *Ibid.,* 412–13.

thor's way of writing fiction underwent a decisive change. *Flags in the Dust* had been turned down by the publisher of his first two novels, and eleven other houses were to reject it before it was finally accepted by Harcourt, Brace and Company. Whatever was going on in Faulkner's mind at the time—and apparently it was a period of considerable emotional upheaval—he seems to have decided to write his new book without any heed to the practical concerns of the literary marketplace. For whatever reason, he said goodbye for the time being to the conventional ways of telling a story and let his imagination run free.

In choosing to tell his story through the eyes of an idiot, Faulkner did something new for him: he took for his storytelling method the flow of consciousness itself. He had read *Ulysses,* of course, and admired it greatly, and it seems likely that without Joyce's novel there might never have been *The Sound and the Fury.* Yet neither the Benjy nor the Quentin section that followed it is stream-of-consciousness as Joyce wrote it: Faulkner was not so much interested in portraying the *act* of consciousness as in *using* its representation as a way to tell a story. What Joyce helped him to see was that it was possible to tell a story from inside the character's mind, not just from the outside and above, summarizing the activity of that mind. And for what Faulkner wanted to do, this was a crucial discovery. For it enabled him to portray the impact of experience, and especially of the past upon the present, in the way that such experience is encountered: *as it impinges upon the process of consciousness.* What he did was to divest himself of the customary authorial strategy of interpreting cause and effect for the reader, so that he could describe the mind in the act of receiving the experience that caused the effect.

Why did he want to show that? Because, I believe, what fascinated him most about human personality was its liability and vulnerability to received experience, whether in the form of childhood trauma, historical tradition, family membership, community involvement, or whatever. For Faulkner the individual does not stand alone and independent, and choose whether to be involved in life: he (or she) is a complex being whose identity is made up of a concatenation of forces, and any freedom of action that the individual achieves in time is in the line of the recognition of necessity. In *The*

Sound and the Fury Quentin Compson envisions the individual as a "gull on an invisible wire attached through space dragged." He remembers his father giving him a watch "not that you may remember time, but that you might forget it now and then for a moment and not spend all your breath trying to conquer it."[21] His protagonists are all compulsive, driven persons. Thomas Sutpen in *Absalom, Absalom!* spends his life ruthlessly seeking the status that as a child he identified as necessary to his self-esteem. In *As I Lay Dying* the iron will of a dead woman, herself driven in life by a force that impelled her to assert her identity, acts beyond the grave to compel her husband and children, each with a different set of motivations, to continue to function as a family until they have taken her to Jefferson to be buried.

Those characters who seek to escape into a place of shelter from the forces that drive them are relentlessly drawn back into the current—as, for example, Gail Hightower in *Light in August,* Ike McCaslin in "Delta Autumn," Bayard Sartoris in "An Odor of Verbena." Having once acted, they set in motion counterforces that are not to be evaded. In *Light in August* Joe Christmas thinks, "I have never broken out of the ring of what I have already done and cannot ever undo."[22]

In Faulkner's fiction, Time is the shape that necessity takes. The writing of fiction itself is a necessity, not a choice. "[I] wrote a book and discovered that my doom, fate, was to keep on writing books," he declared in his introduction to *The Faulkner Reader* in 1954. Whether they would be read was unimportant because "one was too busy writing the books during the time while the demon which still drove him still considered him worthy of, deserving of, the anguish of being driven."[23] Only someone like Benjy Compson seems exempt from necessity, and Benjy is an idiot.

So when with *The Sound and the Fury* he moved into the consciousness of his characters, Faulkner could display that consciousness as it is impacted upon by the elements that comprise necessity.

21. Faulkner, *The Sound and the Fury and As I Lay Dying*, 123, 95.
22. William Faulkner, *Light in August* (New York: Modern Library, 1950), 296.
23. William Faulkner, foreword to *The Faulkner Reader* (New York: Random House, 1954), x.

78

The result of the discovery was that for the first time he could create characters open to the full flow of language. It was no longer necessary to confine his depiction to the language that the character might speak or even think in, or else stay completely outside the character. He would not have to observe the realistic convention of limiting what his people thought to what was appropriate in vocabulary or syntax to their education or cultural condition, for by showing what their thought meant, rather than how they might phrase it, he could as narrator *translate* that thought into whatever degree of complexity was demanded.

For the first time, therefore, he was able to write about the kind of ordinary, unlettered people who lived in the milieu he knew—in Yoknapatawpha County—and endow them with the complex sensibilities of human beings whose consciousness was restricted by their particular situation. As narrator he could move from telling what they were thinking to characterizing what they were feeling.

Thus he could end the Benjy section of *The Sound and the Fury* this way: "And then I could see the windows, where the trees were buzzing. Then the dark began to go in smooth, bright shapes, like it always does, even when Caddy says that I have been asleep." [24] Surely Benjy knows no such language, and commands no such vocabulary; but by thinking and feeling *for* Benjy, rather than describing Benjy from outside as trying to think, Faulkner can choose the appropriate word to symbolize what Benjy *feels*—the trees are "buzzing," the dark assumes "smooth bright shapes," and so on.

This is not to say, of course, that Faulkner could not also make full use of the convention of representing vernacular characters with vernacular language when appropriate. The Jason section of *The Sound and the Fury* is a triumph of just that; the youngest Compson brother's vindictiveness and meanness of spirit are convincingly captured in a spoken monologue that is addressed to nobody in particular and the world in general, as if Jason were engaged in a constant self-justification. It is the technique of a writer such as Ring Lardner, brought off with an eye for nuance and an implied but compelling quality of self-incrimination that far surpasses Lardner's bitter sarcasm. The Jason section is a stunning tour de

79

24. Faulkner, *The Sound and the Fury and As I Lay Dying*, 94.

force, a virtuoso performance by a maturing artist engaged in using and flaunting the capabilities of an extraordinary talent.

If in the novel immediately preceding this one, *Flags in the Dust*, or *Sartoris* as the truncated version published in 1929 was entitled, there were sections that seem self-consciously "literary" and overly poetic, in *The Sound and the Fury* there are no such awkwardnesses. For in discovering the narrative technique that put him in full command of his prose, Faulkner no longer needed to make an artificial separation between his sensibility as author and that of his characters; he moved *into* his characters' minds, and identified his discourse so convincingly with his characterizations that what he said about them was entirely credible.

80

In the same way, abandoning the customary conventions of the narrated novel in order to create the sense of reproducing their consciousness had the effect of virtually eliminating from Faulkner's fiction any elements of local color quaintness and folksy caricature that had been present in *Flags in the Dust*. In getting inside the consciousness of his characters he was enabled to view and present them without condescension; the range of his own sympathies was thereby extended and expanded. The distance between the assorted local-color blacks in *Flags in the Dust* and the characterization of Dilsey in *The Sound and the Fury* is stunning to contemplate.

The discovery of how to write the new novel was a momentous breakthrough for Faulkner. And it was equally significant for Southern literature as a whole, for what Faulkner's great style offered was a way for the Southern author to apprehend and explore his personal and community experience without either condescension or sentimental idealization. Not many of his contemporaries chose to adopt the rhetorical particularities of the Faulknerian high style, which is a good thing. But what they could and did profit from was the way in which the High Sheriff of Yoknapatawpha County showed them how to move among characters representing all degrees of social and cultural sophistication, economic condition, and other distinctions of rank, class, and caste, without ever having to "write down." Faulkner did not have to compose rustic pastorale in order to depict dirt farmers, whether white or black; the annals of the poor are neither short nor simple to him. Neither did he have to adopt the two-dimensional facades of the plantation novel in order to write about the Southern squirearchy. For he had discovered how to get past the facades and surfaces and into the minds and hearts of his people, and the string of great novels that began with *The Sound and the Fury* and did not close out until *Go Down, Moses* fifteen years later demonstrated the richness and the availability of what was there in the Southern community.

He did it through technique, through style. Needing to find a way into his material that would enable him to write what he knew, he discovered the method and the language that could take him there. In a very real sense *his style made him wise.* For like every great literary artist, he learned what he thought and felt by writing it down. He did not come to the creation of fiction with an already-developed set of insights and characters and situations, and proceed to write these down. Rather, it was *in writing about them that he learned about them.*

81

IV

Earlier I noted that on the few occasions when he made public statements, wrote essays, articles, or letters, or otherwise commented on public events, Faulkner did not come across as being notably sagacious or impressive. I also asked, rhetorically, whether the artistry of Faulkner should be described as the product of a kind of "divine raving," the putative madness of the poet that, whether through the intervention of his "tutelary genius" or his muse, as the ancients would put it, or the neurotic compulsions of a driven and frustrated psyche, as we might describe the process today, was made to speak "divinest sense." How, in short, did the "chosen vessel" get chosen, and the genius manifest itself?

I hope it is obvious that the literary breakthrough that I have described, which enabled the author of several interesting but not terribly impressive novels to become the author of *The Sound and the Fury,* was no blundering happenstance, but an act of the highest intelligence, an artistic achievement embodying, in its depiction of the nature of human experience, a genuine wisdom. Faulkner's brand of wisdom was not that of the philosopher or journalist or man of science; it was not abstract, logical, paraphrasable, or even in any direct way usable. Because he was a literary artist, William Faulkner's intelligence manifested itself through and as the technique of story-telling, and his wisdom in the form of works of fiction entitled *The Sound and the Fury, As I Lay Dying, Light in August, Absalom, Absalom!,* and so on.

It is not that these novels "mean" this or that about life, or that they "teach" us this moral or that, or even that they allegorize or demonstrate the "truths" of religion, or history, or psychology, or what have you. They may very well do all those things and more, yet they are not "about" knowledge; rather, they *are* knowledge. The difficulty is that we have been so trained to think of knowledge as being something abstract or usable, or more often both, that we fail to remember that a work of art can be equally something that we "know," and that the knowledge it has to tell us is concrete and particular, not abstract and general.

When Faulkner referred in his Nobel Prize speech to the "old verities and truths of the heart . . . love and honor and pity and pride and compassion and sacrifice," he wasn't discoursing on the moral lessons afforded us by great works of literature. What he was doing was saying what great literature *was*—not what it signified, or counselled, or meant, but *was*. The good novel helps us to recognize our own experience by giving form and shape and order—beginning, middle, end: causality—to an imagined experience created in language. When we read Faulkner's first major work of fiction, what we know is *The Sound and the Fury*. And clearly only a very formidably intelligent and wise person could be capable of providing us with *that* knowledge.

So to return to the matter of William Faulkner's "genius," we might recall that one of the several dictionary definitions of *genius* that were cited was "extraordinary mental superiority; esp. unusual power of invention or origination of any kind; as, a man of *genius*." The sole owner and proprietor of Yoknapatawpha County was clearly such a person. One can account for what he wrote only through recognizing that he must have been, *had* to be a person of tremendous intelligence, and that the intelligence took the form of writing stories for us to read.

Unlike the abstractable and extractable, "usable" knowledge of science or philosophy or the like, each of Faulkner's works of knowledge unites thought *and* emotion, and expresses these in the form of characters and scenes and actions. In so doing it is unique. This is what "genius" means, for a writer. Science, theology, history, philosophy can tell us *about* emotion, can analyze its causes and its effects. But the work of art can *be* emotion for us to know. The paradox of the work of literature is that the more truly particular and unique it is, the more universal and general is its knowledge, the more profound its wisdom. It is not only about us, it is *for* us.

JAMES HENRY HAMMOND, SLAVEHOLDER
"WHY GOD LET US LOSE THE WAR"

(1988)

> You see, I had a design in my mind. Whether it was a good or a bad design is beside the point; the question is, Where did I make the mistake in it, what did I do or misdo in it, whom or what injure by it to the extent which this would indicate. I had a design. To accomplish it I should require money, a house, a plantation, slaves, a family—incidentally, of course, a wife. I set out to acquire these, asking no favor of any man.
>
> —William Faulkner, *Absalom, Absalom!*

James Henry Hammond's recent emergence as a fascinating and important historical figure of the Old South is a remarkable phenomenon. Until a decade or so ago most students of nineteenth-century Southern history knew of him only as the antebellum South Carolina politician who had made the famous "mud-sills" speech in the United States Senate. "No, you dare not make war on cotton," he had informed his fellow senators in 1858 during the Kansas difficulties. "No power on earth dares to make war upon it. Cotton *is* king." All great civilizations, Hammond declared, require menials to perform the drudgery of life; such an inferior class "constitutes the very mud-sill of society and of political government." The South

85

had secured its menials, "a race inferior to her own, but eminently qualified in temper, in vigor, in docility, in capacity to stand the climate, to answer all her purposes. We use them for our purpose, and call them slaves." Both the sentiments expressed and the arrogant confidence with which they were delivered infuriated the North and the Midwest; "Mud-sills for Lincoln," banners at the Republican convention in Chicago in 1860 are said to have read.

Scholars of antebellum Southern literature had some knowledge of Hammond as a friend of William Gilmore Simms. William Peterfield Trent, in his biography of the novelist (published in 1892 and at this writing still the only biography), was eloquent in his condemnation of slavery as the bane of the Old South's society and literature, yet he referred to Hammond as "a capital fellow if one may judge from his letters." Although the publication of Simms's voluminous correspondence, including numerous letters to Hammond, gave an indication of the complexity of Hammond's mind, for many years the sole biographical work on Hammond was Elizabeth Merritt's 1921 Johns Hopkins doctoral dissertation.

How different it is today! Drew Gilpin Faust discussed Hammond to good effect in her stimulating study of a group of Old South savants, *A Sacred Circle: The Dilemma of the Intellectual in the Old South, 1840–1860* (1977). In 1981 Carol Bleser published an enthralling selection of four generations of Hammond family letters, *The Hammonds of Redcliffe,* in which it is no exaggeration to say that almost every cliché and generalization about the nineteenth-century South received implicit contradiction. The picture of Hammond emerging from the correspondence was both fascinating and more than a little appalling. Here was no "capital fellow," no high-minded Southern planter, but an ambitious parvenu of New England parentage who set out to become a gentleman and slaveholder. He was a driving fury of self-aggrandizement, a political ideologue, a highly indulgent sensualist, a tyrannizing father and domineering husband, and also a self-pitying man who flaunted his sensibility and throughout his days personified the deluded Romantic opportunist—in sum, "a tough-minded son of a bitch," as Dr. Bleser put it both accurately and succinctly. The year following *The Hammonds of Redcliffe* came Drew Faust's *James Henry Hammond and the Old South: A Design for Mastery,* an excellent biographical study that convincingly filled in much of the portraiture that was sketched in the correspondence.

Now appears a book that I can only describe as unique among all the historical works ever published about the Old South. It is nothing less than the private diaries, astoundingly revealing, of this extraordinary man. *Secret and Sacred: The Diaries of James Henry Hammond, a Southern Slaveholder,* again ably edited by Carol Bleser, consists of a set of two previously unpublished diaries containing Hammond's private commentary on what was happening in his life and that of his state and nation. Incredibly, despite the inclusion of much revealing and mightily damning discussion of his sometimes scandalous sexual life, they appear to have been allowed to survive almost intact, except for one passage in which Hammond's acerbic comments on a son's recalcitrant ways appear to have angered that son so much that he removed some, but by no means all, of the offending pages. Otherwise, and despite their remaining in the hands of the Hammond family for one hundred years, they seem not to have been censored, bowdlerized, or even emended beyond some light annotation.

As Dr. Bleser notes in her illuminating introductory essay to the book, diarists do not write and keep such documents for themselves only; the diarist expects someday to be read. From time to time in his entries Hammond would address himself directly to his children, as if he intended his diaries to reveal to them what manner of suffering man their father really was. At the same time, it seems likely that he did not plan for such reading to take place until after his death, for he almost certainly would not have wanted much of what he had to say known to them while he was still around. However, neither will it do to characterize these diaries as a coldly calculated rhetorical performance for posterity. Obviously their author used them for purposes of emotional release, venting of spleen, the rehearsal of his own grievances, expression of private hopes and ambitions—as a way of giving a shape to his pent-up feelings such as was not otherwise available to him. Yet he must have presupposed an audience, even if in the future, because the satisfaction that such self-expression provided of itself could not be sufficient; he needed to know that his emotional outpourings would be *read.*

The dominant tone throughout is resentment, anger, lamenta-

87

tion. From time to time there is also an element of self-flagellation involved, but truth to tell, at such moments one has the feeling that the motif of mea culpa is being staged mostly for effect. Hammond will often blame himself for his real or imagined misfortunes, but in general terms only; when he gets down to the specifics, the fault is seen as resting elsewhere.

There is no need here to comment on the specific relevance of the diary material to Hammond's life and career; Carol Bleser's introduction performs that task thoroughly and admirably. A few observations, however, on Hammond's personality as revealed in his diaries might be in order.

88

It may be presumed that anyone who performs the sustained labor of keeping a diary such as these must almost by definition be said to take himself and what he is thinking and feeling very seriously indeed, and also that such a person is not satisfied with the everyday reality of the world he inhabits. He must give it additional meaning through recorded language. Hammond's diaries do not importantly function as a record of events, so much as the occasion for discoursing upon them. As a planter he also maintained an extensive journal, in which, especially at times when he was not also keeping his diaries, his personal thoughts and feelings are sometimes interjected. For the most part the documentation entered in the "secret and sacred" diaries, as he called them, seems intended as a starting point to allow him to extemporize upon their personal significance for his own career and hopes. While anxiously awaiting word that the legislature has chosen him to be governor, for example, he anticipates almost every conceivable kind of betrayal, and is at pains to denounce the motives and impugn the character of everyone who might possibly do him in. His supporters are portrayed as weak and ineffective, his rivals as crass, vindictive, self-serving.

Like many another ambitious politico before and since, Hammond tended to identify his personal advancement with the public weal, and to ascribe motives of narrow private gain to all who opposed him. But in Hammond's instance it goes beyond that. His view of his public career takes on transcendent overtones, involving not merely the assumption of civic virtue in search of recognition and reward but something approaching a conviction that he possessed a fated destiny beyond and superior to what might lie in store for most other mortals. Believing himself unfairly relegated to the political boneyard because of conniving office-seekers and a hypocritical, scandal-mongering electorate, and observing what he considered to be the timidity and ineffectiveness of the South's leadership in failing to oppose Northern threats to the expansion of slaveholding, he deposes as follows (May 12, 1852): "I have done with the Public forever, in every form and shape so far as it is in my power to keep clear of it, unless indeed by some marvellous turn of event I could be placed in the position which I feel myself entitled to occupy—and placed in it *in all respects* and without condition."

What could he have had in mind? The presidency? The military and civil leadership of a seceded Southern Confederacy? A virtual dictatorship such as he noted on another occasion had been given by South Carolina to John Rutledge in 1778? Or more grandiose even than these, an historical role comparable to Cromwell's or Bonaparte's? It would be difficult to pronounce any limits upon Hammond's secret ambitions, or upon his estimate of his own capacity for greatness.

Yet Hammond also recognized, and frequently bemoaned, his inability to capitalize on opportunity when it arose. Repeatedly during his public career he had a way of caving in under pressure, which took the form of coming down with bodily maladies that were surely psychosomatic in origin. Aspiring to the mantle of John C. Calhoun both before and after that powerful political figure was removed from the South Carolina scene, he failed to rise to certain occasions. Not gifted at introspection, and like almost all others in his time largely unaware of the vital relationship between psychic and physical health, he lamented what he believed to be his wretched bodily constitution for its inability to respond to the demands his career placed upon it. Yet it is obvious, too, that he suspected that there was more to the matter than that.

Mainly, however, he blamed external factors for his failure to achieve public greatness—the electorate, crass times, conniving politicos, public pusillanimity, democracy, pettiness, jealous Charlestonian bluebloods, Jews, the unwillingness of the people of South Carolina to defer to true intellectual and moral distinction when encountered, their inability to recognize its incarnation in himself.

Not a religious man in any meaningful way, he did not, however, shrink from ascribing his economic, social, and political setbacks to the Divinity itself, as in this remarkable but by no means isolated outburst of August 30, 1842, upon the occasion of a series of fatalities among his slaves:

> For I am pursued by "Envy, hatred and all uncharitableness." I feel like one hunted down by the jealousy of the world and that every man's hand is against me. I see no *real, sensible, appreciating* sympathy any where. For a mere exclamation of sorrow, which those round me only give and then dismiss the matter, is a mockery, and I avoid it—I reprove it. If God would only allow my negroes to live and thrive and give me reasonable health, I could stand the rest and fight it out with the world. But this he will not do.

90

Several years later (May 15, 1845) comes another such outburst, triggered by agricultural woes, which produces this stirring tirade whereby, following an expression of seeming humility, the diarist vents his true feelings on the accountability of the Almighty to James Henry Hammond:

> I cannot fathom his [God's] purposes I do not know what to do. Sometimes I think my destiny is not here. He proposes me for other scenes. But I see no clue, no light to lead me elsewhere. All is darkness and I am bewildered. That I am not pleasing to him and that my ways and views do not meet his approbation is further shown in that after selecting every experiment for this year that I could believe likely to succeed here, after going to immense labour and expense to put large quantities of peat on the whole snow f[ield] and testing it also elsewhere, after trying plaster, manure, in various quantities, rice, tobacco, potatoes on a new and laborious plan, planting in various ways with different seeds, in short, after doing all that man could do, it seemed to me, when it became necessary for God to aid me, He *failed*.

As might be suspected, Hammond was nobody's gentle and kind slaveholder. He worked his slaves hard, so much so that, particularly at the outset of his career as a planter, they experienced an appalling mortality rate. Hammond's views in the "mud-sills" speech were genuinely held. Africans were in every way an inferior race, designed for his *use*. Proslavery rhetoric to the contrary, there was nothing remotely paternalistic about it, if we are to believe the evidence of his diaries. Indeed, as Dr. Bleser makes clear, not only did such usage include concubinism, but—and nothing could offer greater proof of Hammond's attitude toward the human inferiority of blacks—Hammond took for his mistress an eighteen-year-old slave with a one-year-old female child, and then when the child reached the age of twelve he made her his mistress as well!

What sent Hammond into political eclipse for thirteen years following the end of his term as governor of South Carolina in 1844 was a sexual indiscretion of an altogether different sort. The four young daughters of his wealthy brother-in-law, Wade Hampton II, were accustomed to spend much time with the Hammonds, and eventually Hampton learned that all four of them were in the habit of engaging, apparently en masse, in the most intimate cuddling with their uncle. In Hammond's words (December 9, 1846):

> Here were four lovely creatures from the tender but precocious girl of 13 to the mature but fresh and blooming woman nearly 19, each contending for my love, claiming the greater share of it as due to her superior devotion to me, all of them rushing on every occasion to my arms and covering me with kisses, lolling on my lap, pressing their bodies almost into mine, wreathing their limbs with mine, encountering warmly every portion of my frame, and permitting my hands to stray unchecked over every part of them and to rest without the slightest shrinking of it, in the most secret and sacred regions, and all this for a period of more than two years continuously. Is it in flesh and blood to withstand this? . . . Nay are there many who would have the self-control to stop where I did? Am I not after all entitled to some, the smallest portion of, credit for not going further?

Hammond's outraged brother-in-law, who thought Hammond had gone much too far as it was, thereafter took it upon himself to see that influential friends knew of Hammond's misbehavior, and when a seat in the United States Senate became vacant the knowledge of Hammond's conduct was sufficient to keep him from being elected by the legislature. Typically, although continually asserting his own guilt and remorse, Hammond thereafter filled his diaries with censure of the Hamptons, charging them with every kind of hypocrisy, justifying his own conduct as no more than a regrettable but unavoidable weakness of the flesh, and complaining bitterly that the people of South Carolina had no right whatever to deny him political office merely because of such private goings-on! (Apparently the powers that be, or enough of them, eventually agreed, because when Senator A. P. Butler died in 1857, Hammond was named to fill the unexpired term, and afterward could have been reelected in his own right.)

In almost every respect James Henry Hammond seems to have resembled nothing less than a monster. Yet there must have been more to him than that, for otherwise how could he have gained and held the close friendship of a man like Gilmore Simms, whose moral and ethical standards were of the highest, and who, though likewise a parvenu in the South Carolina establishment, was generous, loyal, compassionate, indulgent to his slaves, and a devoted family man?

Perhaps the diaries that Dr. Bleser has so ably edited may offer clues to the matter that I have failed to perceive. I would, however, in closing note one thing more. When *The Hammonds of Redcliffe* appeared in 1981, more than one reviewer made the point that if one could imagine a counterpart of Thomas Sutpen in William Faulkner's *Absalom, Absalom!* who unlike Sutpen was also highly articulate and gifted at rationalizing away his misdeeds, he would come close to resembling James Henry Hammond. Like the protagonist of Faulkner's novel, Hammond too possessed a "design," and in its service he subordinated all human considerations, including those of family and fatherhood. Hammond used people as if they were commodities, just as Sutpen did. Hammond too was of humble origins, though not so lowly as those of Sutpen. He aspired to the plantation aristocracy, married not for love but in order to advance his social status, fathered children on a slave mistress and would not recognize them, dreamed grandly and failed massively. Like Sutpen, too, however more articulate in voicing his dismay at what was happening to his design, Hammond could not understand where or why he had gone wrong, and sought to explain away his moral transgressions as no more than unfortunate mistakes in tactics. To a degree, like Sutpen he was "innocent"—not in the sense of being blameless but of failing, for all his great intelligence, to recognize that the world did not exist solely for his benefit.

Life, as has been observed, has a way sometimes of imitating art. Isn't it odd that, a half-century following publication of Faulkner's great novel of the Old South, a James Henry Hammond should emerge from unremembered obscurity with a personality, and with recorded deeds, that seem so strikingly to resemble the protagonist of *Absalom, Absalom!* And what is more, readers familiar with Faulkner's fiction will have recognized at once that Hammond's deed of taking first a slave woman and then later her daughter for his mistress constitutes a sickening parallel with the behavior of a character in yet another of Faulkner's works of fiction, old Carothers McCaslin of "The Bear."

Readers of these diaries of James Henry Hammond—and henceforth his diaries must be required reading for anyone who would understand the history and nature of the Old South—will discover that at one point in his career Hammond himself wanted to write a novel. He was quick to plead his lack of capacity for doing so. "The great points of human character have been forced on my consideration," he wrote in his diary on August 28, 1841, "and I have reflected much upon the workings of the human heart. But even if I could convey my ideas of these things fully, I could not make up for the want of minute practical knowledge in the innumerable variety of positions in which men and women must be exhibited in these works." And he concludes, "I wish I could get [rid] of the idea finally, but I doubt if I ever shall until I write and fail, that I think will cure me."

So perhaps these "secret and sacred" diaries that Hammond left for posterity might be said, in a way, to represent *his* novel, his work of fiction. Not an invented tale or tales, perhaps, but "real life" as subject matter to be shaped and formed to his heart's desire. If so, there is no happy ending to the tale, and the protagonist largely fails to gain our sympathy or to achieve a suspension of disbelief. A "typical" Southern planter Hammond was not, but in his naked acquisitiveness, his intense ambition, and his willingness to use whoever or whatever comes to hand to advance his fortunes and achieve his goals, he represents all too aptly the terrible capacity for evil existing within a system that based its achievements and aspirations upon the ownership of human beings as slaves. The question that Harriet Beecher Stowe asked in her afterword to *Uncle Tom's Cabin,* "Is *man* ever a creature to be trusted with wholly irresponsible power?" is appropriate here. But it is not Mrs. Stowe's novel that is likely to come to mind as one reads the Hammond diaries. Rather, it is Faulkner's great tragedy of the Old South, and in particular what young Quentin Compson finds himself thinking as he listens to Miss Rosa Coldfield telling about Thomas Sutpen:

94

> *It's because she wants it told,* he thought, *so that people whom she will never see and whose names she will never hear and who have never heard her name nor seen her face will read it and know at last why God let us lose the War: that only through the blood of our men and the tears of our women could He stay this demon and efface his name and lineage from the earth.*

THOMAS WOLFE
HOMAGE RENEWED

(1989)

Years ago, in a class I taught in contemporary fiction for college freshmen, there was a very good student who almost always had interesting things to say about the stories and poems we were reading. Once after class I asked her why she had not taken part in that day's discussion, which was about one of J. D. Salinger's stories. Her reply was, "It's too personal."

The particular way she chose to phrase it was amusing, but certainly not what she meant. I understand very well what she was trying to tell me. For certain writers seem to speak so directly and eloquently to young readers in particular that they become part of their private lives. When the young reader comes upon such a writer, it is as if a personal voice is discovered, a way of seeing and making sense of the world. For the first time ever, here is a writer who can understand and articulate one's private thoughts and feelings. What until then seemed vague, confused, even unspeakable can take on the dignity of language, and be expressed. The young reader has found an impassioned spokesman.

Anyone who responds to a writer's work in just this way quite likely will turn out to have artistic ambitions of one's own. The young lady who found Salinger's story "too personal" to talk about in public is now a distinguished writer and critic. And an important part of the kind of discovery I have been describing is that one is being shown a way to make art out of one's own experience. Writing is, after all, a mimetic process: we learn how to do it from reading what others have written, and our idea of what constitutes literature derives from the books we have read. The young person becomes acquainted with various works of literature by an assortment of authors, and some will seem to speak to him or to her more readily than others. But when the discovery I have in mind comes, if it does, then it is as if nothing that has been read before has mattered. A writer has been found whose way of writing seems to mirror, to a degree hitherto unencountered, the needs and the circumstances of one's own sensibility: it is nothing short of a revelation.

There is a marvelous sequence in Marcel Proust's *Swann's Way* in which the young Marcel is introduced to the writings of a novelist named Bergotte; the episode is based upon Proust's early experience with reading the novels of Anatole France. The narrator describes how at first Marcel thought it was the story alone that fascinated him, but then as he read other of Bergotte's works he began to recognize the presence of certain motifs, certain kinds of insights that seemed to be uniquely the possession of that writer, and that Bergotte alone could offer him: "He would express a whole system of philosophy, new to me, by the use of marvelous imagery, to the inspiration of which I would naturally have ascribed that sound of harping which began to chime and echo in my ears, an accompaniment to which that imagery added something aetherial and sublime."

Proust's narrator adds: "[When] I happened to find in one of his books something which had already occurred to my own mind, my heart would swell with gratitude and pride as though some deity had, in his infinite bounty, restored it to me, had pronounced it to be beautiful and right." In so discovering that the great Bergotte himself had written things that he too had thought or felt, the young Marcel was profoundly heartened: "Then it was suddenly revealed to me that my own humble existence and the Realms of Truth were less widely separated than I had supposed, that at certain points they were actually in contact; and in my new-found confidence and joy I wept upon his printed page, as in the arms of a long-lost father."

Numerous other writers have described kindred experiences.

After a while, as the young writer proceeds along the road to greater maturity, other and usually more complex and subtler such discoveries will be made. Indeed, by the time the young writer begins publishing his or her own work, the influence of that first thrilling literary discovery probably will have become so fully absorbed and modified by subsequent literary experiences that its presence will be only moderately felt. Proust's mature style did not, after all, much resemble Anatole France's. The impress will by then have ceased to be visible in such obvious ways as style and subject, and will manifest itself in the more subtle qualities of authorial attitude and vision. What the person in question ends up writing will probably not even be along the same lines of genre or form in which the original influence was encountered; the writer may work in poetry, nonfiction, criticism, journalism, or whatever. I daresay, for example, that very little of the influence of the prose style of Ernest Hemingway can be detected in the lighthearted meditations of Russell Baker in the New York *Times*.

97

All the same, that first breathtaking exposure to another person's work sends the young writer along his or her way, and that is what I want to say about Thomas Wolfe. For many young persons of my generation, this was Thomas Wolfe's role. Other and better writers than I have described the phenomenon of a first encounter with the Wolfe novels. Most of us eventually outgrew him; and this is one reason that there has been relatively little good critical writing about the Wolfe novels. The period when their impact is most profound usually comes before one is either equipped or impelled to make significant discriminations and to distinguish between various kinds of literary artistry.

Mark Twain and William Dean Howells were talking once about why they both hated to think about the past. "Because it's so damned humiliating!" Mark Twain declared. Something of humiliation is involved in any effort to look back and to try to understand just what it was about the Wolfe novels that made them so meaningful during one's youth and young manhood. I want to try to describe something of their impact upon me, even though doing so will involve describing certain less than flattering aspects of my life at that time. What follows will scarcely be an exercise in nostalgia.

I was nineteen years old when I first encountered Wolfe, and about as bewildered and confused as might be imagined. It was in the late summer of 1943, and I was finishing up basic infantry training in the army, at Fort McClellan, Alabama. I had entered the army immediately after my junior year of college. If as a student I had been no great shakes, as a foot-soldier I was a disaster. I was just over six feet tall, weighed about 135 pounds, with all the muscular coordination and endurance of a piece of limp spaghetti; I couldn't even walk a straight line; I had no stamina whatever. Plunged abruptly into a demanding training regimen, I was incapable of doing what was expected of me. I tried to do my best, which was very poor indeed. It was a baffling and humiliating experience, the more so because I took both it and myself very seriously. No doubt if I had been willing to accept my limitations and understand that an inept physical performance didn't constitute a moral flaw on my part, it might have been less traumatic; but intellectually and emotionally I was immature, naive, lacking any insight whatever into either my capabilities or my shortcomings.

My training regiment was made up of college and university students who were scheduled to go back to college for specialized training after the basic infantry cycle was completed, and one Sunday several of my friends were talking about a writer named Thomas Wolfe. That afternoon I went over to the post library and borrowed a book entitled *You Can't Go Home Again*. I read some of it, but then we were marched off on a lengthy bivouac exercise in the field, and after that the thirteen-week training cycle was over, to my considerable relief. Within days, several day-coach loads of us were dispatched to Yale University for specialized training in Italian area and language studies.

I had never been north of Washington, D.C., much less to study at a great university like Yale, and I was excited beyond measure. Yet while the program there was infinitely more to my liking than the infantry training, as an Italian area and language student I proved to be almost as incompetent as I had been as a field soldier. I could not focus my attention, was unable to keep my mind on my studies, and was at best a marginal student who almost wasn't even allowed to complete the program.

It was a disheartening experience, the more so because I knew, or felt, that I did have some ability and talent, and I could not be cyni-

cal or philosophical about my inability to make use of my capabilities. Aspects of my personality that later in life have been among my
chief assets were at that time mostly liabilities. Not to be able to use
them, to be incapable of doing the classwork, and yet to *want* so
very much to do what was expected of me and what everyone else
around me seemed able to handle so easily, was devastating to what
little self-esteem still remained to me.

In any event, not long after I arrived at Yale and began my work
in Italian studies, I went over to the Sterling Memorial Library and
took out Thomas Wolfe's *Look Homeward, Angel.* I read it straight
through, and in the weeks that followed I read all the other Wolfe
novels. I had plunged into an imaginative world that I had not even
suspected could exist. Here was a writer who had put into words so
much that I felt and thought—and not simply put into words, but
invested all that he wrote with an emotion and passion that were
given authority through a rhetoric that did not merely assert but *demanded* acknowledgment. Here was my private inner experience—
not only what was, but what I hoped might someday be—being
interpreted and set forth with an assurance that, by virtue of the
obvious fact that it was printed, published, and read by others,
could not merely be shrugged off or denied.

Imagine, if you will, what coming upon and reading a passage
such as the following from *Of Time and the River* could mean for
an undirected, unfocused nineteen-year-old such as I have been
describing:

> A young man is so strong, so mad, so certain, and so lost. He
> has everything and he is able to use nothing. He hurls the great
> shoulder of his strength forever against phantasmal barriers, he
> is a wave whose power explodes in lost mid-oceans under time-
> less skies, he reaches out to grip a fume of painted smoke; he
> wants all, feels the thirst and power for everything, and finally
> gets nothing. In the end, he is destroyed by his own strength,
> devoured by his own hunger, impoverished by his own wealth.
> Thoughtless of money or the accumulation of material posses-
> sions, he is none the less defeated in the end by his own greed—
> a greed that makes the avarice of King Midas seem paltry by
> comparison.

99

And that is the reason why, when youth is gone, every man will look back upon that period of his life with infinite sorrow and regret. It is the bitter sorrow and regret of a man who knows that once he had a great talent and wasted it, of a man who knows that once he had a great treasure and got nothing from it, of a man who knows that he had strength enough for everything and never used it.

100

It would be difficult for an older reader not to scoff at such words; I confess that I find it difficult not to do so. That they are hyperbolic; that the importance of the sensibility involved is not grounded in characterization but asserted rhetorically; and that it is mostly attitude and almost no substance—to a reader who has long since learned that there is considerably more to life and letters than the assertion of a mostly undefined and unsatisfied appetite, a passage such as that will seem all too empty and hollow.

Yet to leave it at that is to do an injustice both to Wolfe's prose and to one's own experience, for what is really at issue is that the premises on which the rhetoric is based can no longer be shared. They are those of a young person confronting the adult world for almost the first time, tremendously unsure of himself, convinced that he is capable of participating in that world yet unable so far to discover a way to do it successfully, and placing so much importance on his apparent failure to do so that both the attempt and the failure are viewed as epochal and transcendent in significance.

The Wolfean rhetoric is part and parcel of the transaction, because what it does is to invest the experience itself with a declaration of its importance and even universality. The failure, the frustration, are magnified until they take on near-cosmic proportions. To say that the sensibility involved is extravagantly romantic is only to describe it factually. If romanticism is the belief in the uniqueness and importance of the individual sensibility and in its limitless potentiality, then the passage from Wolfe exemplifies just that belief, and in a form untempered by cynicism or irony.

To point out that the attitude exemplified in the passage is painfully naive and egocentric is all very well. But we might ask ourselves just *why* either the naïveté or the egocentricity should seem painful. I suspect it is because so flagrant and uninhibited an insistence upon the importance of one's own emotions reminds us all too vividly of our own youthful earnestness and lack of humor about ourselves. How many of us, confronted suddenly with the specter of our youthful selves made real and material again, could manage to endure that presence for very long?

In James Branch Cabell's novel *Figures of Earth,* Dom Manuel, a swineherd who once wanted to make a statue out of clay, has won through to fame, fortune, and creature comfort. But there is a window in his study that he has long left unopened. One day a certain young clerk named Ruric, with white face and wild glittering eyes, comes in through the window, and when Manuel asks him what he has learned out beyond the window, he replies: "All freedom and all delight. . . . And all horror and all rebellion."

101

> Then he talked for a while. When Ruric had ended this talking, Count Manuel laughed scornfully, and spoke as became a well-thought-of nobleman.
>
> Ruric whipped out a knife, and attacked his master, crying, "I follow after my own thinking and my own desires, you old, smug, squinting hypocrite!"
>
> So Count Manuel caught Ruric by the throat, and with naked hands Dom Manuel strangled the young clerk.

If with a trace of wistfulness, Cabell points up the futility and impossibility of reconciling the two viewpoints. Dom Manuel has long since made his choices, and however imperfectly, he has proceeded to live by and with them. To be transported back to a time before those choices were made, just as if there had been no such thing as necessity at work in one's life, but only unlimited possibility, is dismaying.

This experience is akin to what Wolfe's fiction does to us. That is, the experience it not only portrays but proposes to ratify through its authorial rhetoric is of a young man who simply will not accept any limitations upon what he intends to do and be, and who views any and everyone who would counsel adherence to such restrictions as the equivalent of what Cabell's young clerk labels Dom Manuel: an "old, smug, squinting hypocrite." This, in fact, is exactly what Wolfe has his narrator say in *The Web and the Rock:*

The older and more assured people of the world, who have learned to work without waste and error, think they know the reason for the chaos and confusion of a young man's life. They have learned the thing at hand, and learned to follow their single way through all the million shifting hues and tones and cadences of living . . . and they say, therefore, that the reason for a young man's confusion, lack of purpose, and erratic living is because he has not "found himself."

In this, the older and more certain people may be right by their own standard of appraisal, but, in this judgment on the life of youth, they have really pronounced a sterner and more cruel judgment on themselves. For when they say that some young man has not yet "found himself," they are really saying that he has not lost himself as they. For men will often say they have "found themselves" when they have really been worn down into a groove by the brutal and compulsive force of circumstance. They speak of their life's salvation when all that they have done is blindly follow through an accidental way. They have forgotten their life's purpose, and all the faith, hope, and immortal confidence of a boy.

Wolfe is claiming, in so many words, that it is better to be young and not yet know what to do with one's life, than to be older and know what to do. He is voicing an either/or proposition: one is either young and idealistic and unable to focus one's abilities, or else one is older and cynical and able to use one's talents.

Yet paradoxically—and this is one reason why many young readers found his books so exhilarating to read—in making that assertion, in writing the novels that exemplify that attitude, Wolfe in effect is refuting the very premise he has seemingly advanced. For the existence of the novels themselves and the cadenced passion of their rhetoric seem to demonstrate that one can be ardently enthusiastic, remain passionately open to experience, and yet be able to shape feelings into a form that others may read and esteem. You may, Wolfe in effect says, "write about how wonderful and sad it is to be young and lonely and frustrated and unable to find your way—*just as I have so obviously done here in my book.*"

To a young person who feels unappreciated and who cannot discover a vocation or purpose, what Wolfe has to say is that he should hold proudly to his convictions and not be ashamed of his inability to use his talents, because it is he, and not the supposedly mature adult world, who is really on the right track.

That this is reassuring counsel for many young people is clear from the way that others have written about Wolfe. I like the English novelist Pamela Hansford Johnson's description, in "Thomas Wolfe and the Kicking Season," of what Wolfe meant for her and her young friends in the early 1930s:

> And then, one day, *Look Homeward, Angel* burst upon us like the radiance from a lighthouse newly erected upon some very sticky rocks. We ate, drank, and dreamed it. We weren't fools. We had some taste, we knew that some of it was guff. . . . But that book spoke for us: spoke, not in spite of its sprawlings, its bawlings, its youthful yellings and howlings about the family, the silver cord, the "incommunicable prison of this earth," love itself, but because of those things. We were not articulate ourselves, though we had much we wanted to say. Wolfe had far too much to say, but he said it with our voice.

103

As for myself, I read and reread all the Wolfe I could find, identified myself with him wholeheartedly, and yearned to make a pilgrimage to Asheville, walk its streets, and there listen at night to the outbound freight trains whistling in the distance, just as Wolfe once did. Looking toward the time when the war would be done and I would be back in college, I even applied for admission at the university he had attended at Chapel Hill, and if I hadn't been discharged from the army in late January of 1946 so suddenly and unexpectedly that there was no time to make arrangements, I would very likely have enrolled at Eugene Gant's alma mater. As it was, I had to content myself with living at home and completing my undergraduate work at the University of Richmond. Not that I felt deeply disappointed, since simply to be a civilian and back in college anywhere again was a quite satisfactory state of affairs.

At this juncture I should explain that during my last two years in the army I did manage to do at least some growing up. However little I was able to contribute to the war effort, the army eventually placed me in an assignment for which I was not completely unfitted; and by the time the war was over I had even been promoted to sergeant, a development that would have amazed those who had sought to teach me the skills of an infantryman two years earlier. If I learned nothing else during my military career, I did discover finally how to concentrate my attention a little better, with the result that when I resumed my senior year of college I became a much better student— which in turn no doubt amazed those who had been my teachers before I went into the army. Other things had also happened to make me hope that I would not always be a totally incompetent and impractical young man, although my parents and most of my family remained largely unconvinced. But I suppose that if all there was to my love for Thomas Wolfe was an infatuation with the "O lost" rhetoric, I might have lost much of my enthusiasm for him after a couple of years.

104

Other elements in Wolfe's fiction spoke very directly and personally to me as well. For one thing, like Wolfe I had been born and had grown up in a small southern city, as part of a middle-class family without college-educated parents, and although both of us were impatient with and even rebelling against many of the values and attitudes of our communities, we were also imbued with many of those values to a degree that we were not then ready to acknowledge. For different reasons both Thomas Wolfe and myself had been on the outside of the reigning social and cultural establishment, and as with a writer that Wolfe very much admired and that I soon came to admire as well, James Joyce, literature and the life of the mind were a way of extricating oneself from a limiting social situation.

It is no mere coincidence that most of the writers whose work, whether in fiction or nonfiction, is most patently "autobiographical" in subject and form (and it is the form, not the subject, that embodies the autobiographical dimension) have been persons who in their earlier lives were engaged in a process of transcending a middle-class social circumstance. Not only Wolfe and Joyce, but D. H. Lawrence and Marcel Proust come to mind. Their relationship to their earlier community becomes a kind of love-hate affair, and what they eventually learn to do is to transform the middle-class world they grew up in into art.

An episode in *Look Homeward, Angel* that always fascinated me was that in which Eugene Gant and George Graves leave their

school and walk into downtown Altamont. As they do so they encounter the everyday sights and scenes of a small southern city—
they walk by several churches, hear a church choir rehearsing, then
pass in succession a steam laundry in which Negro laundrywomen
are at work, a dentist's office, a funeral parlor, a millinery shop, a
hearse, a medical building, a Packard limousine, a bank, a five-and-
ten-cent store, the Bijou Cafe, a movie theater, a fashion mart.
Among the citizenry of Altamont encountered in the course of the
walk are a street-sweeper, a Negro gardener, a Catholic priest,
an undertaker, a telegraph messenger boy, attorneys and judges
and their wives, a man peering from an office window, a woman
emerging from a jewelry store, an old man, a lung specialist at
the wheel of a Buick roadster, a Jewish haberdasher, a Chamber of
Commerce secretary, a noted politician, a hotel proprietor, a scout-
master and three Boy Scouts, an Oriental-rug merchant, assorted
youths and teen-age girls, two dealers in real estate, a Baptist minister, a school principal, a newspaper reporter, several women, a half-
witted pencil merchant, a milliner, a life insurance salesman, a
wealthy matron, the owner of a clothing store, a judge, a Confederate veteran.

105

From my own experience as a boy and youth growing up in
Charleston, South Carolina, I was able to recognize the equivalent
of almost every sight and every person described in the episode,
which is doubtless indebted to the "Wandering Rocks" chapter in
Ulysses. Yet Wolfe's walk through Altamont is by no means deriva-
tive; he converted his models into his own art. Throughout the episode Wolfe follows each description with a tag-line of poetry; thus
the view of the Methodist and Presbyterian church steeples concludes with the line "Ye antique spires, ye distant towers." The dentist tells his patient "Spit!" and the line that follows is "With thee
conversing, I forget all time." A waxen model in the millinery store
window is tagged "O that these lips had language." And so on, until
at the end the boys enter Wood's Pharmacy and place their orders
for chocolate milk at the marble-slab soda fountain, and the chapter concludes with "O for a draught of vintage that hath been
cooled a long age in the deep-delved earth!"

The function of the tag-lines of poetry, of course, is in part that of
ironic contrast between the mundane middle-class life of Altamont
and the elevated diction of high art. But there is an essential differ-

ence between Wolfe's use of such material and the way that, for example, a writer such as T. S. Eliot uses similar quotations in *The Waste Land*. Eliot quotes the refrain from Spenser's "Prothalamion": "Sweet Thames! run softly, till I end my song," and juxtaposes the celebration of Elizabeth's and Leicester's expected processional down the river with the sordid trysts of typists, carbuncular city clerks, pregnant young women and swiftly decamped sons of city directors, Sweeney and Mrs. Porter, and so on. The intent is to show the degradation of contemporary urban life in a godless, secularized industrial metropolis.

106 Thomas Wolfe is showing no such thing: in tagging Negro laundry workers with a line from Herrick, a shapely milliner with Wordsworth on daffodils, a drugstore fountain with lines from Keats, and so on, he is depicting, humorously, the commonality of human experience everywhere. Just as James Joyce, in adapting Odysseus' travels to the Dublin of 1904, is not engaged in using Leopold Bloom's and Stephen Dedalus' meanderings as an instance of the decline of the Age of Heroes, but instead is depicting the ever-recurring nature of the myth, so Wolfe is celebrating the middle-class everyday life of Asheville as the stuff and sinew of high art. He is doing what Eugene Gant is told to do by the ghost of his dead brother Ben at the close of *Look Homeward, Angel*. "Fool," says Ben, "*this* is life. You have been nowhere." Marble statues may walk by moonlight in Babylon, in Thebes, Eugene argues, but not in Altamont:

> "Not here! Not here!" said Eugene passionately. "It's not right, here! My God, this is the Square! There's the fountain! There's the City Hall! There's the Greek's lunch-room!"
> The bank-chimes struck the half hour.
> "And there's the bank!" he cried.
> "That makes no difference," said Ben.

It was not simply that Wolfe wrote about the kinds of places and people one could recognize: he invested the scenes of everyday American life with the clarity and radiance that gave them the dignity of art. Depicted in their sensory richness, they made one conscious for the first time that what lay all around one was remarkable. Unlike the local-color tourist-trade writings about my native city of Charleston, Wolfe's Altamont was not shown as quaint or picturesque or delightfully old-timey. Neither was it given the drab tones of Midwestern realism. He made his places vibrant and alive: the town square of a North Carolina city took on the solidity and permanence that previously I had thought reserved for more conventionally literary locales. This was Wolfe's intent, and what he said to me, both by example and in attitude, was that *my world, the locales and the concerns of my middle-class experience, were eligible for artistic use!* As he wrote of his autobiographical protagonist in *The Web and the Rock:*

107

> He "knew," for example, that freight cars were beautiful; that a spur of rusty box cars on a siding, curving off somewhere into a flat of barren pine and clay, was as beautiful as anything could be, as something has ever been. He knew all the depths and levels of it, all the time evocations of it—but he couldn't say so. He hadn't found the language for it. He had even been told, by implication, that it wasn't so. That was where his "education" came in. It wasn't really that his teachers had told him that a freight car was not beautiful. But they had told him that Keats, Shelley, the Taj Mahal, the Acropolis, Westminster Abbey, the Louvre, the Isles of Greece, were beautiful. And they had told it to him so often and in such a way that he not only thought it true—which it is—but that these things were everything that beauty is.

When Wolfe wrote about my native city of Charleston, as he did in *Look Homeward, Angel,* he did not discourse in terms of cobblestoned lanes, closed-off gardens, intricately wrought ironwork, narrow winding thoroughfares, and Old World charm; what he had to say about the Civil War and the Confederacy was mostly sarcastic. Instead he described trips to the navy yard and over to the Isle of Palms. And that was the kind of experience that *I* remembered with greatest vividness about the place where I grew up. My boyhood hadn't been centered on the quaint charms of the old houses south of Broad Street, or colorfully dressed Negroes singing spirituals, but on the doings of a middle-class Southern city of just over 60,000 population, in which the soda fountain of the Walgreen's store at King and Wentworth Streets had been the equivalent of Wood's Pharmacy in *Look Homeward, Angel,* which Wolfe had depicted with the sharpness and allure of the Mermaid Tavern. "Souls of poets dead and gone / What Elysium have you known . . ."

Nor was that all. Wolfe's principal characters had not remained in Altamont or Libya Hill. They had gone off to seek their fortunes in the Northeast, in Boston and New York City, just as Wolfe himself had done in the early 1920s. There they had encountered, for the first time, a sophisticated, cosmopolitan cultural establishment that was far more formidable and difficult of entry than anything they had ever known before. They met other young people who had been educated not at colleges and universities in the provinces but at the leading schools of the Northeast, and whose cultural experience and reading were far in advance of anything they had known back home. They had never before really confronted literature and the arts in the guise of a *social* milieu, in which acquaintance and familiarity with whatever was most fashionable and "in" constituted the terms of involvement. Where back in Altamont and even at the university in Pulpit (Chapel) Hill Wolfe's Eugene Gant had been able to view his involvement in literature and drama as lifting him above the everyday middle-class values of his community, in the metropolis the arts themselves were a species of *commerce;* and involvement in them conferred neither uniqueness nor elevation.

More than that, or (more appropriately) along *with* that, there was the vast size, impersonality, and heterogeneity of the metropolis itself, with its extremes of wealth, its emphasis upon conspicuous consumption. Wolfe's autobiographical protagonist had grown up in a fairly homogeneous community whose white population was predominantly of northern European, Protestant stock. The relatively few who were not of that extraction had largely accommodated themselves within it and taken on its mores and patterns. Now, in New York, Eugene Gant found himself in a society made up of large numbers of people of eastern and southern European origin—Jews, Slavs, Italians, Greeks, Armenians, and so on—who had held onto far more of their ethnic and social heritage and whose speech retained the accents and idioms of their cultural origins.

Geographically, emotionally, socially, culturally he was an Outsider in the city. As might be expected his response was provincial,

108

neurotic, often xenophobic in the extreme. He felt lonely, belea-
guered, and frustrated. He raged defensively against the "alien"
nature of the population, the materialism of the wealthy, the inso-
lence of the privileged, the sordid crudeness and viciousness of the
masses; the seeming coldness of the entrenched cultural establishment to worthy but unsponsored young artists from the provinces;
the supercilious hauteur of the devotees of fashionable artistic cults
and movements; and so on.

In Doris Lessing's words (quoted by Pamela Hansford Johnson),
"He did not write *about* adolescence: to read him is to re-experience
adolescence. . . . I have yet to meet a person born to any kind of
Establishment who understood Wolfe, I have yet to meet a provin-
cial who has cracked open a big city who does not acknowledge that
Wolfe expressed his own struggle for escape into larger experience."

109

That both the denunciation and the evocation of the loneliness of
the outsider were more than acceptable to a young Southerner such
as I was should be obvious. I too had gone northward after graduation from college; had lived for a time across the river from New
York City, working as a newspaper reporter; had walked along the
streets of downtown Manhattan feeling very much Outside and en-
vious of all those who were Inside. A broken romance—my first of
any intensity—had sent me back to the South, but after several
years of newspaper work in Virginia I had enrolled in a graduate
writing program at Johns Hopkins. When my little 1936 Plymouth
coupe moved along the Potomac River bridge on U.S. 301 and into
Maryland, I had felt that I was seeking fame and fortune in a foreign land. Just as Eugene Gant had done at Harvard in *Of Time and
the River,* in graduate school I had encountered other ambitious
would-be littérateurs, most of them far more conversant with what
the literary avant-garde was thinking and writing at the time, and
often affecting disdain for the kind of middle-class interests and enthusiasms that came naturally to me. And like Wolfe's, my defensive
response had been to brand them as philistines and aesthetic po-
seurs, and to make a point of my provincial origins and concerns,
even while secretly envying their sophistication and tastes.

It all seemed very silly, just a few years later, and very adolescent
and romantic: Il faut que la jeunesse se passe. Gradually, for a while
imperceptibly, one begins learning—socially, artistically, profes-

sionally, sexually—to make use of the ways of the adult world to fit one's purposes and needs, and vice versa, so that the defenses can come down enough to allow passage from within and without. Throughout one's lifetime they are never totally lowered, of course; but usually they are converted so as to shape and direct rather than to restrict one's involvement. In graduate school, resisting at every step at first, I learned to read Proust and Joyce and Eliot and Auden, and then Faulkner and Welty and Ransom and Tate, Warren and Frost and Yeats and James, and so on.

When I wrote my first book it was on Thomas Wolfe. I wrote it as a book, rewrote it as a doctoral dissertation, then rewrote the dissertation as a book. I reread it the other day, for the first time in years. At that time I was deeply involved in the literature of the South, and what I tried to do was to make Wolfe into a covert Nashville Agrarian. I did a pretty good job of it, too—for he and they were twentieth-century Southerners, and shared many of the same attitudes toward cities, and society, and history, and even language. All the same he was no Agrarian; emotionally, aesthetically, philosophically he was himself only, and this both for better and for worse. But by that time I was trying to shape my own youthful emotional allegiance to Thomas Wolfe's fiction into something more acceptable and appropriate to my sharpened tastes and greater experience of life and letters. The episodes and sections that I found most convincing and skillfully handled were the descriptions of Altamont, the humorous scenes, the depictions of the family, the deaths of Ben and of Old Gant, the descriptive and satirical passages—and impressive episodes and sections they are.

But they are not why I had read Wolfe when he was spokesman, prophet, and solace. It was the Wolfe who wrote of proud loneliness, emotional hunger, the intense ambition to escape from the prison walls of youthful and provincial limitation, and who understood so well the joy that could come when briefly those walls seemed parted, that so drew my attention and that of others like me. He could write like this of a train stopping at a small-town station in the South:

> And elsewhere there were the casual voices of the trainmen—
> conductors, porters, baggage masters, station men—greeting

each other with friendly words, without surprise, speaking of weather, work, plans for the future, saying farewell in the same way. Then the bell tolled, the whistle blew, the slow panting of the engine came back to them, the train was again in motion: the station, and the station lights, a glimpse of streets, the thrilling, haunting, white-glazed incandescence of a cotton mill at night, the hard last lights of town, slid past the windows of the train. The train was in full speed now, and they were rushing on across the dark and lonely earth again.

The train was outward bound, en route to the city, and when Eugene Gant rode aboard it he went *with* time, *toward* a destination, *into* a future; which was all the certainty that a young man dubious of his chances ever to do any of those things could ask. Let others concern themselves as to whether the trip was worth taking, or the destination meaningfully selected, or with what the imagery, examined from a clinical perspective, might reveal. There would be time enough, and occasion enough, for these; as indeed there has been.

111

At least I can say for myself that I did not try to disown him and what his books had been for me, did not pretend that I had not once devoured and taken for access to truth the most outrageously egotistical, the most flagrantly romantic passages. I did not do what Eliot did to Shelley, who had once been *his* Thomas Wolfe: "The ideas of Shelley seem to me always to be ideas of adolescence. . . . And an enthusiasm for Shelley seems to me also to be an affair of adolescence. . . . I find his ideas repellant" (*The Use of Poetry and the Use of Criticism*). One ought, after all, to be able to grow, to go on to other and newer and, we may hope, wiser views without feeling it incumbent to repudiate what is no longer relevant to our needs. For to do so is not merely to put aside what one used to think and feel: it is to relinquish and repudiate the person who was then thinking and feeling. That would be the height of arrogance, and also of ingratitude, since it is only through what we have been in the past that we are able to attain what any future might bestow upon us in the way of greater knowledge, greater wisdom, greater self-understanding.

So I cannot view the writings of Thomas Wolfe as I might come to view the writings of many of the other authors I have since come to know and to admire—and some of whose books now seem to me wiser and better written than Wolfe's. For what I owe to Wolfe, because of what his books were to me at a particular stage of my life, goes too deep for dispassionate critical analysis (not that one should ever cease trying to understand one's experience of books or of anything else).

What Wolfe's fiction offered me, at a time when there was no one else to tell me so and when all the evidence seemed to be to the contrary, was a belief in myself as one who might some day be capable of a vocation. Reading and rereading his books, I was led to feel that my own provincial American middle-class background and experience could be used to help me interpret what was important and urgent about my world, that my own thoughts and emotions might even be worth writing about.

At the time when I read the Wolfe novels, I didn't need someone to teach me how to discriminate, to *not* like this as well as that, to prefer one thing over the other. That could come later. What I needed, and what I received from Wolfe, was the encouragement to try to express my own emotions, rather than someone else's. I cannot claim that what I made of such expression has been considered either important or enduring. On the contrary, all the evidence has been that it has been neither. But for limitations that are beyond my control I decline to accept responsibility.

The novelist Nancy Hale once remarked to me about Thomas Wolfe that "he makes you want to write." Aren't the Wolfe novels, finally, *about* being a writer? And if so, isn't one measure of their literary worth that they communicate the joy of using language so well that many young persons who read them want to write for themselves?

On one occasion I did at least try to acknowledge my indebtedness. Approximately a third of the way through *The Web and the Rock*, George Webber begins, for the first time, to attempt to write about his own childhood:

> For some time, a vague but powerful unrest had urged him on to the attempt, and now, without knowledge or experience, but with some uneasy premonition of the terrific labor he was at-

tempting to accomplish, he began—deliberately choosing a subject that seemed so modest and limited in its proportions that he thought he could complete it with the greatest ease. The subject he chose for his first effort was a boy's vision of life over a ten-month period between his twelfth and thirteenth year, and the title was, "The End of the Golden Weather."

When I was thirty-eight years old, in 1961, I published a novel. Like almost everything else that I have written over the course of what is now at least half a century of consciously trying to write well, it attracted very little attention at the time and none since. But it was about a twelve-year-old Jewish boy who lived with his parents in a house overlooking the Ashley River in Charleston, South Carolina, and the title I gave it was *The Golden Weather*.

113

Tournament was Shelby Foote's first novel. Originally written in 1939 and 1940, when he was in his early twenties, it was the book on which he first learned his craft. It was his first assertion of suzerainty over what would henceforth be his fictional demesne, the history and the society of the Mississippi Delta and adjoining areas. It was composed (as what novel of any young man's in that particular time and place could not have been?) in the shadow of William Faulkner, and despite *Tournament*'s having been rewritten from start to finish before publication in 1949, traces of the presence of the High Sheriff of Yoknapatawpha remain throughout. It was very much a "young man's book," lavish in its expenditure of literary capital that could have made up the consist of three or four novels.

It is to Shelby Foote's later fiction as, say, the Symphony No. 1 in C Major of Beethoven is to the Third, Fifth, and Seventh Symphonies. That is, while architecturally it is not as intricately constructed as its successors, and while it is much more sketchy in characterization, it is complete in and of itself, and no mere omen of things to come. Moreover, it is in *C Major*. I may as well say that in certain respects I prefer *Tournament* to much of the later fiction; I emphasize "in certain respects," for surely it is neither as psychologically complex nor as dramatically realized as what followed. What it does offer, however, is a kind of lyrical, even autobiographical access to its subject matter. There is a communicated delight in the writer's sheer ability to reproduce and re-create places, relationships, and meanings drawn from personal experience and from received family history and legend.

The logic for inclusion is not always based either upon the needs of the plot or the dramatic requirements of characterization. Is there, after all, from the standpoint of strict story line any real need for Foote to tell the story of Abe Wisten's business troubles, other than that he was drawing upon memories of his own Vienna-born grandfather, whose career bore no real-life relationship whatever to the acquisition of Mount Holly Plantation by Huger Foote, likewise the author's grandfather and the model for Hugh G. Bart in *Tournament?* Still, in the imaginative dynamics of Foote's fictional world, Abe Wisten certainly *belongs.* And because so much of what makes the novel appealing is its re-creation of a time and place, the Mississippi Delta of the late nineteenth and early twentieth centuries, it would scarcely occur to anyone to wonder just what the life of Abe Wisten has to do with the central thrust of Hugh Bart's life. Yet, other than the episode's contributing to Hugh Bart's ultimate attitude toward money and material possessions, which it does only in a thematic way, there is no real dramatic tie-in.

116

In his subsequent five works of fiction, Foote's method of telling a story would be mainly through the dramatic and psychological exploration of the interaction of his characters within a known historical context, and this is doubtless what has permitted him to continue to grow and develop as a writer. All the same, *Tournament,* to repeat, is no mere literary rehearsal, and it is satisfying to have it back in print again after so long a time.

Those who have written about Foote's first novel have noted that the story of Hugh Bart constitutes something of a search for a meaning to his life that he proves unable to discover in anything he has done, whether in politics, money making, planting, hunting, trapshooting, poker playing, or as husband and parent. All his engagements ultimately disappoint him, so that at the end there seems to be no explanation left other than that, to quote the words that his grandson Asa hears him speak on his deathbed: "The four walls are gone from around me, the roof from over my head. I'm in the dark, alone." Helen White and Redding S. Sugg, Jr., in their book on

Foote, note that the figure of Asa Bart suggests a "portrait of the artist," though Asa is present only in the prologue, briefly at the end of Hugh Bart's story, and in the epilogue. They assert quite properly that subsuming all else "there is the grand theme which Asa announces and which recurs throughout Foote's work: the loneliness of the human condition and the inherent difficulty of building any kind of satisfactory life at all." Yet it might also be remarked that something goes on in Foote's first novel that functions as a potential qualification of that bleak theme.

Foote has always insisted that one of the most potent influences on his own fiction has been the work of Marcel Proust. When he revised the novel for its initial publication in 1949, he comments in his introduction to the present edition, he was careful to remove "nearly all the Joyce, most of the Wolfe, and some of the Faulkner; what Proust I encountered I either left in or enlarged on." Somewhat strangely, few commentators on Foote's work appear to have paid much attention to his citing of Proust's role. But in the years that have followed publication of *Tournament,* Foote's acknowledged admiration for Proust's great book has in no way abated. It seems to me worthwhile, therefore, to look at certain aspects of his first novel with the example of *Remembrance of Things Past* in mind.

There is a point, close to the end, not long before Hugh Bart's death and after his fortune has declined almost to nothing, when he comes home late at night after playing poker, and lies in his bed beside his sleeping wife. That day, while talking with a peddler, he had been moved to attempt to recount his personal history. Now he thinks: "So there was no one: No one I can tell it to." It seems to him that "his attempt to present the story of his life was like trying to describe a man's appearance by displaying his skeleton. The truth lay in implications, not facts. Facts were only individual beads; the hidden string was what made them into a necklace." Then he adds: "But what kind of thinking was this, in which one minute the skeleton was not enough and the next the string in a row of beads was everything? The abstract was a trap: his brain was not meant for such work."

No reader familiar with Proust can mistake what is happening here. The implications—more than that, the overtly voiced assumptions—of the French novelist's great work are that human existence in time must of its very nature prove unsatisfactory, since it is only a succession of material experiences lacking permanence and devoid of any meaning beyond that of ephemeral sensation. It is only through art—time regained—that the relationships between our otherwise perishable moments of existence in time can be recognized and joined together into a reality that may endure free of chronology. The writer, Proust says,

118

> may list in an interminable description the objects that figured in the place described, but truth will begin only when the writer takes two different objects, establishes their relationship— analogous in the world of art to the sole relationship in the world of science, the law of cause and effect—and encloses them in the necessary rings of a beautiful style, or even when, like life itself, comparing similar qualities in two sensations, he makes their essential nature stand out clearly by joining them in a metaphor, in order to remove them from the contingencies of time, and links them together with the indescribable bond of an alliance of words.[1]

Nothing in Hugh Bart's experience, or within the community in which he has lived out his life, has taught or encouraged him to look for what is real and meaningful in anything other than material possessions and physical experience. But these have, inevitably as Foote sees it, failed to satisfy him, and now that he has used up most of his days, he is left with no coherent explanation for the way he has lived. It is Time that *was* the reality, but how could he ever know it for what it was, imprisoned as he was within its succession of moments? Thus, like all those characters in Proust who have sought their identity in what one of Proust's characters, the novelist Bergotte, referred to as the "inexhaustible torrent of fair forms," he is left at the close without anything to keep for his own.

How could Hugh Bart find a meaning for his experience, he

---

1. The translation here cited is that of C. K. Scott Moncrieff and Frederick A. Blossom in the two-volume Random House edition (1932) of *Remembrance of Things Past*. Moncrieff translated all but the seventh book, which was done by Blossom (pseud. Sydney Schiff) and in which the quotation above appears.

wonders, since "to tell it properly would require as much time as had been required to live it. There was no end to what it would have to contain. All the lives that had touched his own, some of them only slightly, had a share in the telling . . . these and so many others, how could he tell all that? Every one omitted, however, would be a space left blank on a canvas larger than life."

Of course, Hugh Bart cannot "tell it." He has been in succession farmer, sheriff, planter, hunter, parent, trapshooter, gambler; these must inevitably remain no more than successive disguises, each separate from the other in his memory, so long as he cannot discover in them what Proust calls their "essential nature" and succeed in "joining them in a metaphor, in order to remove them from the contingencies of time." And there is not time left to him to do that.

119

But it does not end there. For soon, we are told, "unexpectedly, he found a link." He had until then been so preoccupied with his own doings that he paid little attention to the presence of his grandson Asa. A few weeks before Christmas, however, he notices the boy at the top of the steps. "What are you watching?" he asks. At that "Asa looked up. His eyes were gray-green, the same as his grandfather's." Hugh Bart "leaned down, caught the child beneath the arms, and lifted him so that they looked directly into each other's face. And he held him, looking into eyes that were so much like his own."

What Hugh Bart sees in his grandson is analogous to what, near the end of *Remembrance of Things Past*, Marcel Proust's narrator sees when he beholds the daughter of his childhood friend Gilberte and his now-dead companion Robert de Saint-Loup: in her features she bears the impress of her ancestry—not only of her parents but of her grandfather Charles Swann, her grandmother Odette de Crécy, and of the Guermantes family heritage as well. She is thus the living fusion of certain persons who have played so immense a part in the narrator's own history, the union of what to the young Marcel had seemed the impossibly discrete and separate "ways" of the middle-class Swanns and Verdurins and the aristocratic Guermantes. To the narrator she is "very beautiful, still full of promise. Laughing, fashioned of the very years I had lost, she seemed to me like my own youth"; she is "a measure of the long lapse of years I had endeavored to ignore. Time, colorless and impalpable, had, in order that I might, as it were, see and touch it, physically embodied itself in her and had moulded her like a work of art."

Having identified in his grandson not merely the product but the validation of his having been alive in Time, it is no wonder that when Hugh Bart leaves his house, he "walked with that curious flat-footed stride, guarding his dignity. The gold head of his cane was a dancing gleam of sunlight, flashing on and off and on and off until he passed from sight." When Hugh Bart dies a few weeks afterward it is from a fall from a ladder as he reaches up to place a star at the peak of a Christmas tree he is trimming for his grandson: "Bart lay against the base of the tree, partly covered by the wreckage of cedar limbs, candles still in their sockets, and shards of colored glass. The tinsel star lay by his face."

In the same way, at the close of Proust's novel the narrator declares of an old friend that he "had wavered as he made his way along the difficult summit of his eighty-three years, as if men were perched on giant stilts sometimes taller than church spires, constantly growing and finally rendering their progress so difficult and perilous that they suddenly fall."

It seems clear that it will be Hugh Bart's grandson Asa who will redeem him from oblivion, much as the art of Marcel Proust's narrator will preserve Charles Swann from nothingness. Asa Bart, one surmises, will not himself make the mistake of confusing the "inexhaustible torrent of fair forms" for the reality of time regained, but will write a book *about* his grandfather's having done so, thus confuting the remorseless passage of time through reuniting past and present within the confines of a metaphor—entitled *Tournament*.

Stated thus baldly, it seems a somewhat pat solution to the complexities of human beings in time, place, and history, and in the way that *Tournament* is told, it does appear to be implanted upon the novel, as it were, rather than organically infused throughout the narration. I suspect that this, or something like it, is what Foote means when he describes it as a "young man's novel." It is not that *Tournament* doesn't "work" as a novel; on the contrary, as fiction it works, I believe, very nicely indeed. It holds together well, tells a good tale about an interesting man, and for all the Proust and Faulkner echoes audible throughout its telling, is essentially an original act of the literary imagination. But if we view the direction of Foote's subsequent work, it has not proceeded toward any more such direct portraiture of the artist as a young Mississippian. Rather, the development has been toward more dramatic, "objective" fiction, in which the experience, instead of being drawn relatively straightforwardly out of "real life" (however combined and reapportioned), has been transformed into characters and situations that furnish their own dynamics and set up their own relationships.

Indeed, one might even say of the young Shelby Foote that artistically there were for him two "ways" of discovery, Proust's and Faulkner's, and that what he decided was that for him the route toward realization of his own literary fulfillment lay by way of the latter approach. If so, he would appear to have chosen wisely. All the same, I am not so sure that the option tentatively contemplated in his first novel is meant to be closed out. "Permanently dead? Very possible." And possibly not, too. In any event, not having read a word of it myself, I predict that when the book that he is now engaged in writing, and which is suggestively entitled *Two Gates to the City,* reaches completion, it will be found to contain elements within it that will send the reader back to the "Asa" sections of his first novel, in much the same way that a reader of *Remembrance of Things Past* can look back at an earlier Proustian opus such as *Contre Sainte-Beuve* and see where certain things began.

Moreover, we might keep in mind that just as readers of Proust's great work found that there were really not two separate and mutually exclusive ways to choose from when setting out on a journey, but only one way that encompasses both paths, so a similar discovery may lie in store for Shelby Foote's readers. For the nature of the relationship between Hugh Bart and his grandson Asa in *Tournament* is by no means appropriate to the experience of the author of that book alone. After all, with certain relatively unimportant modifications it was also implicit in the family heritage of the great-grandson of Colonel William Clark Falkner, C.S.A.

121

I'LL TAKE MY STAND
THE LITERARY TRADITION
(1982)

I find myself in somewhat the predicament of the late General Nathan Bedford Forrest, who received for a third time the request of one of his officers for a leave of absence. To which the general responded with the scrawled endorsement, "I told you twicet alredy godamit No." Having written about the Agrarians repeatedly over the course of twenty-five years, including two different introductions to *I'll Take My Stand* as well as a full-length book, I don't know what I shall have to say that I haven't already said before and probably better.

The topic that was assigned to me was "the literary background of *I'll Take My Stand*." Certainly it does have a considerable literary background, not only in other literature but in the writings of the participants themselves. Upon reflection, however, I believe a better title would be "the literary foreground"—for it seems tolerably clear, now that fifty years have gone by, that the importance of *I'll Take My Stand* is principally as a *literary* work. It is an imaginative work on culture and society, and its survival past its immediate occasion is due, I think, largely to its literary quality. That is, its argument is effective because it makes an imaginative, emotional appeal as well as a logical one, through its use of a controlling image.

Sir Philip Sidney, in "An Apologie for Poetry" (1583), seeking to

123

justify poetry in the face of puritanism and the nascent prestige of science, advanced the thesis that the poet is superior to both the historian and the philosopher, in that "hee coupleth the generall notion with the particuler example. A perfect picture I say, for hee yeeldeth to the powers of the mind, an image of that whereof the Philosopher bestoweth but a woordish distinction: which dooth neyther strike, pierce, nor possesse the sight of the soule, so much as that other dooth." Similarly, what has made *I'll Take My Stand* endure, when other writings making much the same argument have long since receded into the domain of historical documentation, does not lie so much in the political cogency or the social appropriateness of the Agrarian program alone, as in the clarity and passion with which it was set forth. And just as in a good poem, the clarity and passion were not just rhetorical strategies added to sweeten and embellish the idea under discussion, but were integral to the formulation of the idea itself. As in other works of literature, the metaphorical possibility helped to shape the form: that metaphor was predicated upon the symbol of the rural South.

But it was *not* a symbol, someone might object (Donald Davidson once so objected to me). The Agrarians *meant* it literally. They were concerned with a particular time and place, and made specific suggestions and criticisms about that time and place. And I know that at least some of the Agrarians, in sober truth, intended just that. Well, but it was a symbol even so, and its survival is due to the fact that it was. Obviously it cannot have been the practical, topical recommendations of the Agrarian program that have made possible the continuing life of *I'll Take My Stand*. For a polemically designed book to speak to an audience a half century after its occasion, when the agricultural dispensation that the book advocated was not only obsolescent at the time but has now been utterly transformed, it must possess an appeal, must make a commentary on something, that is at once more general and more timeless in its relevance.

The ultimate assertion of *I'll Take My Stand* is in the form of pastoral. It is, fundamentally, a species of pastoral rebuke. Like all pastoral, it was written for and by, not shepherds and swains, even of the dirt-farming variety, but a sophisticated audience of citizens who, like the Agrarians themselves, were dwellers in cities.

We know, of course, that the extent and degree to which the indi-

124

vidual Agrarians actively believed in the practicability of a society of farmers differed from participant to participant, and that what they had in mind by "Agrarianism" varied considerably. Stark Young's and Andrew Lytle's notions of what would constitute a traditional rural community were about as far removed from each other as John Ransom's and H. C. Nixon's conceptions of what farmers thought and did and wanted. And so on. We know that the various participants arrived at Agrarianism by different routes, that involvement in the symposium served different needs and played different roles in their careers, and that within a very few years after they jointly took their stand they were headed off in different and sometimes contradictory directions. All this is a matter of record; in retrospect it is in no wise either remarkable or even regrettable.

125

What brought and held them together, then, was something in the Agrarian scheme that appealed to and, for a time at least, filled certain needs for all of them. It involved rural life, and this not only (perhaps not even principally) for its own sake, but for what it symbolized. It involved the South. It involved a cultural and literary attitude toward nature, and toward cities, of many centuries' standing. And it involved these things *symbolically,* by which I mean that whatever Agrarianism was topically, it stood for something else, and not allegorically but as tangible and real in its own right. As Coleridge says of the symbol, "It always partakes of the reality which it renders intelligible; and while it enunciates the whole, abides itself as a living part of that unity of which it is the representative."

It should not be forgotten that the moving spirits among the twelve Agrarians were principally the literary men—Ransom, Davidson, Tate, Lytle, to a somewhat lesser extent Wade. (Warren's involvement was peripheral; he was in England when the plans were being made.) The others were brought into the venture. Critics of *I'll Take My Stand* dismissed it as merely an affair of poets, which indeed it was. But in actuality this was the source of its greatest strength. For if the poem is, as Tate later defined it, "a formed realm of our experience, the distinction of which is its complete knowledge, the full body of the experience that it offers us," then this attitude can be said to have carried over into the Agrarian undertaking, so that, to an extent at least, the book that resulted made its appeal not only through reasoned expository argument but by embodiment of that argument in an image that could not be dismissed merely as having to do with a farming economy. T. S. Eliot would have it that it is not enough for the poet to look into his heart: "One must look into the cerebral cortex, the nervous system, and the digestive tracts." Without insisting that *I'll Take My Stand* is a poem (it is not), I would contend that its conception is significantly *poetic,* as might be expected of a work planned and developed by poets.

Let me look briefly at the literary tradition out of which it came. William Wordsworth, in the Preface to the Second Edition of the *Lyrical Ballads* (1802), made a case for the poetic imagination as being of especial importance in his day. "For a multitude of causes," he declared, "unknown to former times, are now acting with a combined force to blunt the discriminating powers of the mind, and unfitting it for all voluntary exertion, to reduce it to a state of almost savage torpor. The most effective of these causes are the great national events which are daily taking place [*i.e.,* the French Revolution, the Napoleonic Wars], and the increasing accumulation of men in cities, where the uniformity of their occupations produces a craving for extraordinary incident, which the rapid communication of intelligence hourly gratifies." His response as poet was to write poems having to do with nature, the countryside. It was his answer to the Industrial Revolution, and to the increasing specialization of work and narrowing of sensibility involved in modern life as a result of the exploitation of the natural world through applied science.

Now, in part that response involved nostalgia, but it was considerably more than that. Wordsworth set out to write a poetry that "rejoices in the presence of truth as our visible friend and hourly companion. Poetry is the breath and finer spirit of all knowledge; it is the impassioned expression which is in the countenance of all Science. Emphatically may it be said of the Poet, as Shakespeare hath said of man, 'that he looks before and after.' He is the rock of defense for human nature, carrying everywhere with him relationship and love." In short, poetry is to deal with the whole man, not the fragmented personality of the specialist, and the proper locus for that is not in cities but in the countryside, where the fragmentation and dissociation of sensibility have not yet done their work.

Wordsworth was by no means the first English poet to hold up man in nature as spiritual corrective to man in the city. It is a con-

comitant of English poetry from Shakespeare's time onward; it finds
vivid expression in Marvell's "The Garden":

> Meanwhile the mind, from pleasure less,
> Withdraws into its happiness:
> The mind, that ocean where each kind
> Does straight its own resemblance find;
> Yet it creates, transcending these,
> Far other worlds, and other seas;
> Annihilating all that's made
> To a green thought in a green shade.

127

The transcendental implications of the last two couplets in that
stanza, written as they were before the impact of Lockean sensa-
tionalism upon subsequent thought, are, to make a bad pun, indeed
mind-boggling. Generally, however, nature and the rural scene are
attractive because they are more restful, more tranquil and beautiful; the element of metaphysics is not customarily at issue. It is not
until the eighteenth century that urban society begins importantly
to be seen as constituting a menace to the natural world. I am sure
that most of the Agrarians, growing up in the South as I did, were
like myself made to memorize lines from Goldsmith's "The Deserted Village":

> Ill fares the land, to hastening ills a prey,
> Where wealth accumulates and men decay;
> Princes and lords may flourish or may fade;
> A breath can make them as a breath has made:
> But a bold peasantry, their country's pride,
> When once destroyed, can never be supplied.

The poem is a response to the Enclosure Laws and the movement of
the rural population into the factories of the city. By the close of the
eighteenth century, the problem of man in nature had assumed proportions so acute that it could no longer be dealt with, as it was in
previous times, merely as a mode of sensibility. It became part of the
very apprehension of experience itself, forcing a revolution in language, so that poetry, instead of being a commentary upon received

aspects of general human experience, must now endeavor to reconstitute that experience in order to give it a totality of meaning unavailable in other, partial forms of apprehension. And that poetry turned increasingly to nature, to the rural experience, not because it was typical of everyday human life, but because in subject matter and terms of reference it offered an *alternative* to what was fast becoming typical and habitual. Instead of nature being used as a term that included human experience—human nature—it now becomes what is *outside* human consciousness. Nature—physical nature—and the mind are separate entities. The poet turns to nature because, not being man-made, it is *real*. Thus Coleridge, in "Frost at Midnight," addresses his child as follows:

128

> For I was reared
> In the great city, pent 'mid cloisters dim,
> And saw naught lovely but the sky and stars.
> But *thou*, my babe! shalt wander like a breeze
> By lakes and sandy shores, beneath the crags
> Of ancient mountains, and beneath the clouds,
> Which image in their bulk both lakes and shores
> And mountain crags: so shalt thou see and hear
> The lovely shapes and sounds intelligible
> Of that eternal language, which thy God
> Utters, who from eternity doth teach
> Himself in all, and all things in himself.

Needless to say, this newer and more desperate relationship to nature and rurality became part of the American literary experience, for once the frontier had been pushed back to the mountains and the Navigation Acts repealed by the winning of independence, the new nation promptly underwent a rapid recapitulation of the Industrial Revolution, over the course of a few decades rather than across several centuries. Emerson's American Scholar Address is commonly taken as the overt declaration of American literary independence from Europe. Yet what is asserted is precisely the opposition to the fragmentation and specialization of industrial society that so exercised the British poets:

Man is not a farmer, or a professor, or an engineer, but he is all. Man is priest, and scholar, and statesman, and producer, and soldier. In the *divided* or social state these functions are parcelled out to individuals, each of whom aims to do his stint of the joint work, whilst each other performs his. The fable implies that the individual, to possess himself, must sometimes return from his own labor to embrace all the other laborers. But, unfortunately, this original unit, this fountain of power, has been so distributed to multitudes, has been so minutely subdivided and peddled out, that it is spilled into drops, and cannot be gathered. The state of society is one in which the members have suffered amputation from the trunk, and strut about like so many walking monsters,—a good finger, a neck, a stomach, an elbow, but never a man.

129

And to remedy this state of affairs the first recourse that Emerson offers to his scholar is nature. For the rural world can teach him not fragmentation but organic wholeness: "He shall see that nature is the opposite of the soul, answering to it part for part. One is seal and one is print. Its beauty is the beauty of his own mind. Its laws are the laws of his own mind. Nature then becomes to him the measure of his attainments."

For Emerson's friend Thoreau, the condition of man under modern commercial society is considerably more desperate:

Men think it essential that the *Nation* have commerce, and export ice, and talk through a telegraph, and ride thirty miles an hour, without a doubt, whether *they* do or not; but whether we would live like baboons or like men, is a little uncertain. If we do not get out sleepers [cross-ties], and forge rails, and devote days and nights to the work, but go to tinkering upon our *lives* to improve *them*, who will build railroads? And if railroads are not built, how shall we get to heaven in season? But if we stay at home and mind our business, who will want railroads? We do not ride on the railroad; it rides on us.

Which is Thoreau's industrialized version of "Things are in the saddle, and ride mankind."

I am aware that it is considered an act of semi-treason to suggest the existence of important affinities between the Nashville Fugitives and Agrarians and the New England Transcendentalists, and I am quite aware of the considerable differences between what the New Englanders and the Southerners thought concerning what "nature" was, and what man's relationship to it ought to be. There is, for one thing, in the Southerners no transcendental escape from the ultimate duality of matter and spirit. Yet it seems undeniable that implicit in the dynamics of the so-called American Renaissance of the mid-nineteenth century was much the same desire to assert the primacy of religious humanism in the face of the mechanistic positivism of applied science, as is exemplified in assertions like the following, from the "Statement of Principles" to *I'll Take My Stand:*

130

> Religion is our submission to the general intention of a nature that is fairly inscrutable; it is the sense of our role as creatures within it. But nature industrialized, transformed into cities and artificial habitations, manufactured into commodities, is no longer nature but a highly simplified picture of nature. We receive the illusion of having power over nature, and lose the sense of nature as something mysterious and contingent. The God of nature under these conditions is merely an amiable expression, a superfluity, and the philosophical understanding ordinarily carried in the religious experience is not there for us to have.

There were available to the Agrarians, then, powerful literary precedents for thinking and writing about rural society and the natural world as a moral and social corrective to modern urban complexity, for identifying the countryside and life on the land as offering a wholeness of personality and a less mechanistic attitude toward human identity than did urban experience, and for the use of nature as pastoral rebuke to the dehumanizing forces present in mass industrial society. The attitude was part of their thinking, as literary men; the literary tradition to which as young twentieth-century American writers they were heirs embodied that perspective as a mode of language and form.

They were not only young American poets, however; they were *Southerners.* The patterns of their community experience had until recently been almost totally rural. From colonial times onward the South had been agricultural; it had remained so when the North had turned to industry. Its leading philosopher had proclaimed the virtuous husbandman as the new republic's social ideal. "Those who labor in the earth," Thomas Jefferson declared, "are the chosen people of God, if ever he had a chosen people, whose breasts he has made his peculiar deposit for substantial and genuine virtue." As for urbanization, "the mobs of great cities add just so much to the support of pure government, as sores do to the strength of the human body." For more than a century after Jefferson the politics of the South was focused upon enunciating the needs of an agricultural community in opposition to the rival claims of an industrial and commercial economy. The response of the South to the Industrial Revolution had not been the factory, but the plantation system. The planter, not the capitalist, had been the Old South's dominant image. And after the defeat of the Civil War, though the notion of a New South of commerce and industry gained powerful adherents, the region had remained largely rural in economy and social attitude. The loss of the war had the effect of retarding any significant industrial development that might otherwise have occurred in accordance with the dynamics of nineteenth-century society; there was no capital available to build the factories.

131

It was well into the twentieth century before any sizable proportion of the South's population began to derive its income from industrial growth. Thus, the life of cities had come very late to the region, and its hold on the Southern mind was still of recent vintage, while the suddenness of its impact—the years after the First World War were when it first got really into high gear—dramatized the contrast between rural past and urban present. The old ways, however threadbare, still maintained a powerful hold on the imagination; rural life, in a time of change and confusion, still seemed, in several senses, "natural," a farming economy normal, real. It was the life of big cities that represented the new, the unfamiliar. Thus social experience and literary tradition alike offered, to a group of young men disturbed about their section's future and dismayed at the rampant materialism and commercial opportunism of the 1920s, the Agrarian metaphor. It has been pointed out, and rightly, that the revolt against machine-dominated society and mass dehumanization was very much in the air during the 1920s. The poets that the Fugitives read were full of it, whether in Eliot's "unreal city" in which

> Under the brown fog of a winter dawn,
> A crowd flowed over London Bridge, so many,
> I had not thought death had undone so many.

or Pound's "Mauberly" for whom

> All things are a flowing,
> Sage Heraclitus says;
> But a tawdry cheapness
> Shall outlast our days.

or Yeats:

> Locke sank into a swoon;
> The Garden died;
> God took the spinning-jenny
> Out of his side.

The intellectual community of the 1920s was repeatedly being reminded, polemically and diagnostically, that all was not well in the industrialized and progressive Western World. The message was implicit in Lawrence's novels, in *The Great Gatsby, Manhattan Transfer,* "The Great God Brown," *The Sun Also Rises,* "The Second Coming," *The Waste Land;* it was explicit in the disquisitions of Lewis Mumford, Walter Lippmann, Joseph Wood Krutch, Hilaire Belloc, James Truslow Adams, Ralph Borsodi, Dean Inge, Stuart Chase. There can be no question but that the Agrarian venture was part and parcel of the overall protest of thoughtful people against the unchecked disintegrative forces in Western industrial life, forces that would eventuate in the Great Depression that struck just as the Agrarian symposium was coming to fruition.

What the Agrarians had as their own, however, was the tangible experience of the Southern community as it confronted, belatedly and fiercely, the impact of modernity. Thus they possessed an im-

132

age, a focus for their own critique, which not only grounded their response in the actualities of American historical experience but in so doing protected them from the abstract panaceas of Marxism and Fascism that proved so catastrophic to much of the social thinking of the 1930s. If there was an element of abstraction in Agrarianism, as in all ideologies, it was largely held in check by the palpable and tangible social experience of the Southern community involvement that all Agrarians inherited by birth and upbringing. Agrarianism may have been a concept; the Southern community, with its rural ties and historical loyalties, was substantial, a thing of flesh and blood. And if, as young intellectuals of the 1920s, the Agrarians had experienced something of the sense of rootlessness and dissociation that Malcolm Cowley has described as an "exile . . . from any society to which they could honestly contribute and from which they could draw the strength that lies in shared convictions," their response was to assert an identity with a community that for them was not so irretrievably lost that it possessed no meaning except nostalgia. They were moderns, but they were Southerners; they could still think of themselves as having a place to go to.

133

Whatever the literal practicality of Agrarianism might have been at the close of the third decade of the twentieth century, there can be little doubt that it represented, for the twelve Southerners who took part in the 1930 symposium, considerably more and other than an intellectual formulation, a strategic device for developing an argument. It was a *cause,* demanding and receiving of its adherents emotional engagement as well as rational assent. In the long run the decision to use the Agrarian identification may have blunted the force of the participants' critique of industrial dehumanization through exposing it to ridicule because of the anachronistic economics. For it was as a rebuke to the uncritical espousal of material Progress that *I'll Take My Stand* had something important to say to its readers, and not as a social and economic program. We know that Tate and Warren made a last-minute attempt to have the title of the symposium changed so as to avoid the overt Southern identification that came from the echoing of the war song of the Confederacy. The use of that title, Tate warned, would enable hostile critics "only to draw portraits of us plowing or cleaning a spring to make hash of us before we get a hearing." And of course he was right; that, so far as the immediate reception of the book is concerned, is exactly what happened.

The argument, however, leaves out the obvious truth that it was precisely the Southern identification, neo-Confederate associations and all, that accounts for much of the book's cohesion and passion, for it enabled the participants to draw what for *all* of them was a powerfully felt community identification. What the details of the "South" meant for each of them differed from participant to participant, but for all of them it involved vigorous emotional as well as intellectual loyalties, grounded in a common geography, drawing upon a shared sense of social identity, and given form and feeling by a passionately shared historical mythos.

134

John Shelton Reed, in an excellent essay, has described this element as something closely resembling nationalism, which he properly characterizes as one of the central forces of the past several hundred years.[1] I am not so certain that nationalism is precisely the term for what he is describing, however; certainly the Confederate loyalty was present, more so for some than for others, but I do not believe that the Agrarians considered themselves as any other or less than Americans *in* their Southern loyalties. Sectionalism, however much it was considered a "bad" word (the "good" word was regionalism), comes perhaps closer than nationalism: the community identification, independent of the political concomitants usually associated with the term nationalism, is what was uppermost. I can't really see the Agrarians as the equivalent of young Scottish nationalists plotting to steal the Stone of Scone. (Indeed, there have been historians who have declared that even the wartime Confederates were not really nationalists at heart, and that the defeat of the Confederacy was due in important respects to the absence of a true sense of nationalism on the part of the people of the South; the Confederacy has been described as having come into being and subsequently disintegrated because of states' rights.)

The important point, however, which I believe Mr. Reed is getting at, is that anyone who attempts to strip *I'll Take My Stand* of

1. John Shelton Reed, "For Dixieland: The Sectionalism of *I'll Take My Stand*," in *A Band of Prophets: The Vanderbilt Agrarians After Fifty Years*, ed. William C. Havard and Walter Sullivan (Baton Rouge: Louisiana State University Press, 1982), 41–64.

its distinctively Southern character, and fails to recognize that the
Agrarian identification was a powerful and probably essential symbolic element in the involvement of the participants in the common
enterprise, ignores a great deal of what has kept this book alive for a
half-century. The agrarian community provided an image for what
the participants cherished about the South, and the South in turn
constituted a symbol for qualities that were lacking in mass technological society, and that were very much menaced by the forces
of urban industrialism. Stark Young's caveat—"We defend certain
qualities not because they belong to the South, but because the
South belongs to them"—is only half true. In the minds of most of
the young Agrarians, no such distinction could be made.

As for just what those qualities are, Tate has used the term "religious humanism," which is appropriate, I think, but needs to be
supplemented by the word *Southern*. There have been many attempts to characterize the cultural and social ideals of religious humanism in relationship to the South. Tate himself has referred to
"knowledge carried to the heart," and has summarized them in his
description of what Aeneas takes with him after the destruction
of Troy:

> —a mind imperishable
> If time is, a love of past things tenuous
> As the hesitation of receding love.

Earlier, Henry Timrod had offered the following formulation:

> the type
> Whereby we shall be known in every land
> Is that vast gulf which lips our Southern strand,
> And through the cold, untempered ocean pours
> Its genial streams, that far off Arctic shores
> May sometimes catch upon the softened breeze
> Strange tropic warmth and hints of summer seas.

I like best John Ransom's way of putting it:

> True, it is said of our Lady, she ageth.
> But see, if you peep shrewdly, she hath not stooped;

Take no thought of her servitors that have drooped,
For we are nothing; and if one talk of death—
Why, the ribs of the earth subsist frail as a breath
If but God wearieth.

In Ransom's uniting of poetry, religion, ritual, the land, and Southern history in a single developed image, we have, I think, not only the themes of *I'll Take My Stand*, but the underlying values that Agrarianism symbolized. In identifying the Agrarian symposium as a form of pastoral, shaped to remind a modern community of the dangers of dehumanization, I mean to insist that *I'll Take My Stand* is, finally, a poetic work. Wordsworth described poetry as "a homage paid to the native and naked dignity of man, to the grand elementary principle of pleasure, by which he knows, and feels, and loves, and moves." (By pleasure Wordsworth meant not mere sensory enjoyment but the passion and knowledge of the mind of man in nature.) Not all the Agrarians were poets; not all were literary men. But what the terms of the enterprise drew from all of them was the fusion of knowledge and feeling that characterizes the poetic imagination. The cogency of the argument cannot be separated from the disciplined passion with which it is articulated. That is why, fifty years after it was set forth, we continue to read the book.

R. P. W., 1905–1989

(1990)

He was on the literary scene, an active participant, for *sixty-five years*. Think of what an expanse of time that career bridges! When he published his first poems in the *Fugitive* in 1923, Thomas Hardy, Joseph Conrad, Anatole France, Henri Bergson, and George W. Cable were still alive. Mary Cassatt, Claude Monet, and George Bellows were painting. H. L. Mencken was king of the roost, an obscure poem called *The Waste Land* was being extolled by the avant-garde and damned by all right-thinking critics who knew what Beauty was. Nobody much had ever heard of William Faulkner, Thomas Wolfe, or Hart Crane. *The Great Gatsby* would not be published for another two years. Eudora Welty was a thirteen-year-old in Jackson, Mississippi.

He lived to be eighty-four. Yet I daresay that few persons ever thought of Robert Penn Warren as an old man. We recognized, these past few years, that he was in bad shape when we saw him hobbling around with a cane, and saw the flesh on that furrowed, incredibly bony face now drawn as thin as blotched parchment. The russet hair that gave him his nickname had long since lost all trace of redness. Still, he was Red—Red Warren, friend to so many, with that Kentucky drawl that, added to his habit of bunching his words together, could make a conversation with him into an act of interpretation. (That for the last year or so he could scarcely make himself understood at all, only those closest to him, as I certainly was not, knew.)

He had a way of speaking in staccato bursts. In 1969, at the height of the New Left unrest, he came to read poems at Harvard, where I was teaching in summer school, and I was invited to dinner with him, along with a well-known eighteenth-century scholar on the Harvard faculty. (The latter was most affable, full of conversation when in the presence of the poet. The next day, at lunch in the Faculty Club and without Red, he cut me dead.) After dinner we went by the Harvard Commons, where there were hordes of dissidents encamped by day and night. Red gazed at the spectacle of shirtless torsos, lengthy male hairdos, and other desperately contrived imitations of proletarian habiliment on the Commons. "It's *like-a-magnet*," he remarked. "Draws 'em from a *thousan'-miles-aroun'*—."

138

The first time I met him was in 1953, at Johns Hopkins, when he came to give a reading. He had recently published *World Enough and Time,* and he was not thought of primarily as a poet at that time. *All the King's Men* had come out eight years earlier, had brought stunning success, and now he was famous.

He did something that I found astonishing. With his recent bride, Eleanor Clark, he was staying at the home of an emeritus professor who was a cousin of Eleanor's, and after lunch he excused himself and retired to his room to work on a novel. How could anyone on the road like that simply close the door for two hours and write? I wondered. What kind of incredible power of concentration enabled him, amid unfamiliar surroundings, to shut out the world around him like that?

Many decades later, in the 1970s, I was spending the night at his home in Connecticut, and was sitting around at breakfast talking with Eleanor at an early hour when he came into the room in his pajamas and robe. "Well, I got two poems started this morning," he remarked. "Do you mean you've already been up and working in your study?" I asked. No, he said, he had begun them while lying in bed. I found that equally incredible. I could not imagine the act of writing taking place without the actual putting down of words on paper. But apparently he could simply clear his conscious mind of externalities and proceed to think out and isolate images, lines, even stanzas, to be committed to paper at leisure.

He first came into notice as one of the Nashville Fugitives, that brilliant group of poets centered at or near Vanderbilt University who published the little magazine known as the *Fugitive*. Of the four Fugitives who became professional men of letters—John Ransom, Allen Tate, Donald Davidson, and Warren—he was the youngest. Tate always considered him the most gifted young man he had ever known.

The poetry the Fugitives favored, and which distinguished them and their magazine from among the dozens of little poetry groups and societies that were flourishing everywhere in the United States at the time, was controlled, focused, grounded in words—language—rather than ideas. It was objective, complete, fully crafted, not the spontaneous overflow of powerful feelings but the disciplined re-creation of those emotions into words and images. For Ransom and Tate it was an ideal poetics; as poets they could realize themselves fully within it.

139

Warren's early poetry was composed in the same mode, and not without considerable success. A poem such as "Bearded Oaks," so frequently anthologized, is evidence of that. But for Warren it was not really a congenial aesthetic. His imagination was not naturally formal, self-contained, compressed; rather it was expansive, far-ranging, open-ended, and highly personal. Even so, the apprenticeship he served was useful and valuable, for it schooled him in the properties of language, taught him the absolute importance of specific words, the precision of concise metaphor.

It was the telling of stories, finally, that liberated him as poet, but only after a lengthy period of not writing verse. During the 1930s he began to try his hand at fiction—short stories and then novels. He wrote several novels before *Night Rider* was published in 1939. That book, based on the Black Patch War of the early 1900s between the tobacco growers of his native south-central Kentucky and the buying monopolies, was well received, but it was his third published novel, *All the King's Men,* that earned him his first general fame as a writer.

Begun as a verse play only a few years after the assassination of United States Senator Huey P. Long, the Louisiana "Kingfish," in the foyer of the state capitol in Baton Rouge, and written at a time when the dictatorships were seemingly triumphing over the democracies in Europe, *All the King's Men* centered on a charismatic populist politician who knew how to appeal to the otherwise inchoate aspirations, fears, and affections of the mass of people, and who was willing to play fast and loose with the checks and balances of constitutional government as he moved to translate his programs into action.

What Warren's fictional Willie Stark exemplified was the central problem of democracy and representative government: responsible leadership. How to galvanize the mass of voters into recognizing where their own welfare lay and acting to make government genuinely responsive to their needs, while at the same time resisting the temptation to seek and to wield power for power's sake—such was the meaning of the phenomenon of Huey Long and others like him, as Warren saw it. In Willie Stark, Warren created a man whose ideals became inextricably bound in with his craving for power. As Stark came more and more to identify the public good with his private needs and ambitions, compromise became corruption, and success brought tragedy for himself and to all involved.

140

Today, more than four decades after it was published, *All the King's Men* remains the quintessential American political novel, read and taught in both literature and political science classes in many hundreds of colleges and universities. So pervasive is its literary example that almost every political novel written since it appeared unconsciously imitates its approach and echoes its key scenes. Subsequently he wrote seven other novels, making ten in all, several of them highly successful, but none was ever to approach *All the King's Men* in popularity or lasting impact.

As a writer of fiction Warren was a Philosophical Novelist. He defined the genre himself in an essay on Conrad: "one for whom the documentation of the world is constantly striving to rise to the level of generalization about values, for whom the image strives to rise to symbol, for whom images always fall into a dialectical configuration, for whom the urgency of experience, no matter how vividly and strongly experience may enchant, is the urgency to know the meaning of experience."

It was his strength as a writer of fiction—and also his weakness. For sometimes the patterns he evolved to develop his ideas gained precedence over the stories of people that he wanted to tell. A novel such as *World Enough and Time,* for example, is dramatically complete a half-hundred pages before it actually concludes. The temptation to round out his thematic scheme at the expense of fictional probability was all too real. Even *All the King's Men* is flawed by it; would the Anne Stanton that Warren characterized ever have become Willie Stark's mistress?

Almost nothing that Warren wrote is *perfect* in form, because Warren simply was not that kind of writer. He took chances, discovered meanings as he went along, tried new ways, alternate approaches, fresh strategies; his tastes were eclectic, his sympathies wide-ranging. He could never wrap his experience up in neat little packages tied in bows.

Nor was his taste fastidious. There was a coarse, earthy streak to him that was largely missing in the other Fugitives, and that I think helped to make possible his success as a novelist. The documentation of the world did not offend him. Allen Tate and Caroline Gordon in particular felt that he had sold out, and Caroline caricatured him cruelly in *The Strange Children*. I daresay the financial and journalistic renown that came to Red with *All the King's Men* and stayed with him thereafter caused jealousy. "Red Warren always courted popularity," Allen said once. "Read his criticism. He's never written an unfavorable review. He's never attacked anyone." "What about his piece on Thomas Wolfe?" I asked. "That's not unfavorable," Allen replied. It depends, I suppose, on how one defines the word; certainly Wolfe thought the essay was unfavorable, although later he and Warren became friends.

That Red was keenly ambitious for literary success and fame is undoubtedly true. How could anyone not have been who was endowed with so much talent and blessed with so much energy? But— and I think this is important—he was never covetous of the success that others won. He wanted his own books, his writings, to be successful; he wanted to achieve fame through what he *wrote,* not through literary politics and because of who he *knew.*

He had an endless curiosity. Wherever he went, he wanted to see what was there. We were at a conference at The Citadel, in Charleston, South Carolina, once. Apparently he had never visited Charleston before. Almost the first thing he wanted to know was how he could go out to see Fort Sumter. It was a very hot day, and the rest of us chose to sit around the air-conditioned hotel talking. Not Red; he went out to Fort Sumter on the tour boat.

As a critic of literature he was vastly influential. The textbook he

141

wrote with Cleanth Brooks, *Understanding Poetry*, revolutionized the teaching of poetry in American universities and colleges. Read the poem, Brooks and Warren insisted. What does the poem before you actually say? Why did the poet use *these* particular words and images rather than other words and images? What is the relationship between this word in this line and that word in the next line? Critical fashions have changed in the half-century since *Understanding Poetry* first appeared, but it seems safe to say that never again will a teacher, no matter how wedded to concerns of ideology, politics, biography, theology, theory, or whatever, be able to get by without first reading the poem itself, as an artifact, for what the printed words themselves actually say.

142

Yet Red Warren did not consider himself a real "critic." He lacked the conceptualizing talent needed for writing important critical discourse, he insisted, declaring that he wrote criticism as a duty, in order to put bread on the table. Perhaps so. But I don't believe he could compartmentalize his life in such fashion as that.

In recent years the "New Criticism" with which Warren, Brooks, and their friends Ransom and Tate were identified has come under attack, and it has been the fashion to characterize the critical method that they advocated as unconcerned with history, politics, and society and its problems, and even as "elitist," covertly aimed at shoring up the political and social status quo, and "crypto-Anglican." (I have never understood how someone like Cleanth Brooks could be attacked on the one hand for wishing to leave all the history out of poetry, and in the very next breath accused of being an active Confederate sympathizer.)

For some reason, having I think not to do with his critical attitudes but the parlor politics of literature, Warren was usually exempted from these strictures, or else assailed only obliquely. As if *Understanding Poetry* were not at least as much Warren's as Brooks's! As if his essay on "Pure and Impure Poetry" was not one of the seminal documents of the New Criticism!

How anyone could think that a critical method that stressed careful reading and insisted upon the primacy of the text itself was necessarily a prescription for narrowness and exclusivity still escapes me. That it didn't limit Warren's horizons must surely be obvious to anyone who has ever taken the time to look at his critical writings.

What is striking is the range of its sympathies and interests. The same man who could write "Pure and Impure Poetry" (itself a document for *inclusiveness,* not exclusiveness) and "A Poem of Pure Imagination" also published highly appreciative studies of Melville, Faulkner, Dreiser, and Whittier. He was one of the earliest critics to do Faulkner full justice. He wrote history, biography, political journalism, drama, and in the 1950s and 1960s published two books attacking racial segregation. I got a letter from him once written from France, in which he said that he was currently caught up in reading Zola. What a marvelous writer! he declared. Zola? Of all things!

Several years ago, growing weary at some of the nonsense that was being written about the New Critics, I used an assignment to write a paper on Warren's criticism to point out that he believed strongly in the role of the critic as interpreter of a text, placed a premium upon the recognition of complexity and the supposedly "bourgeois distrust of singlemindedness and commitment" (I quote the words of one structuralist polemic), and insisted that the critic must look long and hard at the literary work itself for its own sake. He was highly suspicious of easy, self-serving moral judgments and overly simplified readings. When the book containing the symposium papers appeared, Red was delighted. I won't go into the details of what he wrote, but I recall one remark in particular: "Yale School, my ass!"

143

Not being the sort of person who enjoyed literary controversy, Red didn't get into the structuralist and deconstructionist controversies of the past several decades. He was too busy writing new poems. For of course it was poetry that was Red Warren's real love. Following a hiatus of six or seven years during the 1940s, he moved back into writing it, and for the remainder of his life it was his principal literary activity.

The pivotal book in his career as poet was *Brother to Dragons: A Tale in Verse and Voices,* published in 1953. In the late 1930s he had written several long poems drawing upon folklore and history and with an implicit narrative content, but to tell the story of Thomas Jefferson's imagined confrontation with the nature of evil following the brutal murder of a slave by a nephew, he interposed a dramatic spokesman, labeled "R. P. W.," to argue with Jefferson and to discuss and comment upon the implications of what went on.

Apparently the possibilities inherent in this voice opened the way for Warren to move into a new poetic mode, giving him access to a persona that would enable him to speak for himself more directly and immediately, and allowing him to range into personal and family history, private rumination and comment, historical and political meditation, thus liberating him from the more impersonal poetics of his earlier years.

Whatever it was that made it possible, it triggered a cascade of new poems, many of them long and divided into multiple sections, and that continued throughout the three decades remaining to his life. *Promises: Poems, 1954–1956* was followed by *You, Emperors, and Others: Poems, 1957–1960,* and thereafter every few years saw the appearance of a new book of Warren's poetry.

As might be expected, not all of his verse was of the highest quality. Sometimes it seemed as if, rather than writing poems, he was writing something known as Poetry—which is to say, an ongoing flow of emotive images, lines, stanzas, passages that did not always attain the individualized uniqueness of completed, fully realized literary statements. Again, however, his temperament was such that it worked against tightly compressed, formally perfect entities.

At his best, as in such poems as *Audubon: A Vision,* "Homage to Emerson," and *Rumor Verified,* this gifted, introspective, boldly speculative craftsman of language seemed to be moving from strength to strength, producing poem after poem of breathtaking intensity. Certainly the body of his collected verse represents a sustained creative accomplishment of extraordinary power and beauty.

Future biographers will, and I think rightly, link the wealth and profusion of Red Warren's poetry from the mid-1950s onward to the circumstances of his domestic life. After a lengthy, unhappy first marriage that ended in divorce in 1950, with his marriage to Eleanor Clark in 1952 he entered upon years of enduring happiness as a husband and, finally, in his forties, as a father, that were deeply gratifying to his friends.

For all the public fame and literary renown that Red came into following the success of *All the King's Men,* and that continued thereafter during all his remaining years, he was probably the least affected by it of any writer I have ever known. I never knew him to put on airs, demand special treatment and consideration, or in any way to be other than the friendly, open, enormously kind and considerate person he so thoroughly was. If he ever sustained a grudge, schemed and maneuvered for favor, cultivated the influential and important because of their influence and importance, I have never heard of it. His ambition sought recognition and reward entirely through the merits of his literary performance itself. I never heard him try to put down anybody, or slight anyone. He was endlessly patient, repeatedly generous.

I like to think of him as I saw him once in Nashville, on the occasion of the Fugitives Reunion in 1956, when belatedly Vanderbilt University consented to honor the group of poets who three decades earlier had begun to give it the worldwide fame it enjoyed in literary circles. It was late in the evening, at the old Allen Hotel, after a long day of conferences and ceremonies. By then the celebrities, the distinguished older poets and critics, had all gone off to bed—all except Red. With three or four of us younger people, he sat up—in point of fact Red was lying across my bed—talking about this and that until the wee hours. Stand on his dignity? Expect deference? Not Red Warren. He was having much too good a time just talking.

How could Red have endured that final year when he was scarcely able to talk? One can only hope that he did not fully realize what was happening to him. How he loved conversation! I remember the time when we were both taking part in the program at The Citadel. I had finished giving my talk and was leaving the auditorium before the next program started, when Red noticed it. "Wait a minute and I'll go with you," he said. He didn't want to sit through the next event, either. We went outside and found a bench at the edge of the parade grounds. He then proceeded to talk almost non-stop for fifty minutes.

Now Red is gone. Of the Vanderbilt group, only Andrew Lytle and Cleanth Brooks survive, though Cleanth was younger and never actually a Fugitive. As men of letters their influence was profound. Their coming together, at that place and in that time, was one of those seemingly fortuitous happenings that defy mathematical probability. Of all of them, I think, Red Warren made the most of his gifts, worked hardest and to best effect. His passing diminishes us all.

145

PART II

CRITICAL OCCASIONS

THE MENCKEN MYSTERY

(1991)

If the mystery of what made H. L. Mencken tick is ever to be solved, I am convinced that the services of a psychoanalytically trained critic will be required, and moreover, one with a sense of humor (if that is not a contradiction in terms). Nothing less than full professional competence in getting at the interior man through the exterior facade is needed. The more I read about and by Mencken—an edition of his diary, 1930–1948, edited by Charles A. Fecher, is the latest piece of evidence to emerge—the more convinced I am that the nature of this man, his writings, his life, constitutes a literary puzzle that thus far has gone not only unsolved, but largely without even being investigated.

Despite the fact that he lived his literary life in public, and left an incredible array of papers meticulously arranged for posterity, we know less about the inner Mencken than about almost any other American author of wide repute. Compared with Mencken, our understanding of Mark Twain, say, or Henry James is monumental. To say that Mencken has been taken at face value, with almost no effort made to square what the man wrote with what he thought

Scheduled for publication as a review-essay on *The Diary of H. L. Mencken,* ed. Charles A. Fecher (New York: Knopf, 1989), in the *Sewanee Review* (Summer, 1991).

and did, is to understate the matter. There are enough anomalies, enigmas, and contradictions present and unaccounted for in his recorded personality to keep a literary clinician busy for years. The recent publication of selections from his diary only increases the bafflement.

For starters, contemplate the following:

Item. This vigorous foe of hypocrisy, sham, and cant of every variety seems never to have questioned the social, political, and racial assumptions of a middle-class businessman father whose notions of the true, the good, and the beautiful were identical with those of a well-heeled Saxon burgher of the time of Frederick the Great.

150

Item. This author, who entitled his biographical memoir of childhood *Happy Days,* a phrase that in every sense is an accurate description of the subject matter and approach, seriously contemplated suicide when young.

Item. This most dutiful and admiring of sons, who despite pronounced literary leanings and a strong yearning to become a newspaperman was sent by his father to a vocational high school and then made to go into the family cigar manufacturing business, applied for a job as a newspaper reporter immediately after his father's funeral.

Item. This affectionate, warm-hearted, highly domestic man, for whom family life and ties were of the utmost importance throughout his life and who greatly enjoyed the company of women, did not marry until the age of fifty, and then to a woman whose health was so poor that doctors had accurately warned her she could expect to live only for a few years.

Item. This inventor of a magnificent *bravura* style, the slightest of whose published writings can be counted upon to provide wit and excitement, kept a diary written for the most part in the most uncomplicated and verveless prose.

Item. This man, a majority of whose closest friends were Jews, and who frequented the company of Jews throughout his adult life, generously sprinkled his diary with anti-Semitic comments, made no public complaints about Hitler, was convinced that England had gulled the United States into opposing Nazi Germany just as she had done in 1917, and wrote in his diary at the end of World War II that "the American people will now begin paying for their folly. The bills will keep on coming in for 50 years."

Item. This man whose several volumes of autobiography are notable for the almost complete absence of introspection and of revelations of his private thoughts and emotions, and who left a note asking that upon his death his longtime associates on the Baltimore *Sun* refrain from any notice of it beyond a brief factual announcement, spent much of his later years compiling, recording, and organizing massive records of all his career and writings, and noted with satisfaction in his diary that "not many American authors will ever leave a more complete record" behind for posterity.

Item. The author of this statement, about a Dreiser novel—"it is drab and gloomy, but so is the struggle for existence. It is without humor, but so are the jests of the great comedian who shoots at our heels and makes us do our grotesque dancing"—and of this one, about Mark Twain—"The real Mark was a man haunted to the point of distraction by the endless and meaningless tragedy of existence"—could depose in his diary that "despite some staggering shocks," among them the death of a wife, the loss of a reading public, the frustration of two wars, and a hypochondriacal parade of ailments, "I have had, on the whole, an extremely happy life."

And so on. There is so much contrariety and antithesis to Mencken that anyone who would address the issue can scarcely decide where to begin. I propose to get at the matter through his anti-Semitism, not only because I find it particularly difficult to swallow, but also because that and his attitude toward his father strike me as being perhaps the most puzzling things about this baffling human being.

Anti-Semitism among literary folk can take various forms and manifestations, ranging from a mild prejudice against strangers to the active advocacy of Nazism. Not since the seventeenth century has it really had a theological basis. In its least virulent form it is typically a product of unexamined xenophobia, customarily having to do with a distrust of changing times and a fear of the erosion of inherited status. There was a great deal of it around in the late nineteenth and early twentieth century, for example, on the part of people like Henry Adams, James Russell Lowell, John Jay Chapman, etc., who as survivors of the early Anglo-American upper-middle-class establishment felt threatened by new money and unfamiliar customs, mores, attitudes, and the like.

151

It can also have a basis in more or less abstract political and ideological differences, whether helping to produce such differences or being prompted by them. Thus in the Depression years a dislike of Marxism could evoke a doctrinaire anti-Semitism, because most of the Socialist and Communist ferment of the period originated in the metropolitan Northeast, where many of its participants were Jewish. In certain circles it is the fashion to label persons like T. S. Eliot and several of the more prominent Nashville Agrarians as Fascists, in part because of comments made about Jews during the 1930s. What is wrong with this is that it draws upon the knowledge of what anti-Semitism in hate-crazed post-1918 Europe led to—the systematic slaughter of millions of helpless people—and attributes the emotional motivations behind that slaughter to people who had no such objective remotely in mind and if given the choice would doubtless have died before allowing it to happen. The doctrinaire literary anti-Semitism of the pre-Holocaust period may have been a product of the same xenophobia that in Europe made the Holocaust possible, but to ascribe to most American literary conservatives of the 1930s responsibility for what the Nazis did is about as logical as holding Diderot and Beaumarchais responsible for the Napoleonic Wars.

152

But H. L. Mencken's anti-Semitism was not of this sort. It was not doctrinaire, but visceral and reflexive. Nor was the fact that Mencken had Jewish friends an instance of the "some of my best friends are Jews" kind of anti-Semitism. Mencken did not merely have Jewish friends; he sought them out, he relished their company. His publisher was a Jew, his associate in founding the *American Mercury* and his associate editor were Jews, his drinking companions in New York and Baltimore were in plentiful measure Jews, as were some of the members of his beloved Saturday Evening Music Club.

In a diary entry for January 25, 1935, Mencken describes dinner with Theodore Dreiser: "he broke out in an anti-Semitic tirade, somewhat to my surprise. I asked him why, if his sentiments went that way, he had chosen a Jewish publisher. He answered simply that he had no other choice." Mencken's own publisher, close business associate, and longtime friend was Alfred A. Knopf. Mencken visited Knopf and his wife Blanche repeatedly, constantly read manuscripts for him, was a member of Knopf's board of directors, and for years attended the Moravian Bach Festival in Bethlehem, Pennsylvania, with Knopf. Only two months before the stroke that ended his intellectual life in November of 1948, he went to New York for a Knopf board meeting.

What is the relationship between the man who asked Dreiser that question, the man who was Alfred and Blanche Knopf's intimate associate, to the man who wrote in his diary for July 19, 1944, the following typical entry about a house in the alley behind his own: "The same little house is kept well painted—obviously at the cost of the tenants, for the Jew who owns it never spends a cent on decorations." Or the man who closes an account of a meeting on June 19, 1937, with Gerald L. K. Smith—whom in *Heathen Days* (1942) he would term "the greatest rabble-rouser since Peter the Hermit"— this way: "The Garden City [New York] complaint against him accused him of anti-Semitism. I asked him this morning if he were inclined that way and he denied it. His wife expressed horror at the thought. Nevertheless, I am convinced that Gerald is preparing to get aboard the great anti-Semitic movement now rolling up in New York." (Mencken was quite right.)

153

Beginning in the late 1930s, he used to convene with a congenial group of up to a half-dozen friends to drink a few beers one evening each week. They included a Maryland judge, Eugene O'Dunne, and two prominent Baltimore physicians, Manfred and Alan Guttmacher. At first they met at Schellhase's Restaurant, but their penchant for late hours ended that. When war came Manfred Guttmacher left for the Army medical corps. They tried the Park Plaza but didn't like it. I quote from Mencken's diary entry for November 22, 1944: "Of late we [Judge O'Dunne and himself] have been meeting intermittently, but with increasing frequency, at the Maryland Club, of which we are both members. We can't invite Alan Guttmacher there, for he is not a member, and as a Jew can't become one."

In another episode from his diary—December 1, 1943—he wrote out in detail a story told him by the Maryland Club secretary, concerning a club member who was observed entertaining "an elderly and palpably Jewish gentleman" in the dining room. The guest turned out to be the member's father. It seems that the member had changed his name from Winternitz to Winter, and had been admitted to membership without his ethnic origins being known. The Maryland Club's board of governors decided that nothing could be done about it, but one of the member's sponsors told him of his mortification at revelation, and the member then resigned. Mencken went on to note the Maryland Club's policy of having "no objection . . . to bringing an occasional Jew to a meal in the club, but that this applied only to out of town Jews, not to local ones." The club used to have one Jewish member, but when the last such died, "the board of governors decided that he should be the last of the Chosen on the club roll. There is no other Jew in Baltimore who seems suitable." Maryland Club member Mencken clearly had no objection, and made none.

154

Like most of what is entered in the diary, all this is written factually, without the slightest expression of dismay or disapproval, by the man who replied to a complaint by a correspondent about the behavior of wealthy Jews aboard an ocean liner as follows: "It seems to me that you are generalizing from very small evidence. Certainly it would be absurd to say that the kind of Jews you met aboard ship were the only kind in existence. Some of the most intelligent people in America are Jewish, and not only some of the most intelligent, but also some of the most charming. My own feeling indeed is, that taking one with another, Jews average much higher than Americans. However, I agree with you that the unpleasant ones are unpleasant almost beyond endurance."

This is not merely inconsistency, a failure to practice what one preaches and vice versa. Reading Mencken's diary I grow convinced that on the one hand the man possessed a set of prejudices and attitudes, and on the other he wrote, edited, lived an active social and intellectual life, enjoyed his friends, and so on—*and that the two realms bore almost no conscious relationship to each other.* It is a kind of willed schizophrenia, an apparent denial of any connection between what he thought and did on a day-to-day basis and certain ingrained emotions and beliefs.

Replying to a letter from the writer Jim Tully, apparently in reference to a broadcast debate over foreign policy, Mencken wrote that "the plain truth is that I am not a fair man, and don't want to hear both sides. On all known subjects, ranging from aviation to xylophone-playing, I have fixed and invariable ideas. They have not changed since I was four or five years [old]." He was making a joke, but he also meant what he said; when he contemplated the way of the world, in effect he did so with the social absolutes, including a set of prejudices, bequeathed him by his patrimony.

It is difficult to believe that his intellectual experience made as little impression upon his basic emotional attitudes as seems to have been true. For Mencken's is no instance of an intellect whose premises were shaped early and who thereafter fitted all that he read, heard, and observed into his youthful schemata. The point about Mencken is that he *didn't* do that. Rather, it is as if he kept the two realms strictly separate, sometimes permitting data to circulate back and forth between them but with no absorption allowed with respect to changing or modifying either.

155

The question we need to ask about Mencken is not, Was he anti-Semitic? Or, Was he a political reactionary? Or, Was he this? Or, Was he that? Rather, the question about Mencken has to do with what there was that helped to bring about this enormous gap between certain ingrained attitudes, beliefs, and assumptions to which he consciously subscribed throughout his life, and the very different set of premises on which he clearly conducted that life. This is what is in need of explanation if we are ever to understand his writings, and the personality incorporated within them.

Mencken has been generally depicted as a happy smiter of fools, an exuberant idol-smasher who chastised the hypocrisy and sham of what James Truslow Adams referred to as "Our Business Civilization," a genial advocate of what was genuine in life and art, a social satirist and humorist who was a stylistic virtuoso of the first magnitude, a joyous hedonist, an advocate of the more sensual virtues and thus an unremitting foe to Prohibition, Puritanism, censorship, prudery, and all contemporary varieties of Babbittry. His heyday was the 1920s and his credo essentially one of *vive le bagatelle!*, which served him well in the Jazz Age, but when the depression years arrived and totalitarianism abroad began to signal the oncoming of World War II, he was thereafter out of his element and quite unable to face up to the problems of a world ridden with hate, want, terror and evil. And all that, by and large, is quite true. The question is *How come?*

As noted earlier, a failure of most commentary about Mencken is the inclination to take the Mencken persona at face value, on its own terms, as the comic genius, the happy iconoclast. This is how Mencken wanted it, as in his self-identified "Catechism":

> Q If you find so much that is unworthy of reverence in the United States, then why do you live here?
> A Why do men go to zoos?

William Manchester, in an essay entitled "Mencken in Person," points out the shortcomings of this approach. Noting Mencken's fierce aggressiveness, the satisfaction he took in intellectual combat and in bashing his opponents, Manchester enters, even so, a caveat:

156

> Men who knew him, even many who saw him almost daily, re-call his exuberance and believe his spirits were always high. That is precisely what he wanted them to think. He was a proud man. But in a naked moment he wrote: "Like any other author I have suffered from recurrent depressions." This is an aspect of writing which writers would rather not explore. Theirs is, quite simply, a desperate business. Mencken was cheerier than most in the trade; nevertheless, I have seen him so despondent that he could scarcely speak, when his eyes were moist with unspeak-able sorrow. When the shadow was upon him, he would hoist the drawbridge and struggle back to sanity in his home.

Those "naked moments," when Mencken drops his guard, do exist in his writings. One has to search for them, for he hid them well. But unlike the pre-space-exploration moon, the dark side is visible, if one looks closely. The place to start is with his younger days, with his family and his situation as a literarily inclined German-American in the city of Baltimore, Maryland, in the late nineteenth and the early twentieth century.

Of Mencken's childhood we know only what he told us—which is to say, a great deal, but almost all of it uncritical. That Mencken considered himself profoundly German in his attitudes is well known. His closely knit family, his early schooling, the large and prospering German-American community within Baltimore, above all the formidable role of his father in his life caused him to identify himself with his Teutonic forebears to a striking degree.

"My grandfather, I believe," he wrote on August 27, 1942, "made a mistake when he came to this country. He was an unhappy man himself and his descendants have had many troubles. I believe, in truth, that immigration is always unwise—that is, when it is not enforced. I believe my chances in Germany would have been at least as good as they have been here in America, and maybe a great deal better. I was born here and so were my father and mother, and I have spent all of my 62 years here, but I still find it impossible to fit myself into the accepted patterns of American life and thought. After all these years, I remain a foreigner."

157

With his German loyalties went an abiding suspicion of England and the English. As a newspaper columnist this got him into considerable trouble during the Great War of 1914–1918, because from the outset he championed the virtues of the Kaiser's Germany, including those of a military sort, and as the United States drew closer toward intervention on the side of the Allies he not only would not mute his allegiance but launched a formidable offensive of his own against President Woodrow Wilson. The result was that by the time that the United States declared war on the Central Powers, he had to cease writing about the war at all, and his unpopularity among what he contemptuously termed "Right Thinking People" forced him to lay low until it was over.

It was not, however, the divisions brought about by the First World War that placed Mencken at odds with England and the British. What seldom gets observed about the Baltimore, Maryland, in which Mencken grew up is that as a habitat for a budding littérateur it was highly Anglophile, with its social, intellectual, and artistic life dominated by the old Baltimore families, who were mainly Anglo-American in origins and Episcopalian and Presbyterian in religious affiliation. As the late Frank Beirne wrote in *The Amiable Baltimoreans*, "Although many racial strains are found among its people Baltimore is fundamentally a city with a British background and British social customs." The German-Americans, for all their prominence in music, were decidedly not among the city's social and cultural elect.

As a youth with literary hopes, he cannot have escaped, it seems to me, feeling a resentment for the city's ruling cultural establishment. For although the German-American community was prosperous and self-contained, and by no means inclined to view itself as either socially underprivileged or culturally inferior, the young Mencken's career ambitions soon carried him decisively outside of that enclave and into the larger community.

It would be interesting to know just what the implications were, both social and intellectual, of his father's move in enrolling him at the Baltimore Polytechnic Institute for his secondary schooling, rather than the liberal-arts-oriented Baltimore City College (which was not a college but a high school.) Then as now, the children of the social elite of the city attended the private academies if their families could afford to send them, but a City College education was socially respectable, whereas attending the Polytechnic was decidedly not.

Mencken did not go to college. In the 1890s and early 1900s it was by no means unusual for a young man of intellectual and literary aspirations not to do so, particularly if he were not of the old Anglo-American set and did not intend to pursue medicine or the law. Yet I have wondered sometimes what would have happened if Mencken had been sent to Baltimore City College, where considerable emphasis was placed upon preparation for attending college following graduation.

So far as I know Mencken said nothing about such matters. It is too bad that some of those who knew Mencken during his early newspaper days—the newsman Frank Kent, for example, who covered police courts with Mencken and later became a distinguished author and a political columnist for the Baltimore *Sunpapers*—left no intimate memories of him. Apparently, however, they did not.

When he got his first newspaper job, it was on the Baltimore *Herald,* and as a reporter and then a city editor for that newspaper his principal rivalry was with the *Sunpapers,* which were the respectable, conservative, establishment publication. "At a time when the respectable bourgeois youngsters of my generation were college freshmen, oppressed by simian sophomores and affronted with balderdash daily and hourly by chalky pedagogues," he wrote, "I was at large in a wicked seaport of half a million people, with a front seat at every public show, as free of the night as of the day, and get-

158

ting earfuls and eyefuls of instruction in a hundred giddy arcana, none of them taught in schools." In short, a self-made man, who learned his lessons and earned his laurels in what is known as the School of Life. To paraphrase Melville's Ishmael, a newsroom was his Gilman School and his Princeton and Johns Hopkins as well.

Mencken's youthful milieu, however rich in experience, did not include any commerce with the literati of Baltimore; he knew none of them. Nor did his acquaintance, at that time, embrace the savants of the Johns Hopkins University, who in that era were a conservative, socially distinguished phalanx, of predominantly Anglo-American antecedents. It seems evident that at least some of his notorious scorn for the professorate had its roots in this social schism, and represented the resentment of a self-made German-American at the wellborn, well-connected academic gentleman.

159

Surely Mencken's intense hatred of Woodrow Wilson was greatly fanned by the fact that Wilson represented so much that he himself was not—a Presbyterian minister's son of Anglo-American stock; a graduate of the University of Virginia who took his doctorate at Johns Hopkins; an Anglophile, socially connected with the old Maryland families and Virginia families that gave Baltimore so much of its social tone; and very much the Gentleman Scholar in Politics, given to lofty, idealistic pronouncements, something of a prude, and—when the war came—the man who brought the United States into the conflict on England's side. Equally, Mencken's championing of the novels of Theodore Dreiser before and during World War I owed something at least to Dreiser's German background and to the fact that those critics who denounced him for immorality, loutishness, crudeness, and the like were precisely the Anglophiliac gentry of the Genteel Tradition, many of them college professors. The gist of all this is that socially if not economically, Mencken came from the wrong side of the tracks in Baltimore, and the marks that his origins imprinted upon him lasted all his life.

Until well into his middle years he had two groups of friends: middle-class Baltimoreans mostly of German stock; and journalists and literati, centered both locally and in New York City, many of them Jewish. His literary allegiances during the 1910s and 1920s— the years of the *Smart Set* and the *American Mercury*—were with the authors, mainly the prose writers rather than the avant-garde poets, who had taken on the older literary establishment of the Genteel Tradition of Howells, Brownell, Van Dyke, Brander Matthews, Garland, Boynton, Sherman, etc., and driven it to the wall. Mencken's heroes were Dreiser, Cabell, Joseph Hergesheimer, Carl Van Doren, Carl Van Vechten, and so on. He looked to European literature—Conrad, Hauptmann, Sudermann, Shaw, Ibsen, Mann—rather than to the English classics. The literary, art, and music critic he most admired, James Gibbons Huneker, had championed many of the European virtuosi. His early alliance with Alfred A. Knopf, a Jewish publisher who led the revolt against the older, more staid houses, was significant. Until his middle years none of Mencken's enthusiasms and alliances were with the older, Anglo-American cultural establishment. Significantly, not until 1937 did Mencken apply for and secure membership in the Maryland Club, that bastion of wealth and respectability. Those who Knew Him When were astounded; it was as if Jefferson Davis had joined the Union League.

The Mencken who still gets quoted, who has gone down in the history of the national letters as the Great American Gadfly, whom Alfred Kazin in *An American Procession* describes as "a splendid and highly comic literary satirist just when America needed one," is mainly the Mencken of the 1910s and 1920s. His inability to confront or even concede the existence of the decades thereafter is exemplified in a comment made during the presidential election campaign of 1932, to the effect that unless he was greatly mistaken the principal political issue at stake was the repeal of the Prohibition amendment to the United States Constitution. This at a time when banks were closing, breadlines were a daily feature of city life, mortgages were being foreclosed, downtown storefronts were empty, and bankruptcies were rife. Well might Kazin describe Mencken as one "who never seemed to know that there *was* a depression, and who made light of Hitler as if he were just another redneck demagogue from the Deep South."

From the earliest days of the New Deal onward, Mencken belabored Franklin D. Roosevelt and his administration, and his wrath intensified steadily as the decade advanced. By the late 1930s and early 1940s, as war broke out in Europe and the United States began rearming, he grew positively choleric. Even Mencken's diary entries, until then mostly a bland, emotionless recording of his daily experience, began to smoulder, with his rage and frustration focusing after 1940 on the refusal of the Baltimore *Sunpapers* to oppose what he considered Roosevelt's lust to get into the war on the side of the English. By early 1941 he had ceased to write for the *Sun*, for as in 1917 his complete failure to sympathize with the American war effort had made it impossible for him to publish his views.

He was utterly unable to distinguish emotionally between the Kaiser's Reich and Hitler's. As far as he was concerned, in both conflicts the *Sunpapers*, and the American people, had been hoodwinked by British propaganda. He refused to believe the war news as reported, declaring it a fabric of lies and propaganda. The extent of Mencken's inability to accept the evidence of what was going on can be seen in a diary entry for March 17, 1944, in which, reporting on a meeting with Paul Patterson of the *Sunpapers*, he notes as an example of Patterson's complete gullibility about the British that "he believes that the English captured 300,000 Germans in North Africa." (The actual number was between 240,000 and 275,000.) The *Sunpapers*, Mencken wrote on November 2, 1944, "lead in this patriotic work. Their correspondence from various fronts seldom undertakes to tell precisely what is going on: it is simply rooting for the home team. I long ago gave up protesting against it. Paul Patterson not only believes that it is what the readers of the *Sunpapers* want; he also swallows most of it himself. . . . The American people are now almost wholly at the mercy of demagogues, and it would take a revolution to liberate and disillusion them." As for himself, "So far, no one that I know has been killed in the war, or even injured, and I find it hard to pump up any interest in the tall talk of the newspapers every day."

161

When the German counteroffensive in the Ardennes drove a wedge into the American lines that December, Mencken was convinced that "the Army press-agents are making desperate efforts to turn the German breakthrough into a German rout, but I suspect that even the generality of Americans, as stupid as they are, are beginning to doubt this official optimism." (By Christmas Day, 1944, when Mencken wrote that in his diary, the German drive was stumbling to a halt, there had been no breakthrough, and an American counteroffensive was being prepared. Ultimately, the Ardennes sortie cost the Germans more heavily than it did the Allies.)

He never conceded that his interpretation of the nature of World

War II was flawed. If the revelations of the awesome horrors of the Nazi death camps ever had an impact upon him, he left no evidence of it. As late as October 25, 1945, long after what went on at Buchenwald, Auschwitz, Belsen, Treblinka, Dachau, and elsewhere had become public knowledge, he recorded a meeting with Paul Patterson in which he again berated the *Sunpapers'* publisher for having let the British gull him, declaring that "the course of the U.S. in World War II . . . was dishonest, dishonorable and ignominious, and the *Sunpapers,* by supporting Roosevelt's foreign policy, shared in this disgrace."

162

Did Mencken actually want Nazi Germany to win the Second World War? To ask the question in that way is to miss the point. Mencken was no Nazi. But what he wanted was for the British to *lose*. From childhood on he was anti-English, and when his set of *Ur*-prejudices were involved, he did not discriminate or weigh one element of his experience against another—did not, in short, *think*. He *felt*, and the pros and cons, ifs and buts, on any conscious level at least, did not matter. His choice of a title for the series of collections of his writings from 1919 through 1927, *Prejudices*, was quite apt.

It is as if he went through life equipped with a certain set of attitudes, which were essentially visceral and negative, and whenever these were brought into play, his reaction was reflexive, automatic, and totally predictable. I'm certain that he had no more control over them than if they were so many involuntary muscular responses. What is astounding is not the presence of such attitudes and responses, but the coexistence alongside them of the intelligence, imagination, enthusiasm for new experience, and creative energy that were equally a part of his makeup. The two realms of his consciousness seem to have been able to function side by side, with little or no overt dialogue taking place between them.

That they did in fact impinge upon each other, I have no doubt; but the transaction took place on no conscious level. In another person the result might have been chaos, mental paralysis, even madness. But in H. L. Mencken's instance the result was the brilliant cascade of words, the explosion of language and idea, that made him the exuberant and forceful literary personality that he was.

Personality. The whole of his life's work, the political and social and literary and philological and epistolary activity that makes up his collected output (and uncollected as well, for there must be millions of words of journalistic writing and thousands of additional letters that will never be resurrected), constitutes the intense assertion of personality, a virtuoso performance of incredible proportions, composed with the objective, kept foremost in mind, of saying, *Listen to me! Pay attention to me! This is what I have to say!* Critics have on occasion used the adjective "irrepressible" to characterize Mencken, and that is exactly what is at work. Some force or forces, comprised of the complex interaction of family upbringing, Oedipal compulsion, civic and social experience, historical circumstance, redirected repression, aesthetic need, together with naked creative energy, made this man into the font of galvanic energy that he so marvelously was. He wrote for the same reason that Shriners parade and real-estate promoters drive Lincoln Continentals—for purposes of self-display—and he found delight and profit in being himself in public print.

163

Whatever it was, or whatever the component parts were, however, there seems to have been almost no impulse toward any kind of *doing* things involved in the transaction. Seemingly he was without any urge to lead, to exert a direct influence upon society. He headed no movements, campaigned for no offices, led no crusades, espoused no causes. Indeed, he appears to have regarded the circumstances and conditions of this world as irremediable and irrevocable, even hopeless, so far as ever attempting to do anything about them was concerned. He could, and would, write, talk, rage, asserverate, air his outrage and unleash his ideas in torrents of words, but on no account could he *act*.

This was not merely the behavior of a man who realizes that his forte lies in commentary and who seeks to influence events indirectly through manipulation of opinion rather than by direct action. Rather, it is the manifestation of a profound conviction of the futility of action, the irremediable nature of things as they are. Nor is it a matter of Whatever Is, Is Right. On the contrary, Whatever Is, Is Ineradicable would be more like it. It is as if, early on, he had discovered that there was no way to reconcile what he saw around him with what he might wish things to be, and therefore began developing a set of deeply pessimistic, almost atrabilious attitudes and opinions, to be used as a barrier, a protective carapace against further disillusion.

To assume and to expect the worst is to insulate oneself against disappointment. To guard against a total paralysis of the will to exist by adopting the worst possible interpretation of the human scenario being unfolded before one's eyes is to enable oneself to continue to function. Which, I think, is virtually what H. L. Mencken did, very early on. In effect he out-Teutoned his Teutonic father, adopting all his prejudices, even while conducting his life under very different principles and assumptions, and without feeling the slightest requirement, on any conscious level at least, to seek to reconcile the two, other than through making a joke.

That a function of comedy is to bridge incongruity is well known. It is a way of reconciling—for purposes of acknowledging their existence—two separate and seemingly irreconcilable attitudes. When Mark Twain alludes to "the calm confidence of a Christian holding four aces," he expresses a polarity of attitudes toward human nature that is at the heart of his work. Similarly, Mencken's writings, even his very style, are based on the acknowledgment of opposites.

164

Consider the following passage from one of his most accomplished pronouncements, "The Sahara of the Bozart":

> The New England shopkeepers and theologians never really developed a civilization; all they ever developed was a government. They were, at their best, tawdry and tacky fellows, oafish in manner and devoid of imagination; one searches the books in vain for mention of a salient Yankee gentleman; as well look for a Welsh gentleman. But in the South there were men of delicate fancy, urbane instinct and aristocratic manner—in brief, superior men—in brief, gentry. To politics, their chief diversion, they brought active and original minds. It was there that nearly all the political theories we still cherish and suffer under came to birth.

The technique is to construct one set of incongruous attitudes, and then to appear to reconcile the apparent paradox by a still more startling application of incongruity, building an argument upon that shaky foundation like so many toy wooden blocks, until it finally collapses under the weight of its own improbability. The chasm between the ethical and social ideal and the vernacular actuality— "the political theories we still cherish and suffer under"—is comi-

cally acknowledged, for purposes of laughter, by the seeming paradox that only a genuine aristocrat is capable of democratic belief,
an assertion humorously imaged in the picture of the gentlemanly
founding fathers seeking idle-hour recreation through such things
as enacting the Declaration of Independence, the Constitution, the
Bill of Rights, and so on. One imagines him writing that passage
with much gusto, enjoying his hyperbole as he proceeds.

Like almost everything that Mencken ever wrote, the passage at
bottom is profoundly pessimistic. The actualities of American experience and human nature are measured against a humanistic ideal
and found to be hopelessly inadequate. Behind the humor lies a
thwarted idealism, a devastating conviction of the impossibility of
the True, the Good, and the Beautiful ever being realized on this
earth. It is no wonder that all efforts to better the human condition
through social or political action were quick to draw Mencken's
scorn. Any attempts at reform, any program for improvement, any
and all moves to assert an ethical ideal as a practical social or political goal were certain to touch off a barrage of ridicule and sarcasm
from him. And the more imposing these efforts, the more formidable the impulse to translate ideals into action, the more irate and
savage was his response. For all such things threatened to undercut
the validity of the whole system of disillusion, pessimism, and belief
in the futility of amelioration that he had managed early on to build
up as protection against having to confront the injustice, want, bru-
tality, pain, and ugliness of the human condition—against having
to look evil in the face.

165

It was Mencken's good fortune that following the First World War
an era of disillusion set in, a reaction against the idealism and pro-
gressivism of the 1900s and 1910s, the New Freedom of Woodrow
Wilson, the War to End All Wars. Thomas Wolfe had a character
describe it well in *Of Time and the River:* " 'We're tired of Woodrow's flowery speeches, an' we're tired of hearin' about wars an'
ideals an' democracy an' how fine an' noble we all are an' "Mister
won't you please subscribe." We're tired of hearin' bunk that doesn't
pay an' we want to hear some bunk that does—Do you know what
we all want—what we're lookin' for?' he demanded, glowering bru-
tally around at them. 'We want a piece of the breast with lots of
gravy—an' the boy that promises us the most is the one we're for!' "

What was in vogue intellectually was philosophical justification for the pleasure seeking, and Mencken could provide that, *allegro con brio*. He denounced reformers, uplifters, wowsers, evangelists, demagogues, theorists, fundamentalists, prohibitionists, vice crusaders, politicians, psychoanalysts, bureaucrats, Christian Scientists, faith healers, farmers, sex hygienists, sentimentalists, quacks. Denounced them? He skewered them on the point of his wit, sliced their effrontery into small chunks. Whatever contained sham, pretense, pretentiousness, hypocrisy, fraud, or chicanery was fair game. Nor did he neglect to attack cruelty, ignorance, bigotry, injustice— for Mencken was no friend to these, provided that what was involved were individual instances that did not call for any substantial revision of human nature and society. Thus he blasted away at lynch mobs, the Red Scare, sweatshops, religious intolerance, the Ku Klux Klan, censors, witch hunts of any sort, and the like, and had a delightful time in so doing.

With the advent of the 1930s, as noted earlier, everything was different. The attitudes and interests that in the 1920s had made him popular now worked to precisely the opposite effect. It wasn't that Mencken's own political and social libertarianism changed; rather, it was the attitudes and needs of the American public that had done so. And when Franklin Roosevelt and the New Deal arrived on the scene, Mencken soon lost his sense of humor, for the reason that no longer was the gleeful pointing out of incongruity for the sake of laughter sufficient to handle the widening chasm between the actual and the ideal. Action, political and social, was now called for—and the prospect constituted a dire threat to his need to believe that human nature was incapable of self-improvement and that there was no point in trying to attempt it. Fortunately for him, he was shrewd enough to discern that his opinions were out of fashion, and except for his pieces in the *Sunpapers* he gave up his commentary on the state of national and world affairs and began concentrating on the state of the American language and, increasingly, his experiences during the days of his youth. The past, at least, was still available for subject matter; it need not be acted upon, but only remembered. It was then, too, that he began to keep a diary.

The Diary of H. L. Mencken is one of the saddest, most melancholy books ever published by an important American author. Begun in

November, 1930, only a few months after his marriage to Sarah Haardt and while, despite the deepening economic depression, he was still widely read and very much a public figure, it chronicles events of the eighteen years of decline before the severe cerebral thrombosis of November 26, 1948, which left him permanently unable to read or to write. There is an almost complete hiatus of more than a year and a half, following his wife's death on May 31, 1935, until well into 1937, when save for a few entries he virtually ceased writing in it. During the period of the diary, Mencken saw his popularity experience a sharp dropoff as the depression worsened, Hitler and the Nazis came into power in Germany, and the world began moving toward another war. In 1932 Mencken ceased to edit the *American Mercury*, whose circulation had dropped catastrophically. His connection with the *Sunpapers* went on, and after Sarah's death he joined the board of directors, but in early 1941, to the relief of the *Sunpapers* management, he ceased to write his weekly column. The world was at war, his old friends were dying off, and his own health began deteriorating. After 1945 he resumed his *Sunpapers* pieces, and in 1948 he covered the national political conventions again. In November came the thrombosis that thereafter silenced him. The diary, although its entries deal only very selectively with public events, is a long chronicle of diminution and loss.

167

His anodyne for disappointment was work. Throughout the period he continued writing—magazine pieces, a book, a dictionary of quotations, two supplements to *The American Language,* the set of three memoirs which together with the *Language* supplements earned him a respectable and admiring readership once again, and a selection of his pieces from across the decades, *A Mencken Chrestomathy.* He spent long hours setting his voluminous papers in order, writing an extensive chronicle of his career with the *Sunpapers;* and the *Diary* itself came to some two thousand typewritten pages before it ended. (The present volume is a selection; much of what has been omitted consists of detailed reports on *Sunpapers* labor negotiations, in which he participated, negotiations with the Associated Press, and *Sunpapers* and Knopf board meetings.)

As remarked earlier, the prose in which the diary is written is for the most part flat and factual, lacking the comic fustian and bombast of his published writings. This changes somewhat during the war years, presumably because without a public forum for airing his displeasure and generally expressing his personality in print, it was the best available audience. The editor of the published *Diary,* Charles A. Fecher, in an informative introduction, notes that its entries lack "the highly polished style of the books and articles" as well as "the gorgeous humor which enlivens the public works." He also remarks the triviality of so much of the contents and concludes that "it will be at once apparent that Mencken gave over relatively few hours to pondering the destiny of the race."

There is more to it than that, I think. Diaries are written to be read, if only by the diarist himself. Let me describe a more or less typical entry, that for August 19, 1942, written in Baltimore. Mencken begins by saying that he went up to New York on Saturday, spent Saturday night and Sunday at Alfred Knopf's place in Purchase, N.Y., returned to the city Sunday evening and to Baltimore yesterday. While he was at Knopf's a guest, Ben Stern, came over for dinner, but otherwise he and Knopf just talked. "Among other things, we went over his early history in the publishing business."

Mencken then proceeds to describe Knopf's career, describes his own first meeting with Knopf in Baltimore, tells of Knopf's forming his publishing house, Knopf's marriage to Blanche Wolf, and how he himself got out of a book option contract with John Lane by including a chapter in his next book attacking Lane's star novelist, then joined Knopf and published the book without the offending chapter. He tells about the Knopfs' move to Hartsdale, New York, the birth of their son, and their move back to New York City. He saw them frequently thereafter, he says, and directed numerous books their way. He expresses regret at the loss of most of his correspondence with Knopf before 1921, notes Knopf's first publishing successes, and describes their spritely typography and design, which he says attracted the novelist Willa Cather to the house.

Then he notes that Blanche Knopf had been off in South America, and remarks that a "statesman's complex" has seized her, and that she had hinted darkly of important, mainly depressing, developments in Latin America. She says she found no notable books there, he says, and remarks that when editing the *Mercury* he had never succeeded in securing any interesting material from there, either. "The best I could ever find was almost childish." End of entry.

We have to ask why Mencken wrote all this down. Was it to

168

record information? Yes. But why? I suggest that it was not simply to document his own experience, or that of one with whom he was closely involved. It was also a form of respite, a way to keep his attention diverted. For it is impossible to contemplate the massive amount of "busy work" (I include the compilations that made up the supplements to *The American Language*) that he engaged in— the continuous setting down of the details of board meetings and negotiations, the preparation of an exhaustive record of his *Sun-papers* experience, the elaborate sorting out, organizing, and cataloging of his letters and documents, the habit of answering all his mail on the day it arrived—without coming to suspect that it was being conducted for the purpose of keeping his mind occupied and his attention focused on phenomena, on detail.

169

What he was diverting himself from, unless I am mistaken, was the contemplation of what Mr. Fecher calls "the destiny of the race"—and I suspect that it is this that accounts for the bland, verveless style in which most of the *Diary* entries were written. Mencken wrote in his diary, made his compilations, recorded his negotiations and accounts of board meetings, answered his correspondence, and otherwise kept himself constantly occupied as a way of keeping the enemy at bay—the enemy being the helplessness and despair that arose from the utter irreconcilability of what he saw going on around him with what, as the first-born son of August Mencken, cigar manufacturer, conservative, and German-American paterfamilias, he wanted to believe.

As a child and youth he learned to thrust this contemplation back into the recesses of his mind and away from his conscious thought, so that he could get on with the business of displaying his personality in print. Only in that way could he unleash the tremendous energy that fueled his writings and drove him to the constant, all-out, self-conscious assertion that those writings comprised.

Throughout his adult life he sought to place the worst possible, most pessimistic construction on what he saw and encountered. He did his best to accept and believe the attitudes and values of his father, to view the poor as lazy, the working man as stupid, the English as venal, the Germans as virtuous and wise, the Jews as crafty and scheming, the blacks as inferior, and the world as belonging to the strong—and on any conscious level he did a good job of it. Yet doubt kept breaking in, and he fought it back by telling himself that all effort at reform was doomed, amelioration impossible, action useless, education a waste of time. If he couldn't believe that, then how could he, in good conscience, indulge his personality and properly enjoy life?

Isn't there, after all, something frantic and excessive about all of Mencken's imaginative writings? The endless effort to shock the bourgeoisie, be heretical, iconoclastic, controversial; the rage with which he pummels the high-minded, the idealistic, the reform-bent; the seeming joy in proclaiming the vapidness, stupidity, and avarice of the multitude—the whole breathless, brilliantly innovative and creative performance comprises a single, astounding *divertissement,* a dog-and-pony show of scintillant proportions.

170

Of such was the human comedy presented to us for our enjoyment by H. L. Mencken. As with any other virtuoso of humor before or since, the laughter was only part of the story—the part that he went public with. The other part he sought to keep hidden, and generally succeeded. Yet it was there, and in curious and intricate ways it energized the comedy and drove it on.

What is needed now is a first-rate biography of the man, written by someone with full access to the evidence and capable of identifying and following up the clues. The opportunity is dazzling. Consider Bill Manchester's description of the man himself:

> To be sure, his torso was ovoid, his ruddy face homely, and his stubby legs thin and bowed. Nevertheless, there was a sense of dignity and purpose about his movements, and when you were with him it was impossible to forget that you were in the company of a great original, *sui generis*. Nobody else could stuff stogies into a seersucker jacket with the flourish of a Mencken, or wipe a blue bandanna across his brow so dramatically. His friends treasured everything about him, because the whole of the man was manifest in each of his aspects—the tilt of his head, his close-fitting clothes, his high-crowned felt hat creased in the distinctive fashion of the 1920s, his strutting walk, his abrupt gestures, his habit of holding a cigar between his thumb and forefinger like a baton, the roupy inflection of his voice, and, most of all, those extraordinary eyes, so large, and intense, and merry.

It is the picture of a showman, taking his pleasure in being one. If by 1947 the audience was severely diminished, then he would make what he could of a diminished thing. And, largely, it worked—for a long, long time anyway, almost until the very end. For all his days as a man he did his very best to convince himself that he was not really on the side of the angels, that he didn't care. But he did. And, all things considered, that was the side he was on.

171

ALFRED KAZIN'S AMERICAN PROCESSION

(1985)

When Alfred Kazin publishes a new book, it always receives much respectful attention. He is highly regarded. He writes for the most influential publications, notably the *New York Review of Books*. If there is an American literary Establishment, he is well placed and high up in it. Yet he seems to me, for all that, to be underrated, or in any event not to get the kind of attention his work merits. To my mind he is not just an uncommonly stimulating literary critic but a Presence, a literary Personality such as Edmund Wilson was. Perhaps the reason why he isn't often written about or thought of in that way is that when he discusses a literary work he makes such good sense that what he says seems self-evident. As a critic he doesn't call attention to himself: it is always the literature that he is after.

On the other hand, he has written three volumes of memoirs, and these are highly personal. Surely the person reporting on his own experience in the memoirs is also present in the critical books, even if the presence is not dramatized in the way that someone like Wilson managed to do.

Kazin has no dominant way of reading literature that is distinctively his own; in general he exemplifies T. S. Eliot's prescription for

Originally published as a review-essay on Alfred Kazin's *An American Procession* (New York: Knopf, 1984).

critical methodology: the only method is to be very intelligent. The only group into which he might be placed is that in which he locates himself—the articulate critical phalanx composed of the metropolitan New York literati, most of them Jewish, who have displayed certain traits—political liberalism, a thoroughly urban orientation, intense intellectuality, a disdain for so-called formalist aesthetics, and a hostility toward the academy—that could be said to constitute a school of criticism. In his less inspired, more reflexive moments Kazin does sometimes seem to fit into that context.

Most of the time, however, Kazin thinks, and feels, so completely for himself that ideological allegiances and cultural conditioning aren't permitted to get between him and a work of literature. There is none of Irving Howe's heavy-handed traffic with works of the literary imagination while in pursuit of political goals. Unlike Philip Rahv, he does not view literature as the reification of continental metaphysics. Leslie Fiedler's fun and games, his reckless bourgeois baiting, strike Kazin as either silly or irresponsible, or both. He is at a far remove from Susan Sontag's attitudinizing and general gauziness: he will not oversimplify something for effect. Norman Podhoretz's willingness to approach individual authors and individual novels as tactical pawns in a struggle for power finds no counterpart in Kazin's open admiration for the literary imagination.

Kazin, to repeat, has habitually gone his own way, and done things in his own way. To my mind, however much I may sometimes disagree with him, he is a first-rate critic with a first-rate mind who is decidedly an ornament to our culture. There is nobody else like him.

Almost from the first, in spite of the reflexive Marxism that almost every critic on the New York front shared during the 1930s, Kazin has revealed an unusual talent for recognizing and even sympathetically identifying with other viewpoints, social, cultural, and even political assumptions, that differed from his own. This is not always true, but the thrust of his own imagination, early and later, has ever been toward personal involvement in the literary work rather than imposition of an external system upon it. He has always viewed the language in which works of literature are written not as secondary to the political or social ideas being expressed, but as the testimony of an author whose personality is embodied in words.

I do not mean to imply that Kazin has not viewed literature as social expression, or that he has been unconcerned with its political

174

or social content. He came onto the literary scene as a leftist critic, and his first book was written out of that bias. He was a young man in New York when the depression decade got under way, and the idealistic socialism that was his eastern European immigrant heritage was swiftly and reflexively translated into political radicalism. But Kazin had too fine a mind and too strong a devotion to literature to swallow for long the doctrinaire assumptions of the Communist intellectuals. He did not see ideas—he saw people; and he was quick to spot the phony and the self-serving appeal masquerading as militancy and compassion. Earlier than Malcolm Cowley or even Wilson he could see that the Finland Station was a dead end. He has always been quick to catch the note of hypocrisy and self-delusion in public and private expression.

175

Where did Kazin come by his insight into people? He got it very early in his life, because from the very first he was an observer more than a talker. As a child and a young man he had a bad stammer. It was not in him as a youth to be able to compete with the glib, the facile, the virtuosi of the spoken word. So the youthful Kazin listened, observed—and learned very early to detect the false, the hollow, the evasive. And he read, and wrote; in books he could find the written words that expressed the excitement, the joy, the emotion-charged response to experience that otherwise went so maddeningly unasserted. In his own writing he could struggle to say it for himself.

Reviewing Kazin's *An American Procession* in the *Nation* for June 23, 1984, Mark Shechner notes how "Kazin writes competitively, trading [Henry] Adams sentence for sentence, image for image, cadence for cadence, like a boxer. Kazin's watchwords are intensity, compression, vehemence, energy, style, intoxication, force, avidity, ecstasy, frenzy, acceleration, delirium, relentlessness, power . . . which guide our attention toward Kazin himself. . . . We needn't seek far to observe how closely Kazin's thesis expresses his conception of himself: as an isolato, an ecstatic, a word-intoxicated writer." This is no doubt more true than false, but I don't think Kazin is competing *with* the writers he chronicles so much as he is striving to make his report parallel that of his subject in enunciating what the writer being examined is saying. Kazin's great gift lies precisely in his ability to see and feel experience along with the writer under scrutiny.

Kazin's first book, which in its scope and solidity so firmly established his credentials as a leading analyst of our literature, was *On Native Grounds: An Interpretation of Modern American Prose Literature* (1942). Written as it was in New York City in the late 1930s and early 1940s, it offered an interpretation that was both nationalistic and, not unexpectedly and in no reductive fashion, politically activistic. The proper inclination of the national letters was seen as toward the left, but the book was characterized by an eagerness to explore the complexities of a wide variety of fiction, by no means most of which was politically Marxist or even Progressive.

The place of this book in Kazin's career has been misunderstood. *On Native Grounds* has been seen as an effort to force American literature and the experience it chronicled into a Progressive, activistic political and social stance. The truth is that it was the other way around. What Kazin was engaged in doing was attempting to fit the Progressive bias which was his by birthright into the heritage and meaning of American literary history. When one or the other had to give way, it was the politics and not the literature that did the accommodating. Kazin was involved in discovering the potentialities of the literature for himself. Because I am an American, he was saying, I am part of all this. *On Native Grounds* was an act of identification: the title of the book asserts the claim. He might well have subtitled it *An American Possession*.

In a deeply revelatory episode in *A Walker in the City* (1951) Kazin describes how as a boy he longed to get beyond the neighborhood he lived in in Brownsville, to go into the downtown city, to move into New York's nineteenth-century past, to explore the possibilities of the life that lay beyond the physical and social boundaries of his Orthodox Jewish immigrant neighborhood. In a manner reminiscent of Thomas Wolfe he prefaces a set of recollections of his longing to escape what Brownsville represented with the repeated word *Beyond*: "*Beyond* was anything old and American—the name *Fraunces Tavern* repeated to us on a school excursion; the eighteenth-century muskets and glazed oil paintings on the wall," and so on. "Dusk in America any time after the Civil War," he says, "would be the corridor back and back into that old New York under my feet that always left me half-stunned with its audible cries for recognition."

As an impoverished Jew in an immigrant neighborhood, he was

apart from all this, and the exclusion galled him. "Why did they live *there* and we always in 'Brunsvil'? Why were they *there,* and we always *here?* Why was it always *them* and *us,* Gentiles and us, *alrightniks* [middle-class Jews] and us? . . . Jews were Jews; Gentiles were Gentiles. The line between them had been drawn for all time. What had my private walks into the city to do with anything?"

Late one day, however, while in Manhattan with a school class, he became separated from the group and decided to walk home across Brooklyn Bridge on his own. He watched the evening rush traffic, the excitement, the growing darkness, the look of the towers of Wall Street, and then he climbed up to the observation platform. Below were automobiles, trolley cars:

177

> Then a long line of naked electric bulbs hung on wires above the newsstands and hot dog stands in the arcade, raw light glittering above the flaky iron rust, newsboys selling the *Evening World,* the smell of popcorn and of frankfurters sizzling on the grill. And now up a flight of metal-edged wooden steps and into the open at last, the evening coming on faster and faster, a first few flakes of snow in the air, the lights blue and hard up one side of the transparent staircases in Wall Street, dark on another; the river black, inky black; then the long hollow boom shivering the worn wooden planks under my feet as a ship passes under the bridge.
>
> Dusk of a dark winter's day that first hour walking Brooklyn Bridge. Suddenly I felt lost and happy as I went up another flight of steps, passed under the arches of the tower, and waited, next to a black barrel, at the railing of the observation platform. The trolleys clanged and clanged; every angry stalled car below sounded its horn as, bumper to bumper, they all poked their way along the bridge; the El trains crackled and thundered over my right shoulder. A clock across the street showed its lighted face; along the fire escapes of the building were sculptured figures of runners and baseball players, of prize fighters flexing their muscles and wearing their championship belts, just as they did in the *Police Gazette.* But from that platform under the tower the way ahead was strange. Only the electric sign of the Jewish *Daily Forward,* burning high over the tenements of

the East Side, suddenly stilled the riot in my heart as I saw the cables leap up to the tower, saw those great meshed triangles leap up and up, higher and still higher—Lord my Lord, when will they cease to drive me up with them in their flight?—and then, each line singing out alone the higher it came and nearer, fly flaming into the topmost eyelets of the tower.

All his subsequent youthful walks into the city, as well as all his walks back across that bridge after he had left Brownsville, were efforts to understand that "single half-hour at dusk, on a dark winter day, the year I was fourteen."

178

Consider what might have been involved in that particular memory. For the young Kazin the bridge, with its ascending cables, was a way of connecting where he comes from, the Jewish neighborhood of Brownsville, with what he aspires to be part of and to possess— the skyscrapers of Manhattan, the opportunities open to him there for escape from his confined, immigrant Jewish neighborhood and into full participation in American intellectual life, one that unlike life in Brownsville would be of the mind, involving reading, knowing, writing, expressing himself. Moreover he sees, in the bridge's design, the strong cables and their mounting ascension, not just a sense of almost endless possibility but also an inevitability, a linking connection that is at once secure and daring, practical and beautiful, aesthetically pure and powerfully sexual.

But what of the electric sign "burning high over the tenements of the East Side," which "suddenly stilled the riot in my heart"? There is an earlier sequence in which the youthful Kazin remembers being "first seized by that bitter guilt I always felt in the movies whenever there was still daylight outside. As I saw Monte Blue being loaded into an Iron Maiden, it suddenly came on me that the penalty for my delicious reveries might be just such a death—a death as lonely, as sickeningly remote from all human aid, as the one I saw my hero calmly prepare to face against the yellow shadows of deepest Asia." Whenever the theater door opened, he says, "a hostile mocking wave of daylight fell against the screen." He could hear the movie projector clicking and the noise of the traffic outside, and

I instantly saw in that ominous patch of light the torture-box of life-in-death, some reproach calling for punishment for my sin.

> A sin, perhaps, only of my own devising; the sin I recorded
> against all idle enjoyment, looking on for its own sake alone;
> but a sin. The daylight was for grimness and labor.

(What a Freudian might make of that punitive Iron Maiden and "a sin, perhaps, only of my own devising" is another matter.)

What is significant is the proposed equation: life in the old neighborhood promises only grimness and labor; yet the attempt to escape from it through the use of one's imagination involves retributive punishment, a living death, which will take place in "deepest *Asia*" (remember that Kazin's parents were Russian Jewish immigrants).

Immediately following that remembered incident appears the memory of having once ventured into a Protestant church, the only one in the neighborhood: "One afternoon on my way back from school my curiosity got the better of me despite all my fear of Gentiles." What he saw was "the plainest thing I had ever seen—not, of course, homey, lived-in, and smelling of sour wine, snuff, and old prayer books, like our little wooden synagogue on Chester Street." The church's interior is so "varnished-clean and empty and austere, like our school auditorium." He is impressed by "the number of things written in English. I had associated God only with a foreign language." Finally: "Suspended from the ceiling over the altar was a great gold-wood sign on which the black Gothic letters read: I AM THE RESURRECTION AND THE LIFE. I remember standing in the doorway, longing to go all the way up the aisle, then suddenly running away. The distance from that doorway to the altar was the longest gap in space I had ever seen."

The episode, by itself, would seem to warn him, especially in conjunction with that with which Kazin immediately precedes it, that the only way to escape from the spiritual death of everyday toil and grimness in Brownsville into the full potentiality of American life must be by sloughing off his identity as a Jew. The sign over the altar is in English, not Hebrew; it offers escape from the walled-in social and intellectual ghetto of Brownsville into a life as an American. (A few pages later he describes that school auditorium and the sense of America it offered, with its photograph of Theodore Roosevelt and his family at Oyster Bay; it is seen as one of "thorough varnished cleanness.") To achieve that promise, however, he fears, would be to give up the familiarity and warmth of what he knows

179

and is part of, in exchange for something that is impersonally and almost antiseptically plain and remote from his experience.

The experience on the observation platform of Brooklyn Bridge, by contrast, is so exhilarating and so reassuring because it tells him that no such renunciation, no abandonment of the complex textures of his own social and religious heritage, will be required of him. To be a Jew from Brownsville and also to be fully and imaginatively an American, participating in American life, in possession of American history as *his* birthright—*his* native grounds—is not a mere fancy, a delicious reverie secretly wrenched from the grim reality of daylight. It is solid, real, actual. The electric sign rising high above the East Side tenements, a feature of the cityscape and rightly and proudly present in his vision of the city, proclaims the transaction. What it boldly advertises is the *Jewish Daily Forward*.

180

In *Starting Out in the Thirties* (1965) Kazin describes his entrance into New York City's literary and intellectual life, beginning with an incident in which, on an impulse, he cornered John Chamberlain at the New York *Times*. Chamberlain, then a highly activist leftist, had reviewed a book about the young proletariat, a review that irked Kazin because of its smugness and abstract Marxism. The upshot was that Chamberlain recommended the young man to the *New Republic* as a reviewer, so that at the age of nineteen Kazin began his career as commentator on the American literary scene.

Starting Out in the Thirties offers some delicious portraits of intellectual and literary New York during the period, but it is the third volume of memoirs, *New York Jew* (1978), that contains most of what Kazin has to say about New York intellectual and literary life during his half-century of involvement in it. It opens on a high note: Kazin's memories of the time when, recently married and doing some teaching and book reviewing, he was spending most of his days at the New York Public Library, reading the documents that were to make *On Native Grounds* so rich an evocation and interpretation of the late nineteenth- and early twentieth-century origins of modern American writing. The sense of sheer wealth he felt in having at his beck and call the vast collection at the library became almost intoxicating. "Even the spacious twin reading rooms, each two blocks long," he writes, "gave me a sense of the powerful amenity that I craved for my own life, a world of power in which my own people had moved about as strangers."

Kazin publishes his book, becomes known and famous, and makes his way to a position of solid power in the literary life of the metropolis. He Makes It in Manhattan; thereafter, except during forays into the hinterlands or literary missions to foreign countries, he spends his time almost exclusively in the company of the famous, the intelligent, the influential. The sense of total immersion in culture and the cultivated is overwhelming. Here, for example, is Kazin vacationing at Cape Cod in the 1960s. He has been describing Edmund Wilson, dressed formally as always, preparing to go for a walk.

> The beach was full of interesting and notable people to talk
> to. There, on any August afternoon in the mid-1960s, could be seen Arthur and Marian Schlesinger, Gilbert Seldes, Allen Tate and Isabella Gardner, Edwin and Veniette O'Connor, Richard and Beatrice Hofstadter, Robert and Betty Jean Lifton, Irving and Arien Howe, Harry and Elena Levin, Daniel and Janet Aaron. At times there could also be seen Stuart and Suzanne Hughes, Jason and Barbara Epstein, Philip and Maggie Roth, Marcel and Constance Breuer. Once there was a view of Svetlana, daughter of Stalin, accompanied by the Georgian writer Paul Chavchavadze, whose wife was a Romanoff and who herself often modestly made her way to the South Wellfleet post office to receive letters from her cousins in Buckingham Palace. It was said that Svetlana and Mrs. Chavchavadze had even compared notes on what it was like to live in the Kremlin.
>
> On the beach sat television producers, government and UN advisers from the social scientists and psycho-historians, professors by the dozen—people all definitely "in." There was so much important, authoritative writing going on in Wellfleet that one professor's wife, trying to hush the neighborhood children, put her head out the window and said pleadingly to the children, "The professor is writing a book review. I'm sure all your fathers and mothers have reviews to write, too!" The children of another writer, left to themselves on the beach, were playing a game with a ball devised by the witty novelist Edwin O'Connor. It was called "Schlesinger," and consisted of trying to knock over a beer can propped up on a little sand hill. If you failed the number of times there were letters in "Schlesinger," you had to

pay a forfeit thought up at the last moment by O'Connor, which usually consisted in walking around some of the lesser discussion groups on the beach and mocking the Hungarian psychoanalyst and the graphic designer from Yale.

Each to his own, as they say. One might as plausibly expect to look up one afternoon and espy the Verdurin carriage coming down from La Raspelière to exhibit the Faithful and drum up an additional dinner guest or two. Had I been there I think I would have desperately sought out the company of a charter-boat captain, a baseball coach from the Cape Cod Summer League, or even a barber—anything to provide relief from all that immense and relentless intellectuality. But Alfred Kazin absorbs it as an oyster absorbs tidal water; it is his meet and drink, one might say.

Was this what that fourteen-year-old boy dreamed of while on the observation platform of Brooklyn Bridge? And was the meaning of that joyful act of possession in the New York Public Library, "the powerful amenity that I craved for my own life," no more than this? One might fear so, if one had not also read Kazin's latest book, *An American Procession*. For Kazin, much like the young Marcel who was observing and chronicling the goings-on at La Raspelière in Proust's great novel, had a vocation.

What Kazin writes best about is the American *writer*—how the writer perceives himself or herself within the literary work. He has a genius for identifying, within the dynamics of the written work, the concerns of the writer as American. Perhaps the most impressive quality about his new book is the range of Kazin's sympathies, the extent to which he can put himself in the place of so many different and even contradictory imaginations.

Kazin's basic premise about American writers is that, from the early nineteenth century onward, each sought to locate within the private individual sensibility the absolute and unmediated relationship to the universe, whether expressed in terms of God, history, nature, society, the church, Darwinian selectivity, whatever, that in Europe could be located *within* the nature of those institutions themselves. Failing to find that access to ultimate reality, the American writer has pursued various absolutes, yet that pursuit remains a highly personal affair at all times. The American writer must begin everything anew.

This is a different and far more radical transaction than the predicament exemplified in the well-known complaint uttered by such writers as Cooper, Hawthorne, and James that American life lacked the social and historical materials from which the literary imagination can shape its imaginings. In Kazin's view the availability of the materials was not the source of the difficulty: it was the writer's attitude toward such materials. For the American writer they were not the incarnation of any ultimate reality, but only a set of properties with which he could work out a private and essentially lonely quest for identity. (Something like this is what Robert B. Heilman must have meant when he once described Allen Tate as remaining "the most protestant of Catholics.")

183

To select one among many examples, *The Waste Land* does not depict the chaos and degradation of modern civilization but represents Eliot's struggling *with* that civilization. Eliot's famous paean to the past in "Tradition and the Individual Talent" could not have been written by a European, Kazin says: "Only an American—and this in 1919—could have wished any 'existing order' to be 'complete.' Religion now was less a matter of God than of culture. Emerson's direct experience of divinity had indeed been replaced by the sacred wood. But only the visitor, the outsider, importuning the sacred wood for refuge, would have sensed so well that this ground was shaking and its towers were about to fall."

The way that Kazin can get inside the writer through the writings, and show us what the imagination is engaged with in the act of writing, is remarkable. Consider what he does with Emily Dickinson, about whom much nonsense has been written. Kazin describes her poetry as a cry for life, the expression of a solitary personality existing in a restrictive community in a time and place in which a theological tradition had evaporated into little more than propriety and exemplary behavior. In its utter intensity her poetry seeks to push consciousness to its absolute limits, to wring the last drop of awareness out of the limited social fabric. Her predilection for writing about death is the attempt to hold onto the extremes of life: "In the day-to-day struggle that made up her life and became her text, death was the great weakening, the most intimate diminution of the strength necessary to her frail body and uncertain morale. . . . In the end consciousness, struggling with itself (as always) to endure, to keep *some* victory for itself against the superior universe, has its say, its last say." For, Kazin says, "the frail Dickinson gives us a sudden sense of the most that we can know. We are with it, all the way. There is no blinking anything." Isn't this close to what seems most important, most visceral about the poetry of Emily Dickinson?

Or Henry James: "Obviously James identified his better characters, especially his favorite ones, with his own solitariness. Hence their mental precautions (sometimes it is positive fright) before other people, their frustrated interchanges, the desperate conjectures which the 'witty' dialogue brushes over. The voyeur is prominent among James's characters as outsider, gossiper, prurient innocent. A tribute to James's power, his underground conduit of feeling, is that he was able to get so much interest and even suspense out of characters shut up in their own minds." Europe for Henry James was an imagined country, Kazin says, in whose social possibility he could saturate himself. "What James demanded for himself, and eventually thought he had found in England, was a class, a style of life, the presentation of which would produce its effect." No wonder then, when August, 1914, came and the destructive element revealed itself, Henry James experienced a personal devastation that lasted until he died in February, 1916.

Kazin's insight into Ezra Pound, a writer whose vicious anti-Semitism strikes at the heart of what Kazin would wish for his own life and his identity as an American, is nonetheless so keen that it illuminates the nature of that writer's imagination more skillfully than any criticism I have ever seen. Pound is in almost all respects quite unlike his friend Eliot: where Eliot is vulnerable and highly personal, Pound's poetic personality is "bewilderingly impersonal, slashing, hard." He is not merely unreligious but literally pagan in his intoxicating identification with the energy in nature. "Pound detected in himself powers of divination, attributes of the shaman, the medium through which he touched a great mystery." The mystery was "the secret of style." Pound's gift for language was so astonishing that it was delusional for him: "poetry possessed him to the point of autointoxication"; it "drugged him, blurred the distinction between poetry and the active world." His belief was that "the language of poetry is not primitive emotion but secret knowledge. The shaman was more important to Pound than the bard." Pound, concludes Kazin, "was the last to believe that the poet does have authority. His manic power reminds us why Plato feared the poets and wanted them out of the perfect Republic."

This seems to me perhaps the most extraordinary of all the discussions of writers in *An American Procession.* I cannot understand what Mark Shechner means when he writes in the *Nation* that "*An American Procession,* then, makes virtually no contribution to our *thinking* about American literature." Apparently American literature is something separate from and of a different order from the American writers who created it. Because Kazin does not develop a formulaic, theoretical structure that can fit literary works into categories does not mean that he is not doing a great deal of thinking about his subject, or that he is (as has been said) no more than a critical impressionist. Indeed Kazin's is the *best* kind of thinking about American literature, in that it deals not with vast cultural abstractions but with writers and their books.

The writer that Kazin finds most instructive, most profoundly representative of his notion about the American writer's being bent upon discovering a private, personal relationship to truth, is another noted anti-Semite, Henry Adams. Adams the historian, sensing the function of power as the force that drives civilization, sees himself as having been personally deprived of any public role in the exercise of power because democracy and industrialism have rendered obsolete his historical right to such a role. So he depicts his personal situation *as* American history. "What Adams could not find in his own culture he found only in the imagination of time past and of society-as-friendship that he so brilliantly sustained by his autobiography and letters. . . . As in a novel of manners, the *Education* makes you identify with the author's irony the standard of values by which to judge everybody else. . . . Civilization has a center at last, and you know where it is—with the author's control." He was a sardonic, selfish, even a vicious man, but what Henry Adams aspired to be and the needs that his aspirations reflected lie within Alfred Kazin's range of sympathetic identification.

Like every other good literary critic, of course, Kazin is reading the Book of Myself. He recognizes what the author is doing because he sees himself in the imagination at work in the book. Certainly the premise he develops about the American writer's radical insistence upon confronting ultimate reality within his own personal sensibil-

185

ity, without the mediation of institutions or even of history, fits not only the historical experience of the New World in general, but especially that of a second-generation American of Russian-Jewish parentage raised in a largely unassimilated enclave of New York City and propelled into modern secular America. As we have seen, Kazin's passion for his country's literature was an act of identification, made all the more intense because he was yielding up not merely a theology but the social and institutional community that Judaism had been forced to develop during the long centuries of enforced separateness in the Eastern European ghetto.

186   Was what he found beyond Brooklyn Bridge a satisfactory replacement? If one reads the later chapters of *New York Jew* (a title chosen so deliberately and ironically in order to represent the ambiguity of his situation), the answer would have to be that although the transaction was inevitable and, in terms of power and status, extremely profitable, the emotional satisfaction it offered and offers is ambivalent. The New York City of the 1960s, 1970s, and now the 1980s is no Promised Land. There is no doubt of Kazin's disgust with American politics of the Vietnam and post-Vietnam era, the loathing he feels for the nihilistic opportunism of the New Left, his discomfort with the way that fashionable literary and cultural life in New York, ever commercially oriented, remains flourishing, still exerting its might while the troubled, slum-ridden metropolis itself declines. "The other New York," he calls it, "the capital of words, the chosen city that is even more splendid, chic, glittery and excessive now than when I dreamed of entering it." Brooklyn Bridge is falling down, falling down; "we are," he writes, "the best historians of our own death."

There is no turning back. Brownsville and what it represented is gone: "the place looks worse than the East End of London after the blitz." After the Holocaust, recapturing the identity his forebears knew is impossible. Israel is no solution: he is an American. His last view of Israel is of the West Bank not long after the 1967 war. Arab families are huddled in a field. "When I asked how long they might be sitting there like that in an empty field, with their belongings, my driver cried out, 'Don't forget how many refugees *we've* had!'"

"In Manhattan's West Eighties, where I live, there is nothing to write about but people. 'Nature' hardly exists, and the architecture, when it is not simply eccentric, can be seen from the street as representing nothing but the calculation of how much money can be squeezed each month out of these cubicles." Kazin writes this in beginning the final sequence of *New York Jew*. He closes with an episode that occurs high over Lincoln Center at a party. Everyone present is "arguing about movie reviews, Lina Wertmüller, the 'neurotic guilt of survivors'" of the Holocaust. Across the Hudson River in Weehawken is a fire on the piers. With difficulty he succeeds in calling it to the attention of others. "As they finally turn around and see it, a new party excitement takes over in the face of that blazing insistency over Jersey. The sky is all red, crazy-red. People reach out, feel each other hungrily. The sky over our heads has been loosened at last. I want to love again. I want my God back. I will never give up until it is too late to expect you."

What is impressive about the episode is the intensity of emotional hunger that it expresses. The reaction here goes beyond the excitement of a good five-alarm fire. It is preceded by a description of the "nature"-less city; its commercially functional architecture; the freaks, junkies, and misfits of its streets and parks; the "charged, busy, tense" quality of life; the appalling wreckage and squalor of present-day Brownsville; the shrill rage voiced against slum landlords; and then the "splendid, chic, glittery and excessive" cultural life in "the capital of words"; and finally a description of the "funny and wonderful" strangeness Kazin feels in teaching Yeats to "a shy black girl from the West Indies." "Even in its 'last days,'" Kazin says, "the secret of New York is raw power, mass and volume, money and power."

It is as if, in an urban environment in which all that is tangible and outside of oneself is either garishly bizarre, comically incongruous, or else burnt-out and dying, those who can rise above it (in the most literal sense) by virtue of money and cleverness—"those lighted skyscrapers of so many clever men, so many stirringly liberated women"—can do no more than feverishly divert themselves with indiscriminate chitchat about topics fashionable and twice-removed from real experience. Then, happily for them, a thing that is material and sensuous and immediate, outside of and different from them, occurs, and all else is forgotten. It is "over Jersey" and so cannot directly impinge upon them, but they turn to it in gratitude and

187

awe, for in contemplating its sheer otherness they feel alive and human. Across the Hudson River in Weehawken, something real is happening.

The episode reminds me of "The Party at Jack's," a novella by Thomas Wolfe. In Wolfe's version the fire takes place in a fashionable apartment building in Manhattan itself, and the partygoers are evacuated from the building and watch from the street. Rich and poor, fashionable and humble mingle, seeing each other as human beings for the first time in years, joined together now in their common plight and their awe at what is happening. For Wolfe the fire symbolizes the Great Depression. For Kazin it is a religious symbol—a Holocaust is a fire, and although it happens across the water it is apocalyptic, an emblem of the passion that consumes merely living things. "I want my God back." "Oh it won't be water, but the fire next time."

Thomas Wolfe was a Southerner who chose to live in New York City. His attitude toward what he termed the Enfabled Rock was compounded of admiration and hate, and his provincial xenophobia can be seen at its worst in his depiction of New York Jews. Apparently Kazin never met Wolfe, but he did spend time in the company of another Southerner, Allen Tate, who, "with his unconvincing absolutes about the Old South's slavery and religion, furiously began every conversation as if I personified the liberal New York Jewish enemy."

The power of sympathetic identification that I have noted as Kazin's strongest critical virtue apparently works only in literature, not in life, at least when Southerners are concerned. "The Southerners I met," he writes, "were generally disturbed by Jews—obsessed, condescending, always just veering off with a smile from some irreversible insult." In his attitude toward the South and Southerners Kazin fails signally to move beyond the same kind of 1930s-style reflexive Liberalism for which in other situations he taxes his fellow New Yorkers. At best he is patronizing, at worst forthrightly hostile. General William Westmoreland, he says, is the "Perfect Southerner."

The two American minority groups who mounted the most determined assault upon the older American literary Establishment during the first half of the twentieth century were the Southerners and the Jews—and for very much the same reasons. Both were, by

188

virtue of their citizenship in modern America, in the process of being expelled from a tradition-laden closed community and into an industrial secular world. Each community had offered to its members as powerful, and as defensive, a sense of identity as the other did. Because of the strong community origins, members of each group tended to view outsiders with suspicion and to feel uneasy in their presence.

Allen Tate and Alfred Kazin were, when they encountered each other in the late 1930s and early 1940s, rival operators. Each was in search of literary influence and power. Tate, however, was operating on Kazin's terrain—the literary milieu described so vividly in *New York Jew*. The power and the advantages were mostly in the hands of Kazin and his friends. But Kazin doesn't see the relationship between that simple fact and his experience with Southerners such as Tate. He writes of Tate that "like all the Southern writers I ever met *in New York,* he had a homesickness for the South he no longer lived in that made him see everything in New York with derisory eyes—especially Jews" (italics mine).

189

What he ascribes to "homesickness" on Tate's part was something more complex. Tate was in New York not because he wanted to be, but because to earn his living as a critic he *had* to go there. Both the Southerners and the Jews were *arrivistes,* but as Kazin shows in such detail, the latter were quickly able to take over, and thereafter could set the terms on which acceptance was to be gained. The East River proved to be considerably less a barrier than the Potomac. Then as now it was the New York Literary Establishment that prescribed what was to be admired, praised, and rewarded. And—I don't think this ever occurs to Kazin—the set of political, cultural, social, and literary views and attitudes that he describes at such length in his memoirs represented, to those Southern outsiders, fully as formidable an array of prejudices and hostilities as those he ascribes to Tate and the other Southerners.

Reading through Kazin's memoirs again, as well as some of the book reviews in his several collections, I have the impression that in a sense there are two Alfred Kazins. The one that matters is the interpreter of American literature, the brilliant reader of our country's great literary texts, possessing a matchless ability to enter into the concerns of the American writer and see what impels him as writer, and equipped with powers of sympathy that permit him to get beyond surfaces, see through defensive gestures born of frustration and fear such as Adams' and Pound's anti-Semitism, and recognize the human being grappling with the deepest problems of identity as an American and an artist.

The other Kazin is the ambitious littérateur who, having made his way out of Brownsville into the cultural Establishment, has long since come to see the nature of the evasions, oversimplifications, self-serving strategies, and sentimental naïveté that characterized what was both a search for freedom and opportunity and a drive for power. This Kazin, whose experience is bounded by the corporate and intellectual limits of the particular American city that except for brief forays elsewhere is all that he has ever known as a place to live, still employs reflexively the assumptions, prejudices, responses, and defenses appropriate to a struggle for power and influence that was won decades ago. He snipes at the Southerners, castigates the academy, sneers at the New Criticism with the lingering vehemence of a time when these seemed to threaten his own hopes for fulfillment. And it is this Kazin who, surrounded now by a city in disarray and seemingly in decline, looks out at it, thinks that there is nothing to write about but people, and, in his hunger for what is real, declares that he wants his God back.

It is absurd. For his God, in that sense, had never left him. The Kazin who can enter into, sympathize with, and participate in the imaginations of those American authors whose works constitute *An American Procession* needs no access to reality beyond the quest illuminated there. Like them and with them he is engaged in what he says was Herman Melville's endeavor: "to seek truth in the confrontation of man with the elemental and in the terrors of his own heart." At the risk of seeming terribly and naively Southern, I would note something else that Kazin says of Melville: "In the New York of the Gilded Age and the Brown Decades, the landlocked sailor was more than ever alone with himself. It was his nature to rebound on himself as the desperate quest. But his strangest association with New York was that living *there* did not matter." I think of Kazin in that glassed-in enclosure high above Lincoln Center, watching the fire on the Weehawken piers and feeling as if the sky had loosened over his head.

Not too far upstream from that burning wharf there is a bridge. Beyond it there is still every bit as much to know and to wonder and to write about as that fourteen-year-old Brownsville boy saw on that late afternoon fifty years and more ago. To paraphrase the conclusion of *An American Procession* with a quotation from *A Walker in the City,* this is because American writing is still personal—like this:

> Somewhere in the deadness of the park the water gurgled in the fountains. In the warmth and stillness a yearning dry and sharp as salt rose in me. Far away a whistle hooted; far away girls went round and round the path, laughing. When we went home, taking the road past the cemetery, with the lights of Jamaica Avenue spread out before us, it was hard to think of them as something apart, they were searching out so many new things in me.

TORY FORMALISTS, NEW YORK INTELLECTUALS, AND THE NEW HISTORICAL SCIENCE OF CRITICISM

(1980)

There is an anthropological theory to the effect that in the pre-historic past, before the invention of the wheel and the Ptolemaic system, our remote ancestors used to place stones over the graves of the deceased in order to make sure that they would remain properly dead and buried. This is apparently the origin of the tombstone, and also of the Jewish custom of tossing pebbles on graves. If so, one can understand the impulse. Nobody likes to have ghosts walking around the place, and no matter how beloved the departed, the new generation must have its day in the sun.

I get the distinct impression that something of the same sort is going on in literary critical circles today. There seems to be almost an entire industry devoted to piling rocks on the grave of the New Criticism. One scarcely reads an essay in a journal such as *Critical Inquiry* without encountering the impassioned assertion that the New Critics have, like Albertine in Proust, *disparue*. The statement is always made with great confidence. And yet—methinks the Hartman doth protest too much. The Sweet Cheat may be Gone,

Originally published as a review-essay on Grant Webster's *The Republic of Letters: A History of Postwar American Literary Opinion* (Baltimore: Johns Hopkins University Press, 1979).

193

but the boys seem just a little nervous about it. That is, they go to such lengths to reassure themselves that nobody is going to appear at the door to the classroom and say "Yes, that's all well and good, but what does the poem itself say? Why did the poet use this image instead of another?" that one has the uneasy impression that when they go strolling by the graveyard at night, they are apprehensive that the ghost of Brooks and Warren may not have been safely exorcised after all. (As well they might be: I understand that the fourth edition of *Understanding Poetry* still sells at a respectable rate.)

In any event, if the New Criticism is, like the Judeo-Christian tradition, dead (Hillis Miller has declared them one and the same, and pronounced the obsequies on behalf of French structuralism), it is remarkable how often the fact appears to require proving. Here, now, is one more such demonstration. Moreover the author doesn't stop there. He throws in the New York Intellectuals for good measure. Both movements are dead, it seems. So dead, indeed, that they can be treated in the manner of a paleontologist attempting to record the life history of the brontosaurus. Here is where it evolved, here is how it flourished, these are the conditions under which it became obsolete and disappeared into the Texas mudflats. With this difference: the paleontologist sees the story of the dinosaur as an adaptation to external conditions of climate and such, while Grant Webster, in *The Republic of Letters: A History of Postwar American Literary Opinion*, appears to believe that both the New Critics and the New York Intellectuals were completely autonomous in inception, promulgation, and decline.

Borrowing a schematization from Thomas S. Kuhn's *The Structure of Scientific Revolutions*, Mr. Webster first sets up what he calls a Paradigm or Charter for classifying and encapsulating schools of literary criticism. It begins with an Ideological Period, develops into a full-fledged Critical Revolution, enters upon a period of Normal Criticism and passes into Superannuation, encounters a Crisis in Criticism, and finally reaches Obsolescence, at which time it strives to become part of history. *Ave atque vale, Cleanthes.* It is all very Hegelian, with a little Vico thrown in.

In this volume the Kuhnian Complex is applied to the New Criticism, under the rubric "The New Critics as Tory Formalists," and then to the New York crowd once clustered about the *Partisan Re-*

view and the *New Republic,* who are labelled "New York Intellectuals: The Bourgeois Avant-Garde." In addition Webster promises
us that his New Historical Science of Criticism, as he calls it, will
subsequently produce studies—"by examining the charters"—of
psychological and myth criticism, structuralism, hermeneutics,
American studies, the counterculture of the 1960s, and—since presumably Mr. Webster is still a reasonably young man and by the
time he finishes cleansing these particular stables of their Augean
refuse there will have arrived new charters for his systematizing—
whatever may lie ahead.

There is a fine air of the abstract about Mr. Webster's enterprise.
He uncovers a paradigm. Into this paradigm he places his data.
Wheels whirr, tabulators click, and Presto! out comes what had
been a half-century of confusing critical *sturm und drang,* neatly
packaged and remarkably easy to clean. It probably should have
been done by a Frenchman, except that it is a little too heavy-
handed for that. Even so I am reminded throughout of an anecdote
that seems to sum up the spirit of so much of this sort of business. It
seems that at the production of the Goncourts' *Henriette Maréchal*
in 1865 there was a full-fledged riot. What triggered the riot was
someone shouting "Subscriber to the *Revue des Deux Mondes!*"

195

Whatever its cerebral qualities, Mr. Webster's is a brave undertaking. One thinks of Immanuel Kant as he settled in at Königsberg
to begin his great Critique of the scope, limits, and modes of all human knowledge, or perhaps of the late Laura Lee Hope when she
first sat down at her desk to undertake the opening volume of the
Bobbsey Twins series.

In thus faring forth, Mr. Webster does not travel without ideological armament. Certain assumptions are implicit in his scheme of
inquiry. What they are can be glimpsed through an inspection of a
few of his pet words. Take the word *revolution,* for example. Webster, via Kuhn, is ostensibly using the word to mean nothing more
or less than a period when a new and original critical view displaces
an older, outmoded one. But Webster is also using that word at a
time when it bears certain palpable political and social connota-
tions. And one has the feeling that when Mr. Webster writes about
his paradigms and charters, what he has a fond vision of is not
merely a transaction in intellectual history, but the broken wall, the

burning ivy tower, and Brooks and Warren dead. In other words, like the voltage of an electric chair, his science is not so much theoretical as applied.

Or take the word *formalist* as applied to critics, whether or not preceded by *Tory*. Ostensibly it means one who is concerned with literary work in terms of its form. But *formal* also means—I quote from the Merriam-Webster *Second International Dictionary* (not to be confused with the Third International)—"prim; stiff; ceremonious; set." (Or "How unpleasant to meet Mr. Eliot! / With his features of clerical cut.") Down with the Tory Establishment! Or "bourgeois"; here it gets pretty obvious. The principal difference between being "middle class," which most of us college professors including, I suspect, Grant Webster are, and "bourgeois" is that the latter is definitely a Bad Thing. Thus the New York Intellectuals, for all their onetime flirtation with parlor Marxism, are, in shifting from revolutionary to nostalgic politics, guilty of an issue-avoiding bourgeois intellectualism that has failed to ground itself in the social and scientific reality of our time. That, I believe, is what is implied when you go around calling former Marxists "bourgeois intellectuals."

Mr. Webster doesn't quite put it that way, of course. I'm not sure that he even consciously *thinks* of it that way. It is just that he *likes* those words like *revolution, Tory Formalist, bourgeois,* and a few other such neutral critical terms like WASP and *elitist*. His use of those words is reminiscent of the way that the behavioral psychologists use the word *meaningless* to describe those fields which are not concerned with quantifying meaning—*i.e.,* the humanities. What they really mean is that the humanities are a waste of anyone's time.

Mr. Webster's case against the New Critics—or the Tory Formalists, as he calls them—is pretty much what one might expect. They are a bunch of "crypto-Christians" who would make the study and criticism of literature independent of the involvement of real life, because they feel helpless and alienated in the face of modernity. "Only when one sees Formalism as a flight from the war, the science, the urbanism, the condition of modern man, does such a rejection [of author and historical context] make any cultural sense." Their goal is thus either a covert pleading for Christianity (in Eliot's instance it becomes overt), or else a way of insulating themselves

196

from all distasteful involvement in the concerns of *hoi polloi.* The Southern Agrarian wing of the movement, disabused of its hopes of political power [!] when Agrarianism failed in the 1930s, moved to take over the universities, and succeeded all too well. That notorious elitist version of *Das Kapital* entitled *Understanding Poetry* was the weapon with which the Messrs. Brooks and Warren, acting at the behest of the resolutely antiscientific John Crowe Ransom and the quasi-paranoiac Allen Tate, tried to keep America safe for the Christian gentleman. Mr. Webster knows all about the Fugitives and Agrarians, of course; he has read Alexander Karanikas and John L. Stewart on the subject—which is something like turning to the Book of Joshua for an unbiased account of the inhabitants of Jericho. Webster really appears to believe that the leading Agrarians hoped to gain control over Southern society! And that it was only when they saw that they couldn't do it that they turned to a more realistic goal of merely taking over the universities.

197

Paradoxically, though the Tory Formalist New Critics attempt to isolate literature from life and historical involvement, and to treat it upon purely formal grounds in order to keep from having to confront the condition of modern man, they are also guilty of the most flagrant kind of patriotic flag-waving regionalism. Cleanth Brooks, as one might expect, is the topmost villain. He is even quoted as having remarked once that "our most authentic literature has been coming from the provinces and not from the great metropolitan centers."

Why would Brooks say so absurd a thing as that? Could it be that he might have had in mind such writers as Faulkner, Yeats, Joyce, Eliot, Frost, Hardy, Lawrence, Pound, Warren, Fitzgerald, Huxley, Dreiser, Auden, Crane, Durrell, Wright, Welty, MacLeish, Mencken, O'Casey, Ransom, Tate, Roethke, Thomas, and a few dozen others? But enough—clearly Brooks should have known better. Moreover Brooks, that Formalist escapist from the vexatious relationships of time and place into a timeless haven of poetic form, is simultaneously castigated for having written a book about William Faulkner in which the work of that novelist is interpreted in terms of the life, society, and history of the American South. (If there is any element of contradiction there, it doesn't seem to bother Mr. Webster. Apparently, genuine social reality exists only north of the Potomac and Ohio rivers.)

One might wonder why the New Critical Formalists are branded as Tories. (Ransom, for example, was a New Dealer.) If so, on page 83 one finds out. "Such a view [as Eliot's] of literature is Tory in its construction, for it assumes that the form of literature parallels the conservative view of the form of life—good and evil locked in struggle." In other words, the reason that we know Eliot is a Tory is that he views life as a contest between good and evil. By this criterion, other noted Tories would include Karl Marx, Mao Tse-tung, and the Reverends Matthew, Mark, Luke, and John.

Not all the Tory Formalists were Southerners or Anglicans, however. There are also a few such as R. P. Blackmur, who in his "hankering for lost aristocracy . . . reminds one of Edmund Wilson, who came from the same WASP patrician class as [Henry] Adams," and Kenneth Burke, who is mostly "an old-time American crank inventor who might have been Edison except that his work lacks any relation to society outside his own mind."

Happily, however, the domination of WASP Tory Formalism is over. As a critical movement it has passed the point of Superannuation and is now well into Obsolescence. For proof of that, Mr. Webster says, examine the *Sewanee Review*. It has "kept the faith, has tried far more consistently than any other magazine to provide a unifying center for culture. But what its editors consider to be the center has in terms of the general culture become a dead center, a graveyard of issues of the past. As such, it stands as most faithful and most forlorn of the Formalist magazines, with the irony of the criticism it expresses being itself judged by the irony of history." It is, in short, stone cold dead in the literary market. I pick up the most recent copy of the *Sewanee* that I have at hand, and in it I find pieces dealing with, among other topics, structuralist criticism, the Holocaust, literary biography, Marxist literature, George Steiner, semiotics, transactional discourse, Philip Rahv, F. R. Leavis, Jacques Derrida—O death where is thy sting, O grave thy irony?

So much for Tory Formalism. When Mr. Webster moves on to his next paradigm or charter, that of the New York Intellectuals, complete with schematic diagram showing their dual allegiance to "Bourgeois Liberalism" and "Avant-Garde Radicalism," he seems more at home. That is, though he views them as dreadfully dated, and even comes to suggest that maybe they didn't acquire a legal

198

Critical Charter at all but only a kind of stylistic license, obviously they don't disturb him as much as the wicked Formalists, in that at least they didn't go around trying to flee from the modern world by insisting on reading poems as poems.

The New York Intellectuals were of two kinds: Jews and Ivy Leaguers. Thus, whether owing to a disadvantaged immigrant real-estate condition or the lingering heritage of the old Calvinistic American values, they shared a strong compulsion to Succeed. Mr. Webster quickly decides that despite the claims of Norman Podhoretz, Alfred Kazin, Irving Howe, and others, Jewishness had relatively little to do with what they were about. Instead what we have, centered on the *Partisan Review,* the *New Republic,* Columbia University, and (until Stalin disillusioned them all by making temporary friends with Hitler) the Finland Station, is a group of very bright people who have a pledged allegiance to (a) bourgeois liberal politics and (b) avant-garde literature. This somehow produces a dialectic between social reality and the literary imagination, which works very creatively for a time.

199

Unfortunately, however, the whirligig of time e'er works *its* way, and the literary avant-garde becomes the "derrière-garde," while bourgeois liberalism is replaced by the New Left: "Rise of counter-culture, N. O. Brown, Reich, Leary [Timothy, not Lewis], McLuhan, etc., Weathermen, Panthers, New Left, political avant-garde." Meanwhile the New York Intellectuals accept sinecures in the universities, or else grow rich through writing for the mass media ("Just for a handful of silver he left us, / Just for a riband to stick in his coat"), and instead of remaining Intellectuals they become merely the Intelligentsia. Sic transit Gloria Swanson, as they say.

In such wise are the divers careers of Lionel Trilling, Dwight Macdonald, Irving Howe, Philip Rahv, Richard Chase, Alfred Kazin, Delmore Schwartz, Norman Podhoretz, etc., traced, summarized, and embalmed. There are variations, of course—Schwartz merely went crazy—but in the main, this is what happened to them. Failing to find continued nourishment in the tension between society and the imagination, they moved more and more out of the mainstream, and were finally left ruefully contemplating their lost youth and the death of their hopes.

Thus Irving Howe, middle-aged now, writes: "Yet, precisely at this moment of dispersion, might not some of the New York writers achieve renewed strength if they were to struggle once again for whatever has been salvaged from these last few decades? For the value of liberalism, for the politics of a democratic radicalism, for the norms of rationality and intelligence, for the standards of literary seriousness, for the life of the mind as a humane dedication." To which Mr. Webster's comment is, "For God, for Irving, and for St. George! Howe is quite right in affirming that freedom is essential to the avant-garde Intellectual, but he is less aware that in gaining tenure he has lost his own avant-garde position." Thus "one must then conclude of the Intellectuals that their careers as critics are best understood as parts in an avant-garde play; they have played, and played well for the most part, roles in a drama that is now concluded." (Does Mr. Webster know of a better way of conducting operations any time than what Howe has proposed? If so, will he please go ahead and propose it?)

200

In any event the comedy is finished. There remains only to look at old Edmund Wilson, the squire of Talcottville, who, having interpreted the avant-garde for the bourgeois reader and then had his fling at Marxism, retires into the American past, sets himself up as a figure of the eighteenth-century Enlightenment, and writes for the *New Yorker*. He has failed to give his world the order of the avant-garde and of the political radical; henceforth he will devote his efforts to the creation of a persona who will provide the order of his own personality. Since, unlike the Jewish critics, he did not have to acquire the American experience as an act of the will, but "had it in his bones, he can and does serve as our gold standard for journalistic criticism in the Republic of Letters." (Mr. Webster is too charitable to add that we have been off the gold standard since 1933.)

What does all this amount to? If we leave out the envy and the malice, what is viable in Mr. Webster's analysis is mostly old hat, not much improved sartorially by its resurrection in the form of paradigm and charter. Other formulations for what Mr. Webster thinks he is discovering are of hoary antiquity. Golden age / silver age / bronze age / iron age was one way of expressing it. The rise-and-fall image, by Spengler out of Hegel and Darwin, was another. There are many more such. The insight that intellectual movements begin in enthusiastic conspiracy, have their day, and end in a superannu-

ated establishment is surely a commonplace in the history of literature. Somewhere I have read a story in which the poet Rouget de
Lisle, now grown middle-aged and conservative, goes to a window
during a street disturbance and returns to report to his friends: "It
looks bad! They're playing the *Marseillaise!*"

It doesn't strike me that much new light is shed upon the matter
by adapting Kuhn's *The Structure of Scientific Revolutions* for these
purposes. The New Historical Science of Criticism looks very much
like the Old Historical Study of Literature to me, only with the
literature left out. There is little in this book that couldn't equally
well have been set forth without any reference at all to the system of
schematization. Indeed, seeing the matter as a self-contained paradigm is a positive disadvantage, in that it leaves out the element of
antecedents and of continuing influences.

201

The truth is that this is really a history not of criticism, but of
groups of ambitious critics, told in terms not of their critical ideas
and insights so much as of their politics and allegiances. When
Mr. Webster does discuss what these critics actually did as critics,
what seems to interest him is principally the social implications, as
he sees them, of the criticism, not the literary implications. It is
Sainte-Beuve with a vengeance, Van Wyck Brooks with a scowl. Alfred Kazin, in *Starting Out in the Thirties,* has a funny anecdote
about Philip Rahv, who as an editor of *Partisan Review* once asked
a writer who was submitting a story to him, "Who's in it?"
Mr. Webster's new Historical Science of Criticism seems to be
roughly of that sort.

The real difficulty with Mr. Webster's undertaking lies in just
that sector. At the outset I noted that he approaches literary criticism as if it were an autonomous enterprise, produced for its own
sake. In viewing the New Critics and the New York Intellectuals as
he does, he is almost never prompted to examine their critical activity in terms of the kind of literature they admire, espouse, and
even produce. But a great deal of the impulse behind literary criticism and critics arises precisely from the desire to understand and
interpret a body of literature. In other words, in order to understand the vogue of literary critical movements, one must consider
the kind of literature that they choose to criticize. Thus it is impossible to comprehend the role, influence, and history of the New
Critics without seeing that a crucial part of their reason for being

arises out of the need to understand and interpret the particular kind of poetry written in English during the first half of the twentieth century. Their success in "taking over the universities," as Mr. Webster would have it, was owing not to their conspiratorial skills—it took Allen Tate twenty-five years to gain a tenured position—but to the existence of that poetry and the need to learn to read it well. It was not the social and cultural philosophy of "Tory Formalism" that made the New Criticism so influential, but the fact that it offered a *method* for reading twentieth-century verse. And that method has apparently become a permanent part of our way of dealing with poems.

202   In somewhat the same fashion, the role of the so-called New York Intellectuals would seem to have been in large part that of introducing our reading public to the literature of the European continent, together with the ideas that influenced that literature. We needed to learn how to read Proust, Mann, Kafka, Malraux, the Russians; we needed the kind of idea-criticism that would enable us to deal with what they were about; and we needed to learn how to apply those literary ideas, too, to American and British literature. For just so long as that need was urgent, a criticism that was poised between the two continents, based at the port of entry, was in great demand. Thanks to it we now possess that literature for our own. In other words, without the presence of a body of "avant-garde" literature that demanded interpretation, the group that Mr. Webster characterizes as the New York Intellectuals would have been far less important.

The point is that it is the *literature,* not the critical talent as such, that calls forth the criticism, rather than the other way around. Thus a history of literary criticism, new or old, can be made to make sense only if the criticism is discussed in relation to the literature—or else perhaps in terms of purely theoretical aesthetics alone, in which instance it will be a history not so much of criticism as of the aesthetics of literature. To discuss it exclusively in terms of its politics, or even of the relationship of the criticism to society and its problems, as Mr. Webster mostly does, will tell us little. For it is not criticism that is at issue, but *literary* criticism.

At one point in his dissection of Tory Formalism, Mr. Webster must deal with René Wellek; he does so under the category of "The Age of the Theorists," which on his evolutionary diagram comes along close to the point of the ultimate extinction of the species. He quotes Wellek on Samuel Johnson in order to demonstrate Wellek's bias in favor of teutonic theorizing: Johnson, Wellek says, "is one of the first great critics who have almost ceased to understand the nature of art, and who, in central passages, treat art as life. He has lost faith in art as the classicists understood it and has not found the romantic faith." But Wellek isn't talking about Johnson's failure to be a theorist. He is pointing out that by the mid-eighteenth century the neoclassical assumption that the purpose of art was to teach and to delight had come down so heavily on the instructional side of the equation that the identity of art as play was almost ignored. Johnson tended to judge literature in terms of its moral statement about life, without taking sufficient account of its transformation into art.

203

This is quite a sensible observation to make about Johnson, and when Wellek then goes on to note that Johnson is even so a great critic of literature, it isn't an admission that critical theory is unimportant for a critic (which Mr. Webster says contradicts Wellek's own teutonic bias), so much as an admission that a man's critical principles may be sounder than the theory he believes he is using. Surely this is an appropriate observation to make about a critic who could see through the psychological irrelevance of the neoclassical unities in his reading of Shakespeare, yet be incapable of participating in the pastoral convention of "Lycidas." In the one instance his fundament of good common sense, which was part of his critical stance, aided him; in the other it worked against him.

Wellek is able to recognize this, because for all his vast involvement in critical theory he doesn't miss the essential fact that it is criticism *of* literature that is at stake. Mr. Webster, by contrast, has written an entire book about the rise and fall of two schools of literary criticism without attempting to work out any real relationship between the critics, the criticism, and the literature they criticize. That is why I say that it is very much like old-style literary history of the pre–"Tory Formalist" era—*i.e.*, the equivalent for criticism of a history of literature that is written without ever considering that criticism as literature.

Is Mr. Webster, however dubious his methodology, correct when he pronounces the obsolescence and demise of the New Criticism? As I noted at the outset, it is being announced all the time. My response would be that if the New Criticism as a movement is concluded, it is because its job has been done: it has made us read poems closely and in their own right, so that we could gain access to the poetry written in English during the first half of the twentieth century. But I remain unconvinced that it is kaput, because I don't see its job as having been done. Certainly its faddishness is over; it is no longer a novelty. But in ceasing to be New it has not thereby become Old Criticism. Instead it has become simply criticism. And the best criticism of literature, so long as it is criticism *of* literature, will have to be that which starts with the text and, no matter how far it may stray or whatever it brings to the text, will find its validity in the text. The numerous proclamations of its demise, therefore, the stones being heaped so lavishly upon its grave to keep the ghost from walking, might turn out to be wasted effort. Because somebody is always going to say, eventually, after the New Historical Scientist or the structuralist or the Marxist or reader-psychologist or whatever has erected his glittering paradigm or simulacrum or manifesto or document or who knows what: "Yes, but how do you *know* it's so?" And the only convincing response will have to be "Let's look at the text."

204

BERNARD DEVOTO ALL TOLD

(1975)

Whatever the forces, psychological, economic, reverential, or otherwise, that make people write, there is usually more compulsion about the way that they operate than we like to admit. I propose to deal here with a topic that as I confront it I realize is pretty compulsive. It has to do with the late Bernard DeVoto, sometime journalist, critic, novelist, historian, conservationist, teacher, and—most of all—controversialist, whose biography Wallace Stegner has now very ably composed. He has been dead for these fourteen years, and though it cannot be said that he left behind him an enduring reputation as literary maker and finder, there are those who remember his work, and what he represented, very well indeed. They will greatly enjoy Mr. Stegner's biography, as I did.

Let me insist at once that DeVoto's major literary contribution was his books on Mark Twain. That is what he will be remembered for, though during his lifetime (1897–1955) he was perhaps best known as a corrosive critic of life and letters. I first took up the topic of DeVoto some twenty-four years ago, in a review-essay on his book *The World of Fiction* (1950). However, it wasn't really DeVoto as such that concerned me at the time, so much as his un-

Originally published as a review-essay on Wallace Stegner's *The Uneasy Chair: A Biography of Bernard DeVoto* (Garden City, N.Y.: Doubleday, 1974).

charitable attitude toward Thomas Wolfe, first and most notably expressed in his famous polemic "Genius Is Not Enough" in the *Saturday Review of Literature* back in 1936, and alluded to from time to time in *The World of Fiction*. His indictment of Wolfe was perhaps his most famous piece of literary demolition. The burden of "Genius Is Not Enough" and of DeVoto's later remarks was that though Wolfe possessed a considerable quantity of literary talent, he was not only ignorant of the art of fiction but utterly incapable of distinguishing between the immature, vaunting assertion of his own genius and the dramatized rendering of experience in the form of fiction. Among Wolfe scholars the attack is customarily credited with touching off Wolfe's decision to separate himself from Maxwell Perkins and Charles Scribner's Sons, to join up with Edward Aswell at Harper and Brothers, and to discontinue his autobiographical protagonist Eugene Gant in favor of the only slightly less autobiographical George Webber. DeVoto thus became the bête noire of the partisans of Thomas Wolfe, and most of them have sought at one time or another to denounce him for his base scurrility and his manifest insensitivity to true genius.

The specific terms in which DeVoto's polemic was framed were calculated beautifully to infuriate anyone (such as myself) who tended to view the matter of youthful self-acknowledged genius versus the prosaic society of philistine getters-and-spenders along the same lines that Wolfe's protagonists did. That nasty-tongued man seemed to exemplify so much that was awry in the literary situation: his contempt for rhetorical exuberance; his dogmatic insistence that nothing was worth reading that was not ordered, proportioned, and expertly shaped; his infuriating air of commonsensicality and his contemptuous unwillingness to accept the supremacy of Feeling over Thinking; and above all else, the crass way in which he dismissed Wolfe, and those who thought fondly of Wolfe's more romantic literary outbursts, as being simply *immature*.

So we hated DeVoto. And we feared him. Yet, when the chips were down, I for one could not dismiss him. When I read *The World of Fiction*, I bridled when I came upon the statement, appended to a choice item from Wolfe's rhetoric: "Just why should we waste time upon a critic's imperatives about the social and esthetic obligations of fiction when he admires such stuff as this?" Even so, I

206

was forced to recognize that the man had a good deal to say about writing, that he did understand many of the reasons why people wrote novels and did not underrate what fiction could and could not do, and that for all his surliness of disposition he had thought to good purpose about the art of fiction and knew how to write about it. It was difficult, therefore, to square one's resentment at his man-handling of Wolfe with the fact that much of what he wrote made considerable sense. In the review-essay that I prepared, I tried my best to come to grips with this contradiction, wound up denouncing DeVoto's bad manners while generally approving his principles, then insisted (I quote) that "the person reading *Look Homeward, Angel* is well aware that he is reading not pure narrative, nor even pure 'fiction,' but a unique mixture of communicated narrative and exposition, fact and fancy, and is quite content to do so." In other words, it was a mistake to judge Wolfe by the same rules one employed for judging other writers.

Needless to say, DeVoto survived this critical onslaught. My essay was a naive enough performance, though I remember slaving desperately over its every phrase, and I resurrect its wan ghost only because I desire to lay my cards on the table and not to pretend that my views on Bernard DeVoto and his work are the outcome of a long experience of disinterested objectivity. For myself, reading Mr. Stegner's excellent biography is like seeing the other side of the story: the man who so irked me once, who seemed to personify so much that I disliked about the literary "Establishment," and whose personality and position seemed so entrenched and so unassailable, so formidably self-contained, now turns out to have been a quite distraught fellow, insecure of position, writing his contentious criticism as much out of anxiety as of inner conviction, and in no way impregnable in his critical bastion. *The Uneasy Chair,* Mr. Stegner entitles his biography of the man, punning on the title of the department that DeVoto conducted for *Harper's Magazine* for so many years. How, then, could he ever have seemed so formidable?

Yet he did. Looking back on what he was and what he wrote, I see that he symbolized a way of viewing the writing of fiction and the province of the novelist that had the result of impoverishing my own experience of reading novels. Why this was, I could not articulate. Though about Wolfe he was rather more on target than I could then grasp, and I much too ingenuous to be able to explain my own objections to what he said, my discomfort with his approach to fiction was considerably more sound than I knew. What was so frustrating was that he put forth his own position very well, while I could not get at what was wrong with it. What I was really coming up against, of course, was a much more complex and fundamental matter than the literary criticism of Bernard DeVoto. Thomas Wolfe's fictional flaws only elicited it in an especially obvious and crude way. It had to do with the nature of the fictional experience.

In *The World of Fiction* what DeVoto had to say was clear, precise, well worked out. Essentially he viewed fiction as dramatized illusion. Distinguishing between the art of the dramatist (as presented in simplified form in a puppet show) and that of the novelist, he declared that "there are no actors, no photographs of actors, no dolls; there are only words printed on a page. The reader is not present at the event, for there is no event. The novelist must persuade him that an event is occurring, that he is present at it, and that *what in the theater happens in mimicry before his own eyes is happening in a place which exists only by consent of his imagination.* When the persuasion succeeds, the illusion of fiction is established" (italics mine).

In saying, as I did then, that Wolfe's fiction was a "mixture of communicated narrative and exposition," I was quite right, though for the wrong reasons—I was trying to make a special case for Wolfe, and, truth to tell, defend some passages which were every bit as overwritten as DeVoto was saying. It was not that Wolfe's fiction was any such unique affair as I was claiming; other and greater novelists also offered up that kind of "mixture." Instead I was letting myself accept DeVoto's quite limited, albeit closely reasoned, definition of fiction as dramatized illusion, when the truth was that the "illusion" of fiction involved a dimension that DeVoto did not apprehend. What he was leaving out of his aesthetic was authorial language—what Wayne Booth was later to call the "rhetoric of fiction" and what I would denote as the "authorial personality."

No novel, no matter how dramatic its technique, is merely an imagined three-dimensional drama. It is *told*, by a story teller, and the personality of the storyteller, whether effaced or (by DeVoto's definition) intrusive, is an essential element of the experience of fiction. The *language:* that is what matters most. That is how the meaning is communicated. But for DeVoto language did not really count for very much at all. He went at *Ulysses* in an effort to demonstrate how, at the outset, Joyce puts us in Stephen Dedalus' imagination, so that we see the scene through him and also see Stephen: "The reflection of one character through another makes both more alive." A little later on he cites a passage in which Joyce tells us, from the outside, what Stephen was thinking: obviously DeVoto preferred the first procedure. Joyce did the latter, he suggested, only when necessary. But the truth is that even though in one instance we see the story through Stephen, while in the other we see Stephen through Joyce, the novelist is equally present for the reader, as storyteller, upon *both* occasions, and is telling a particular kind of story through his choice of language; and though we assume his presence and take it for granted, we never forget it is there, for that is how storytelling works. James Joyce, as master of the revels and virtuoso user of words, is never absent from one's experience of *Ulysses*. It is only when, as sometimes in *Stephen Hero* and (I think) in the aesthetics chapter in *A Portrait of the Artist as a Young Man*, James Joyce as author forces his own biographical concerns into his story so that the storyteller's logic is violated, that he can be said to intrude.

209

When things went wrong in Wolfe's fiction, that was what was happening, not what DeVoto thought. It was not because they did not dramatize ideas and emotions that the more windy, self-assertive passages failed: in the best of Wolfe there was just as much rhetoric, just as much authorial "intrusion" (in DeVoto's sense) as in those rhapsodies that DeVoto rightly condemned and labeled placental. The difference did not lie in the dramatization, but in the fact that in the successful work the rhetorical assertions by the author conformed to the logic of the storyteller's story, and vice versa, while in the passages DeVoto didn't like the relationship was unbelievable because not justified by the logic of the story.

In truth it wasn't merely Wolfe that I was advocating so clumsily and awkwardly in my long-ago essay: mostly without my knowing it, it was also the art of Proust, and Joyce, and Cervantes, and Sterne, and many another author who didn't write DeVoto's brand of tidy dramatic fiction. And though DeVoto expressed his strong approval of Joyce and Proust and Sterne, in actuality he didn't really recognize why or how their fiction worked for him. He took in the rhetoric, but tried to make it out as a form of internal characterization. The best he could do was to introduce the metaphor of the tragic chorus, and attempt to assign that function to what the novelist said apart from his dramatizing; he did not see that the novelist was performing the function of the chorus just as surely when dramatizing his characters as when commenting on them. "A passage of fiction," he declared, "that is intended to give the scene reality, a passage of analysis that is intended to interpret the behavior of characters, or a passage of exposition that is intended to give significance to the action, is fiction clumsily written." That is, the catechism chapter in *Ulysses*, "Swann in Love," the author's comments on what Lambert Strether would later be thinking about having encountered Chad Newsome and Mme. Vionnet in the boat in *The Ambassadors* are clumsily written fiction! But in Proust and Joyce and James and the work of many another master of the art of fiction such passages are not only not at all clumsy, but are as much fictionalized as the straight dramatic passages. The fiction lies in the total experience of the language, not in the narrative sequences alone, and the storyteller is speaking directly to the reader as much during the action as during the so-called analysis or exposition.

210

Fiction *isn't* drama, as DeVoto himself insisted; but having said that, he did not accept the implications of the statement, and most of his formidable technical expertise was exercised as if fiction were imagined dramatic illusion. A craftsman of sorts with language himself, with a talent for abusive rhetoric reminiscent of his mentor H. L. Mencken (who, however, also had humor, which DeVoto did not), he nevertheless did not apprehend the absolutely primary position of language in the art of fiction, and never saw that because it was done through written words, the art of storytelling had a relationship between story and reader that was centrally different from theatrical illusion, and in certain important ways close to that of lyric poetry. What Thomas Wolfe was doing, however stumblingly at times, was writing fiction which was very much in the artistic tradition of Cervantes, Fielding, Sterne, Twain, Stendhal, and Joyce; it was not dramatic in the way that the fiction of James and Richardson and Dickens and Hawthorne was usually dramatic, yet it was every bit as much "pure" fiction as the so-called dramatic novel. It was based much more directly and obviously upon the functional presence of the authorial personality, who told his story in virtuoso fashion and let his role as master of the revels become an overt dimension of the celebrated Representation of Reality. Far from pretending to be invisible in order to accomplish a fictional sleight-of-hand trick, such authors held center stage, and with their flourishing rhetoric played openly with and upon the reader's sensibilities and guided his responses to what was going on.

Reading *The World of Fiction* today, almost a quarter-century after its publication in book form, one thinks how completely at sea DeVoto would have been with some of the more creative new forms of fiction in our own day. He would never have been able to enjoy John Barth's *The Sot-Weed Factor,* for example. The whole thrust of the "anti-novel" movement would have baffled him. Indeed he felt more than a little uncomfortable with such virtuoso stylists as Faulkner and Hemingway, and did not really understand what Proust was doing with a first-person narrator who could move so completely into the minds and lives of Charles Swann and others, and also have so much to say about what he was doing even as he did it. He tried to make it into simple point-of-view characterization, which it wasn't at all.

Isn't it odd that this critic, who prided himself so much upon his practical approach to problems of technique and who thought so extensively and in detail about the requirements of craft, should have had so limited a realization of this central rhetorical dimension? Rereading *The World of Fiction,* which once had so intimidated me in its technical authority even as it cut to ribbons the one novelist who meant most to me as a young man, I was struck by its narrowness of vision. DeVoto was one of those writers about fictional technique—one of the more skillful of them—who, able to descry that, say, J. P. Marquand and Marcel Proust are employing a similar technical solution to a problem, can deftly analyze and interpret the technical problem, but have no critical tools for getting at and explaining what makes *Remembrance of Things Past* a classic while *B. F.'s Daughter* is a run-of-the-mill novel. He was writing about the "world of fiction," and it is significant that he saw that world as involving problems of biography, psychology, reader re-

211

sponse, and dramatic method, but not of imagination or of language. He could, in other words, deal with the *why* of it, but before the *how* and the *what*, the main show, he was silent. It is no coincidence, I think, that though DeVoto wanted very much to write good fiction, as a serious novelist he was a failure, but as a hack novelist writing serials for the slick magazines under a pseudonym he was a considerable success. He knew the way to put a plot together, but he didn't know how to use his skill as a means of discovery; *as a novelist* he had almost nothing to discover. Thus he couldn't understand how the technique in really good fiction was placed at the service of discovery, and was not method in a vacuum but used in order to reveal experience. A critic for whom Marquand and Proust are akin in technique can only view such technique apart from what is being revealed, as a skill, rather than approach it as a means of revelation, as an art. DeVoto seems always to have assumed that the novelist already knew his story and its meaning, and chose his technique to communicate them; he did not see that it was through the technique that the author discovered his story and its meaning.

So that poor Thomas Wolfe, for all his fustian and self-assertion and addiction to "placental" rhetorical passages, will survive in literature because he had something to say and when at his best possessed the technique to uncover it, while Bernard DeVoto, exponent of the craftsmanship of fiction, is all but forgotten because he had nothing, finally, to say beyond pointing out rules. Genius may not be enough; but unless one understands that the genius consists of a technique for discovery of one's experience through language, one is likely both to miss the genius and to view the technique only mechanically and superficially.

Reading Wallace Stegner's biography of Bernard DeVoto was a moving experience for me, and reminiscent of what happened with the reputation of the public Hemingway. For many years the portrait of Hemingway that we got was that of the tough guy, the hard-as-nails, sun-bronzed, wound-scarred professional who disdained the neurotic intellectual weaklings who wrote about him, and who composed his prose and viewed his world as an arena for slugging it out with death and destruction. This was how he projected himself, and many readers took the public projection for the artist. Then, prompted by Philip Young, we suddenly realized how carefully

212

and desperately cultivated was the hard-boiled, he-man, big-game-hunter role, and that behind it was a man who was a bundle of nerves and compulsions, who was struggling bravely against some terrible fears, and whose every work of art represented a momentary stay against catastrophic doubt. When he remarked that his own psychoanalyst was Portable Corona Number Three, he wasn't merely taking a swipe at those effete weaklings who depended upon psychiatric counsel: he was making a statement about his art, which was incredibly and tremendously revelatory of what was going on inside him. As a friend of mine once said, the Ernest Hemingway who ultimately emerged was not only more believable, but also far more attractive and worthy of one's admiration than the one we used to know.

213

In the same way, the DeVoto that Mr. Stegner shows us is a very different man from the one we thought we knew through his "Easy Chair" pieces and his books on fictional techniques, literary fallacies, and the like. An Establishment figure? Not at all, really. Here was a man who throughout his life felt that he didn't quite belong, either in Utah or at Harvard or in critical circles or as journalist and editor. From his beginnings out in Ogden and throughout his career he was considered not quite respectable, and he felt it keenly. His pose as advocate of the healthy, red-blooded, commonsensical westerner who scorned the fads and neurotic flagellations and defeatist preciosity of the Anglo-Catholic Waste-Landers and effete intellectual parlor pinks of the Europeanized East Coast was without any real basis whatever in the facts of his own life. When he lived in the Far West he detested its cultural barrenness and suffered from its insensitivity, desired nothing so much as to depart forever, and yearned for the good life in and about Harvard Square. The man who scoffed at Thomas Wolfe's depiction of Eugene Gant in pain over criticism of his book spent much of his time agonizing over his own failure to be taken importantly by reviewers. There was all too much recoil and sour grapes to his vitriolic savaging of the Eastern Establishment—by which is meant whatever group, coterie, movement, professional conjunction or combination of individuals that proved unappreciative of his worth. Tough-minded, stoical? Repeatedly and stridently he insisted upon the deep-down sanity of art. Art was no product of neurosis, no result of wound and bow, no compensation for failure to cope with the Real World: it was an affirmation of control, health, maturity. He had to insist upon that; for he feared for his own sanity at all times, was ravaged by deep depressions, constantly underwent psychoanalysis—to give in to such fears, to concede the irrationality of much that he thought and felt, would surely mean madness.

Clearly what enraged and frightened him about a writer like Wolfe was that author's naive disregard of consequences. The author of *Of Time and the River* didn't care that others might think him egotistic or romantic or immature; he trumpeted his own uniqueness and superior sensibility, hesitated not at all to expose his ardent emotions and ambitions and longings. The nerve of him! What did he think he was, anyway, a genius? DeVoto would therefore take down Folsom Man of the Asheville Site a peg or two; and he did. And there *was* more than a little truth in what he had to say about Wolfe. But what he was really doing was exorcising just such demons from his own mind. What he recognized and loathed in Wolfe was himself: that was the way *he* had felt about the world and Bennie DeVoto.

Only such a process can properly account for the savageness with which he attacked Wolfe, a savageness that went beyond literary criticism and into psychological pronouncement: "Superfluous and mistaken things are lovely only to a very young writer, and the excision of them is bloody carnage only if the artist has not yet learned to subdue his own ego in favor of his book. And the same juvenility makes him prowl 'the streets of Paris like a maddened animal' because—for God's sake—the reviewers may not like the job." This is not the analysis of an author's fiction: it is the clinical dissection of the autobiographical compulsions of the writer.

Thus DeVoto. His biographer does not fail to note and document what made the man what he was and was not. Whatever the arrangements involved in Mr. Stegner's undertaking to write this biography, they clearly did not involve the necessity to pull punches. But even so—perhaps because so—it is a biography written out of compassion and admiration for its subject. What Mr. Stegner recognizes, proclaims, and cherishes in DeVoto was the man's true independence of spirit. From the beginning out in Ogden and all the way through his career, he did things his own way, and he thought

214

for himself. He wanted faculty status at Harvard, but on his own terms (and God knows he was worth his asking price). He wanted fame as a writer of fiction, but he never tried to write anyone's kind of novel but his own. He asked no quarter, buttered no biscuits, toadied to nobody. Robert Frost, it is true, took him in for a while; it was not until that tormented egotist lost all control over his own vanity in public that DeVoto broke with him and ceased to champion him as the Sole Apostle of Sanity in the Waste Land of Defeatists and Cultists. That was DeVoto's single lapse into subservience; the rest of the time, before and after Frost, he was his own man.

What does an independent like DeVoto do, in our literary situation? He couldn't stay home and write his fiction, as Faulkner did; he was too much the critical journalist, too needful of intellectual companionship. He couldn't follow the academic road; not only did he not have the professional credentials at first, but he desired the hurly-burly of the front line too much. The New York scene wasn't for him; though he liked publishing and editing, he wanted more substance and solidity to his ideas than were available in the fashions and fads of the marketplace. His response to the Expatriates and the Popular Front was to berate most of the better writers of the 1920s and 1930s for their ignorance of America and their negativistic attitude toward American middle-class culture. In so doing he came preciously close to the philistine ethos: as Mr. Stegner notes, "It is hard to see where he got the notion, for instance, that Eliot, Dreiser, Anderson, and their younger contemporaries Hemingway, Fitzgerald and Wescott knew neither the Middle West nor the middle class." Yet, as Mr. Stegner adds, such assertions "contained a legitimate corrective of much excess on the other side, and in 1936 it was exhilaratingly bold. He crawled into a cave packed with bears, and shined his insolent flashlight around, and growled."

Cambridge, Massachusetts, not Manhattan, was his métier. But in Cambridge, President Conant's university was at the center of things, and DeVoto was too much the maverick and middlebrow to catch on there permanently. So the man constructed his own literary circle, more or less. He gathered around him persons he admired and who admired him, and he made do with these.

The one place where he was happiest, for a time at least, was the Bread Loaf Writers' Conference. This is a damning thing to have to

215

say, but it is true. How he could not only endure, but take seriously and even exult in the curious blend of hucksterism, commercial opportunism, uplift, and how-to-do-it aesthetics that constitute that intellectual dog-and-pony show is more than I can understand, but he did. So do others, persons I respect. DeVoto grew eloquent about it, loved it; he spoke in hushed tones of the good life on the Mountain. For once in his life, I suppose, he felt that he fully Belonged and was Appreciated. Alas, it too wore out for him.

Well, we may allow him that. We may even allow him that taste for self-conscious Heartiness and Camaraderie, that delight in Good Companionship that produced so terribly and consciously cute a book as *The Hour*, written in celebration of the 3.7-to-1 martini at eventide. ("And under it, through it, behind it," as Mr. Stegner notes, "forcing its creation and threatening every minute to interrupt or destroy it, was the panic from which in his whole life DeVoto never escaped for long.") It is reminiscent of Mencken's oft-vaunted taste for shared pilsner at various metropolitan bistros—another driven man, but that one a genius. Or of Mozart's laboriously worked-out dirty songs, of which Karl Schumann writes that "one feels the striving towards pleasant companionship on the part of a man who, deep down, felt completely alone." But for Mozart and Mencken such things, however doggedly enforced at times, were diversions. For DeVoto they came close to being the main show.

On November 13, 1955, his biographer reports, he came down to New York to appear in a television show about the West, and afterward, at the six o'clock cocktail hour he loved, he sat in his hotel room and talked with his young friend and physician, Herbert Scheinberg. Epigastric pain set in, with vomiting, diarrhea. It was his heart that gave out. His pulse was very poor. "It's bad, isn't it?" he asked. He was taken to a hospital. His blood pressure was 190 over 110. "What does it mean?" he asked. A minute later his heart stopped beating. Then it began to beat again. He opened his eyes and looked around. Then he lost consciousness and died.

I wrote a newspaper editorial about him when his death was announced. I do not remember what I said, but I am sure it had to do with his cantankerousness and his worth, both of which were considerable. When I wrote it I did not know about the "migraines, sleeplessness, dreads, panics, and fits of suicidal depression." I did not know, until I read Mr. Stegner's biography, just how appropriate was the characterization of DeVoto by his wife: "the bravest damn man I ever knew." When I think about him and his work, he remains, if far less formidably, as vexing as ever to me—as I am sure must be obvious. As the historian of the Far West, which I gather Mr. Stegner sees as his greatest accomplishment, he does not strike me as particularly important. It is for what he was able to recognize about Mark Twain and write about him that he will survive as a literary figure; that, and for his attack on Thomas Wolfe, which has become part of literary history. He goes into posterity, in short, for what he had to say about two American writers. For my part, though I have long since wavered in my addiction to the romantic excesses of Wolfe, DeVoto remains in many ways the Literary Antagonist, the Smart Aleck who knows it all. If so, it is because he so often and so willingly cast himself in that role. As man and as critic he was not one about whom it is possible to be neutral. But Mr. Stegner's fine biography makes it impossible not to admire him.

217

MR. EPSTEIN DOESN'T LIKE IT

(1986)

Joseph Epstein, author of *Plausible Prejudices,* has a few of them. He doesn't like modernism. He doesn't like English professors. He doesn't much care for Renata Adler, Svetlana Alliluyeva, John Ashbery, John Barth, Jonathan Baumbach, Ann Beattie, Walter Benjamin, Harold Bloom, Francis Brown, Walter Clemons, Robert Coles, Robert Coover, Malcolm Cowley, Joan Didion, E. L. Doctorow, John Kenneth Galbraith, Richard Gilman, Paul Goodman, Doris Grumbach, Joseph Heller, Ernest Hemingway, Daniel Hoffman, Irving Howe, John Irving, Elizabeth Janeway, Diane Johnson, Jack Kroll, John Leonard (he hates John Leonard), Dwight Macdonald, Norman Mailer, Bernard Malamud, Joyce Carol Oates, Cynthia Ozick, Maxwell Perkins, Richard Poirier, Orville Prescott, Thomas Pynchon, Adrienne Rich, Philip Roth, Robert Stone, William Styron, Ronald Sukenick, John Updike, Gore Vidal, Gerald Weales, Virginia Woolf, and so on—up through page 132 (there are 411 pages in the book, but, in the words of the late Uncle Remus, too much is a plenty). He doesn't like contemporary fiction. He doesn't like political liberalism. He doesn't like Feminism, Lesbianism, Homosexuality, Black Studies. He doesn't like graphic sexual descrip-

Originally published as a review-essay on Joseph Epstein's *Plausible Prejudices: Essays on American Writing* (New York: Norton, 1985).

tion in novels. He doesn't care for *People, Publishers Weekly, PMLA, Diacritics,* or *Wisconsin Fiction Studies.* He doesn't like structuralism, deconstruction, semiotics, or television. He doesn't like Jewish novelists and critics who talk too much about being Jewish. He doesn't like creative writing programs. He doesn't—but I trust the point has been made.

Mr. Epstein teaches at Northwestern University and is editor of the *American Scholar,* a title taken from an essay by Ralph Waldo Emerson, whom Mr. Epstein also doesn't like. Under his editorship the *American Scholar* is one of the most consistently interesting magazines on sale today. This is because as an editor Mr. Epstein has catholic taste and an eye for good prose on whatever the subject. From reading *Plausible Prejudices,* however, you would never guess it.

With only a few exceptions I happen to share Mr. Epstein's dislikes. From analysands and Emerson to Ramses IX and the Rosenbergs, I am with him more often than not. The question before the house, then, is Why, given the congruence of so many of my dislikes with Mr. Epstein's, does this book put me off so? Or, as he writes about John Simon's efforts to preserve the well of English from further contamination, why is he "the sort of writer who, when one finds oneself agreeing with him, makes one instantly want to reconsider one's own position"?

The subtitle of *Plausible Prejudices* is *Essays on American Writing:* a more descriptive phrase would have been *Essays on the Decline and Fall of American Literary Integrity.* In the first section of his book Epstein presents essays on the literary situation today. We are inundated with mediocrity, banality, special pleading, intellectual dishonesty, cant, liberal do-goodism, left-wing thinking, voyeurism, and exhibitionism, and are otherwise in danger of drowning in the sea of our own troubles.

The ten essays in the second part treat the individual sinners. Our literature is apparently suffering owing to the failures of the Messieurs and Mesdames Stone, Irving, Malamud, Updike, Beattie, Mailer, Ozick, Roth, Adler, and Didion. There is also the matter of Gabriel García Márquez, who according to Mr. Epstein writes quite well but is much too fond of Fidel Castro.

In part three we come to the writers that Mr. Epstein does like;

they are designated as "The Older Crowd." They are: Van Wyck Brooks (egad!), Edmund Wilson, A. J. Leibling, Willa Cather, John Dos Passos, and James Gould Cozzens. Not only are they older: they are all dead.

The fourth and final section of Mr. Epstein's book is a kind of catchall, in which are included essays on the abuse of the language by the overeducated, overindulgence in explicit sexual description, the difficulty of working up a list of great books (given Mr. Epstein's approach in this book, one can readily understand that), and the timely elevation of the familiar essay to its present literary preeminence (one can also readily understand that).

What is wrong with all this? Let us consider the two literary critics that Mr. Epstein seems most to admire, Edmund Wilson and H. L. Mencken. Both gentlemen, Mencken in particular, were pretty good at literary demolition. But both of them genuinely *enjoyed* literature. Wilson made the case for the early modernists: he taught his readers how to read Joyce, Proust, Eliot, Hemingway, Fitzgerald, Cummings, and many another new writer. He was constantly discovering or rediscovering neglected or forgotten authors of merit. And when, in his fifties, he realized that he lacked the requisite sympathy to appreciate the generation of authors that followed after his own, he had the wisdom to move backward into the premoderns and explore his ties with them, rather than to spend his remaining years belaboring the writers of the 1940s and 1950s for failing to duplicate the work of their immediate predecessors.

Wilson was a critic with wide-ranging interests and never-ending curiosity. An egotist to the core, much given to surface arrogance, he was ever unwilling to accept received opinion: he had to read everything for himself and make up his own mind. It would be difficult to imagine Wilson penning a sentence like this one by Mr. Epstein: "I have felt no need to read Carl Sandburg's monumental biography of Lincoln because of Edmund Wilson's crushing attack on it in *Patriotic Gore*." Wilson would have read it and decided for himself—and if Mr. Epstein ever recants and reads *The War Years,* the final four volumes of the six-volume work, he may discover that Wilson's "crushing attack" was quite off the mark, however appropriate to the first two volumes. (Incidentally, since we are speaking of the use of the English language, is Mr. Epstein saying in that sen-

221

tence that while Wilson's censure of Sandburg's biography might have caused others to read it, that wasn't why *he* intended to read it? Or that Wilson's attack made it unnecessary for him to read it? Grammatically it could go either way.)

As for Mencken, savagely though the Sage of Baltimore could lay about him with a club, throughout his best work there was a zest in the belaboring, a fine relish for the endangered cause of the True and the Beautiful. Mencken enjoyed many things, from beer to Beethoven to Bishop Cannon; and even his most devastating demolitions were customarily carried out in the service of an implied but genuine devotion to what was *not* tawdry, meretricious, or hypocritical. The great Henry—the man who wrote the criticism of the 1910s and 1920s for the *Smart Set* and the *Mercury*—was almost never narrow-souled, petulant, mean-spirited. The literary task before him was the removal of the debris left over from the dismantling of the Genteel Tradition at the hands of Dreiser, Crane, Eliot, assorted Europeans, the Chicagoans, *et al.* The razing was done by the novelists and poets; it was Mencken's part to clear away the rubble so that the new construction could be properly admired, and he did his job admirably, even though it turned out that he possessed relatively little insight into the literature of modernism that superseded that of William Dean Howells, Henry Van Dyke, Clayton Hamilton, and others.

While appearing to be *against,* Mencken was actually *for*—for the genuine as opposed to the fake, for the deed as opposed to the pretense, for the right of young authors—writers who, as Eliot once put it, felt that the language of Shakespeare was not only good enough for them, but far too good—to image their experience in the terms and language in which it presented itself to them. To pick up at random a volume of Mencken's is to discover how many things he *liked.* Consider the leading essay in *Prejudices, First Series:* he dislikes abstruse literary theory and timid literary critics, but he likes Spingarn, Wilde, Dreiser, Goethe, Carlyle, Lessing, Schlegel, Sainte-Beuve, Hazlitt, Bahr, Brandes, Huneker—the whole thrust of his essay is in the direction of opening doors, removing blinds, letting the light in.

Mr. Epstein's prejudices, by contrast, are door-closing all the way, and—in a fashion that Mencken as literary critic was not—truly reactionary. There are few things he likes: mainly he dis-

222

approves of just about everything that has happened literarily since the death of Warren Gamaliel Harding. His manner is sometimes Menckenian; but his matter is more along the lines of the late Paul Elmer More. Like the New Humanists, he has no yen for immersion in the destructive element: he would keep his feet dry at all costs. Unfortunately the cost of preserving oneself from contamination by the real world can come pretty high.

What I find unpalatable about Mr. Epstein's way of approaching the literary world is precisely that quality of almost total lack of sympathy for anything now going on. It isn't, to repeat, that I don't share many of his antipathies: on the contrary they are usually mine as well. The same goes for most of the very few things he says he likes and approves of. Not only, for example, do I concur with his estimate of Edmund Wilson, but I was pleased to discover that what he had to say about the absurd preface to *Patriotic Gore* was almost exactly what I said about it in this magazine more than two decades ago. But perhaps what is missing is the attitude toward poetry that Marianne Moore expressed so well some years ago: "I too dislike it"—yet it has its uses, which nothing else can supply, and while not mistaking the false for the real thing we would be advised to dwell upon its advantages until we have something better to serve up in its stead. One need not adopt the critical stance of Pollyanna in order to accept the fact that our own time and place are the only time and place available to us to inhabit, and we had better go ahead and concede their existence.

What, I ask myself, is *wrong* with the way that Joseph Epstein looks at the contemporary literary scene? The particularities of his indictment are not without validity, taken individually. Where does he go off the track? He tells us in his introduction that "literature, considered as an institution, is in important respects a barometer that measures the quality of the culture as a whole." Perhaps that is it: literature is being approached as an institution, rather than as an assortment of novels, stories, poems plays, essays, and so on. Instead of reading each book as a work of the imagination, on its own terms, and then moving to fit it into the larger cultural generality and to look for the patterns and relationships, Mr. Epstein views each book and each author as items in an entity known as Contemporary Culture.

Several times he quotes approvingly a statement by Desmond

223

McCarthy that "it is the business of literature to turn facts into ideas." That may be true for philosophers: it is scarcely the job of poets or novelists. This may help to explain why Mr. Epstein works with so narrow and, if I may say it, so drab a canon of representative American authors. He is in something of the situation of the leading magazine critics and reviewers of the 1930s, who were so preoccupied with the ideology of Marxism, Fascism, the class war, etc., that they scarcely knew that William Faulkner, immeasurably the most important American writer of the period, even existed. Faulkner was concerned with people, situations, history, but not with naked ideas as such.

224   Another favorite quotation of Mr. Epstein's is Stendhal's famous remark concerning the presence of politics in a work of literature as being like the firing of a pistol in a theater: one's concentration on the play is spoiled. But I have the uneasy feeling that what Mr. Epstein really objects to is not the pistol shot as such, but its target. That is, the politics he objects to is that of the radical Left. Well, I too dislike it, as they say; I have never forgiven the utter irresponsibility of the *New York Review of Books* in publishing a diagram of how to build a Molotov cocktail on its front cover, back when it was the fashion in New York City to grow beards, refrain from wearing neckties or taking showers, and be Revolutionary. But Mr. Epstein's way of reading fiction seems even so to be very much conditioned by his politics, not in a positive so much as in a negative sense. That is, he objects to certain excesses, elements of implausibility, unconvincing characterization—and in almost all instances such objections are based upon political assumptions. What I find myself wondering is whether, if the political assumptions were different, he would still consider such elements excessive, implausible, unconvincing, since it's the political assumptions that seem to guide him in his perception of them.

He devotes an entire essay, for example, to John Irving. *Hotel New Hampshire,* he tell us, is profamily and antirape. It is, he concludes, so popular because it is so shallowly optimistic. But—and more centrally—*Hotel New Hampshire* is also full of unconvincing characterization, tawdry sentimentality, and implausible motivation; and these failings, and not its ideological stance or its philosophical assumptions, are the reasons why it is so trivial a work of fiction. What I want to know is, if you are going to characterize the post-1945 literary scene, where are writers such as Eudora Welty or Walker Percy? Where are any of a dozen interesting young novelists and short-story writers who are currently producing fiction—fiction which has little or nothing to say about "the shape and fate of culture" as an abstract concept?

The essays in Mr. Epstein's book were originally magazine pieces, many of them book reviews, composed with but one exception for *Commentary* or the *New Criterion* or the *Times Literary Supplement.* To an extent, therefore, the choice of subject was prescribed. Yet generally one reviews the books that one wishes to review, and I can only assume that the authors Mr. Epstein has chosen to write about are those that he considers of greatest significance, and that this also works in terms of those he has omitted taking up.

Of course it is true that the lack of sympathy, the negative quality of Mr. Epstein's way of dealing with literature, would be less evident had I read these pieces one by one in the magazines that first published them, with suitable intervals between readings. Grouped together in one book, however, as he has done here with them, they make up a formidable chunk of nay-saying. Certainly nothing is wrong with a good, sincere, wholehearted literary ax job: anyone who when recognizing crap does not proclaim it as such is derelict in his duty toward the Future of the World and the Destiny of Mankind. Yet a whole book of looking down one's nose at one's contemporaries is a great deal too much of same.

When Mr. Epstein berates the attempt to turn the late Willa Cather into a practicing lesbian, I am with him. When he scores Norman Mailer for making all the ancient inhabitants of Egypt into active sexual freaks, right on, I say. When he savages the cliquishness, faddism, and complacent insularity of the N.Y.C. literary Establishment, I applaud. But enough is enough—and to make a literary career out of one's feelings of contempt for, resentment of, and superiority to almost all others is to deprive oneself of a life of one's own.

Joseph Epstein is witty. More than that, he is at times genuinely funny. On Norman Mailer, for example, he deposes as follows: "He is at his worst when he is being Norman Mailer, the modern thinker. He is, that is to say, a serious writer except when he is think-

225

ing, and the trouble is that over his long career he has been thinking a very great deal." But the humor, the wit, seem almost always to be at the expense of somebody or something. I didn't believe that it was possible for me to feel much sympathy for most of the writers whom Mr. Epstein savages, but after reading witticism upon witticism at the expense of this or that novelist, I found myself doing just that.

One feels like saying—or in any event I feel like saying—to Mr. Epstein something like the following:

"Sir, you write extremely well, you have the requisite instinct for identifying the meretricious and phony, you have the energy to search these out. Yet what we need in these uneasy and mendacious times is not merely dismissal but discrimination. We need help in recognizing, identifying, and encouraging what is worthy and in need of encouragement. If as seems clear you cannot find writing and writers worthy of your admiration in the places where you have been looking—the fashionable literary enclaves of the Northeastern cities—then what you must do is look elsewhere. There are writers—young ones and some who are no longer young—living and at work elsewhere in our confused country who need and deserve your help. Pay less attention to the Literary Situation, and more heed to the literature they are writing. For that was what the critics you admire so, Mencken and Wilson, were doing back in the 1910s and 1920s.

"Try it; you'll like it."

ADDENDA

THE NOTEBOOKS OF
DESMOND GOOHOOLIGAN
EDITED BY LEONIDAS O'DELL

(1975)

Editor's note   *The central role of Desmond Goohooligan in the intensely creative ferment that in the 1920s gave America its most exciting and accomplished literature is well known. The reviews and chronicles he was writing in such leading periodicals as the* Bell Telephone Times, *the* Proceedings of the Perth Amboy, New Jersey, Historical Society, Cap'n Billy's Gee-Whiz, *and above all, in the* Fulton Fish Market Daily Announcement Bulletin, *later collected in such magisterial compilations as* The Beaches of Sodom, To the Delaware Lackawanna and Western Station, *and* The Womb and the Beau, *not only defined the life of the decade as it occurred but provided a crucial form and substance to the otherwise mostly unharnessed and undisciplined imaginations of the writers of that day. Indeed, one comes to realize that without Desmond Goohooligan there might not have been any 1920s at all. We might have leaped straight from the Volstead Act to the Great Depression without so much as a raccoon coat, a hip-pocket flask, a smuggled-in copy of* Ulysses, *or a monkey trial. Sinclair Lewis might never have published* Babbitt *and* Elmer Gantry. *There would have been no* Waste Land *(on the other hand there might also have been no* John Brown's Body*). America would never have known miniature golf*

229

or mah-jongg. Babe Ruth would not have hit sixty home runs. And so on. The thought is terrible to contemplate. Let us be thankful that Desmond Goohooligan was—and thus that the twenties were. [L. O.]

Introduction   *Desmond Goohooligan was born in Vincennes, Indiana (some say Illinois), on July 4, 1895, of prosperous parents. The elder Goohooligan operated a livery stable, and was of a philosophical bent: his son later recalled him as having a habit of staring up into the skies from time to time and remarking, to no one in particular, "It won't be water but fire next time." It was his mother who made by far the deepest impression upon young Desmond, however. A dominating woman, she once entered his third-grade classroom to scold his teacher for having awarded him only a B+ on a composition (years later Desmond admitted that his mother had actually written the composition for him), and when the teacher objected, she picked up an inkwell from a desk, fired it through the open window, and forthwith removed the young Desmond from school. It turned out that this was fortunate, for the inkwell struck the school bully squarely in the chest, and had young Desmond remained in that school he would quite possibly have had the tar flailed out of him during recess. Shortly after this the Goohooligans entered young Desmond in St. Stanislaus Military Academy, Shawnee, Indiana, a highly prestigious school of the day. There his mother once again embarrassed him by calling him by his pet nickname, Snookums, right in front of the entire corps of cadets, eighty-one youths strong, and the nickname stuck to him for the rest of his life.*

Upon graduation from St. Stanislaus the young Desmond was enrolled at Cairo State A&M College and Normal School. Desmond was, as might be expected, an excellent student, and it was at Cairo State that he came, as it were, into his own. Swiftly establishing his intellectual superiority, he was elected as a freshman into the exclusive Robert W. Service Literary Society; was pledged to Alpha Sigma Sigma, the campus' most elite social fraternity; was appointed an editor of the campus literary publication, the Pharaoh; *was awarded the coveted Salmon P. Chase Medal for hortatory declamation; and in his senior year joined with F. Marion Crawfish in*

230

writing the annual musical production of the Square Club, which they entitled "Twenty-Three Skidoo; or, The Plucked Chicken Inspector."

It was at Cairo State, of course, that he first met the future novelist Crawfish, and they became lifelong friends. Crawfish, with his contagious innocence, his infectious smile, and free spirit, looked up to Desmond for guidance and critical expertise. "Snookums Goohooligan was everything to me," Crawfish later said. "At that time I could not spell c-a-t: he had won the Indiana State Spelling Bee. I had done no reading of contemporary authors whatever; he could quote entire sentences from Ben-Hur: A Tale of the Christ, *and recite the poems of Edmund Clarence Stedman from memory. My favorite magazine was the* Sporting News: *he subscribed to* Delineator, *the* Police Gazette, Grit, *the* Congressional Record, *and other highbrow literary publications. Though he was something of a social neophyte, there seemed nothing in the intellectual world that he did not know about."*

231

In June, 1918, the young Goohooligan was graduated from Cairo State summa cum laude, *and was set to go to New York in pursuit of a literary career when a communication from Local Selective Service Board No. 3, Vincennes, forced an abrupt change in his plans, and he was inducted into the service of his country. Fortunately Desmond had learned to play the flute in high school, and he was straightway assigned to the 110th Regimental Band, Camp Lee, Virginia, where he rose to the rank of musician third class, and regularly played the obbligato in "Stars and Stripes Forever" until mustered out of service in February of 1919.*

Proceeding to New York, where his friend F. Marion Crawfish was then working for an advertising agency, he too began looking for employment, and secured a position as assistant editor of the Fulton Fish Market Daily Announcement Bulletin. *For that publication he soon began writing the regular feature entitled "Neptune's Nuggets," which quickly established his reputation in the literary life of Manhattan.*

Something of the fervor of the literary life of the dawning 1920s may be seen in the comments he now began jotting down in the journal he began keeping, the first of 273 such volumes, each consisting of twenty-four ruled pages, bound in blue paper, with the words EXAMINATION BOOK: CAIRO STATE A&M COLLEGE AND NORMAL SCHOOL: Pledge *printed upon the cover, that he was to fill during the years until his death.*

F. Marion Met F. Marion for lunch today at Automat. He is writing a novel. Says his girlfriend at Cairo State, Ophemia Mulligan, won't marry him until he has $250 in the bank. Poor guy, thus to prostitute his art. Marion has zest, Marion has talent, Marion has, one might even say, genius. But Marion lacks discipline. And Marion loves Ophemia.

232

Kaskaskia Began work on final portion of epic poem last night. There are those who say the epic is dead for our time. Little do they know. I have written three-fourths of one already, and the concluding section will be the best of all. Homer wrote his *Iliad,* Virgil his *Aeneid,* Milton his *Paradise Lost,* Longfellow his *Evangeline,* and I am writing *Kaskaskia: A Tale of the Clark.*

Hoboken Ferry Crossing Hoboken Ferry today: towers of Manhattan like gigantic molars, canines, and bicuspids in the yawning mouth of the universe. *S. S. Berengaria* passed us en route, huge, four stacks, bound for the fabled places of the world. Stentorian blast of her whistle: a guttural bullfrog growling its "brekekekex co-ax co-ax" to the tugboats and lesser craft. Gulls dipping, diving, dancing astern, a-one, a-two, a-three: Welcome O life.

Wild Party Strange party at the Clancy T. Ogburns' last night. F. Marion, Ophemia Mulligan, others. Ophemia a bit giddy: insisted upon drinking champagne from F. Marion's shoe. (F. Marion wears size 11½ C.) Got terribly drunk. Climbed upon piano and began singing "Rocked in the Cradle of the Deep" in falsetto. F. Marion somewhat embarrassed. Asked him how it felt to step into shoe recently filled with champagne. "Like diving into a bowl of warm oyster stew," he said. Must remember that. Afterward we all rode subway to Jones Beach, walked under stars. En route Ophemia Mulligan and F. Marion disappeared in direction of deserted bathhouses. Caught up with us half-hour later. Must have had something to talk over. Poor Marion. He doesn't even *like* champagne.

Conan Doyle on Gosse   Overheard fascinating literary anecdote while lunching at Nedick's today. A. Conan Doyle and Joseph Conrad were walking along pathway in Hyde Park when Edmund Gosse came by. After he passed out of earshot, Conrad turned to Conan Doyle and asked his opinion of Gosse. "You mean that cad?" Conan Doyle replied, and pointed down to the ground where Gosse had just been walking. "Mr. Conrad, those are the footprints of a gigantic hound!"

Marion Crawfish   F. Marion and Ophemia are engaged to be married. James Rodney & Sons has accepted Marion's novel, offered $250 advance, will publish in spring. Marion in fine spirits. One can only hope . . .

233

Burlesque   Went to Minsky's last night. The women bumping and grinding, the men looking on. The vacant gaze in the eyes of old men at burlesque: of what are they thinking? Of their lost youth? Helen of Troy? Jewish comedian comes out, tells smutty stories. In his weary features the long sad history of Semitism. The girls. Each attired in spangled scanties, with silk fringe along edges. Large bosoms all. Voices from the balcony: "Take it off! Take it off!" They will never take it off, not all of it, and that is the fascination. A nervous titter runs through the audience. "A shudder in the loins engenders there / The broken wall, the burning roof and tower / and Andrew Mellon dead." (That is not quite right; must look it up.)

Nature and Art   If Art is Mimesis, *i.e.*, imitation, then what is life? We learn through imitating others. So if we live through imitation, is life art, or is art life? *Cf.* Wilde: Nature imitates art. Holding the mirror up to nature, etc., and vice versa. The artist in our commercial industrial civilization is thus forced to imitate models of business, financial success. Why not, say, poem on crossing into New York City on ferryboat? Certainly as poetic as climbing Matterhorn, seeing Eton College. Hmmm. Why not?

> *Crossing Hoboken Ferry*
> Crossing the harbor where gulls dip and dive
> let us fret not nor worry—

but be glad to be alive
for the sour past is o'er—
The flood tide crests the shore
and the Woolworth Building towers
where once were leafy bowers.
What of Egypt's crumbled walls?
Does the dust lay thick in Tara's halls?
Crossing over from Hoboken
What care I if Troy be broken?

Pretty good for a start. Could make a fine poem of this, I think.

234

Walt Whitman   Told Marion and Ophemia Crawfish of my poem. Ophemia, in her usual know-it-all fashion, insisted poem already written on approximately same subject by W. Whitman. Oh, well. One can't always be original. Will try something else.

Virginity   Ophemia C. asked point-blank last night if I was a virgin. Told her none of her business. Poor Marion. [This entry is, to say the least, enigmatic. Was Desmond still a virgin? The evidence, to the extent that there is any, indicates that it is possible. But one never knows. L. O.]

Desmond Goohooligan's lifelong enthusiasm for languages is manifested in the incident that follows. Before his death, he was to know no less than seventeen languages and a score of dialects as well.

Gullah   Puzzling encounter with Negro at fish market today. Was helping out behind counter when a large broad-shouldered black approached. "E hab eny pawgie?" he asked. (I reproduce the sound as best possible.) I could not make out what he wanted. "Pawgie," he kept saying, "pawgie, pawgiefeash. You en gnaw pawgie? Disy size." He spread his hands to indicate a length of about seven or eight inches. "Pawgie en too fat tru e belly, but e tall dough," he said. "E ab fawktail, yellow pless side e cheek. E berry good. Sweet like swimp." Try as I could, I was unable to make out what he wanted. Tried to sell him some tautog but he would not buy. "En go eat no pizen Yankeefeash," he said. "Buckra eat um mebbe." Or something of the sort.

Later consulted Professor Trent at Columbia. He identified speech as something called Gullah, which he said is commonly spoken on sea islands along coast of South Carolina. Considered to include African survivals, Devonshire English, West Indian vowels, diphthongs. Fascinating to think that within geographical boundaries of this nation a language unintelligible to most Americans survives. Also discovered that there are not one but two states in Union named Carolina—North and South. Very odd. Would be interesting to investigate strange political events that brought this about. Wonder if same species of English is spoken in both?

The arrival of the poetess Ellen Sestina O'Shea in New York sent many of the city's literary folk into a tizzy, among them Desmond Goohooligan, as the several entries that follow indicate.

Ellen O'Shea   Party at the F. Marion Crawfishes. Interesting girl there. Writes poetry. Offered to show her some of mine, said would be most interested. Very demure, but given moments of oddness, as when abruptly grasped candle from mantelpiece, borrowed my penknife, cut away tallow from butt end to expose wick, lit both ends of wick, and grasped center of candle between teeth much like dog carrying bone. Before evening was out, did same with every candle in the house. Strange. But charming, all in all.

Ellen O'Shea   Invited Ellen O'Shea to dinner at Child's—wanted to show her I appreciated gourmet food. She dressed in white gown with black spots, much like leopard pelt. Straw hat. Brought ms. of my epic poem, *Kaskaskia,* to read to her. She suggested we go to my place afterward, and would read it there. When we arrived, she removed shoes, took seat on couch, asked me to read. Sat on chair opposite her, began, she stripping butt ends off candles and lighting wicks all the while. (I had laid in a supply of several dozen candles in event of this possibly happening.) Said I read divinely, but voice was too low; would I sit next to her on couch so could hear better. I did so, continued reading. She objected to overhead electric light, said hurt her eyes. She held double-lit candle between teeth, suggested I place head on her lap, read from there. Felt awkward, though found could read, but melting wax from candle kept dripping onto ms. Requested she tilt candle in other direction. Would I prefer she blow it out entirely? she asked. I said could not read very well in the dark. She said if candle tilted other way, wax would drip on her new dress. Did I mind if she removed dress? I said all right. She removed dress, replaced candle in teeth; I resumed reading. After awhile she said candle about to burn out at both ends. Told her not to worry, had plenty more. She said she was tired, would I object if reading continued in bedroom. She lay down on bed, lit up another candle. I drew up chair alongside. She said could hear better if I lay down next to her with head on pillow. Did so. She said light hurt eyes, would I mind if blew out for awhile. I said could not read in dark, suggested she place handkerchief over eyes. She said tired of poetry for now. I said I also had draft of novel, could read that instead. She said never mind, was getting late, must be going. Replaced dress, shoes, I escorted her home in taxi. Thanked me for memorable literary evening. [A footnote to Desmond's relationship with Ellen Sestina O'Shea may be found in a cryptic comment made by Ophemia Crawfish in letter to Sara Murphy, dated May 2, 1924: "Ellen O'S. says spending evening with Snookums G. was like taking of tiffin-and-tea with Pope Pius XI." *L. O.*]

Slang   Overheard this use of American vernacular while riding Fifth Avenue bus:

> "Hot today."
> "You know it."
> "It's not the heat, though, it's the humility."
> "That's what they say."

Amusing Repartee   Heard this story. Nicholas Murray Butler and William Dean Howells were lunching at Century Club and Butler was telling about a Greek tailor who did his mending for him and with whom he always held converse in Greek. He had torn his pinstripe trousers getting out of a taxicab, he said, and he carried them to the tailor the next day. "Euripides?" the tailor asked. "Yes," Butler replied. "Eumenides?"

F. Marion   The following song was composed by Marion Crawfish, with some assistance from me. A good deal of the effect depended

236

on the appropriate gestures that accompanied every line, and on the impersonation of William Jennings Bryan, who was supposed to be singing it. Bryan, for some reason I do not understand, always seemed to Marion somewhat comic.

It was back in old Nebraska
'Bout half way to Alaska
That I started my glorious career
I was left out in the cold
Till I thought of the Cross of Gold
   (you've heard about it)
You could hear all those Democrats cheer.

Oh I'm William Jennings Bryan
My heart is like a lion
And I'm running for Pres-i-dent
And I'm very, very fri'ndly,
But I sure hate Bill McKinley,
So it's Bryan for Pres-i-dent!

It was by the river Platte
Where I knew that I was at
That my words first excited all the town
And they sure did have some fun
When I yelled, 'fifteen to one!'
   (oh don't you know it)
Going to tear that Gold Standard down!

Chorus: Oh I'm etc.

Whether or not Desmond was indeed a virgin in his earlier career in New York, as Ophemia Crawfish has hinted, we can say with assurance that this no longer remained true after November, 1927. For in his journal for that date and for several entries afterward, Desmond describes what is clearly a sexual liaison with a girl whom for simplicity's sake we shall call Inez, though that was not her name. She was, as we shall see, of working-class background— and it seems undeniable that it was this that made it possible for

Desmond to enter into a physical relationship with her. All his other female acquaintances had been, like himself, from the upper reaches of society, and one guesses that the formidable influence of Desmond's mother was not without its role in his inability, at this stage in his life, to develop intimate relationships with any of them. Now for the first time Desmond encounters a girl of plebeian up-bringing, and the result is a tender and happy interlude in his otherwise mostly unfortunate love life. Indeed one could wish that Desmond's background and social assumptions had not been such as to preclude a more lasting relationship with Inez. It is interesting, too, that within four years after Ulysses *was first published, and while D. H. Lawrence was still employing euphemisms, Goohooligan's boldness in describing his sexual experience foreshadows much of the explicitness of latter-day literature.*

238

Inez   Had for some time become accustomed to having dinner at Bijou Restaurant, and had struck up acquaintance with waitress named Inez. Petite, olive-hued, sly smile, large round eyes, quaint manner of speaking, *e.g.,* "How about a lamb choppie, old chappie?" "Better have some of that lemon meringue. It's awfully good for your rang-a-tang-tang!" "Wanta second cuppa cawfee to drive away the collywobbles, dearie?" etc. Was raining tonight, and happened to be taking taxi just as she was leaving. Offered to give her lift. "You know," she said after being seated, "I like you." I replied that I was flattered that she did. Wished to know if I had what she referred to as a "steady girl." I said not at present. "No fooling? What do you do when you w**t y**r a***s h****d?" I explained that I lived in an apartment house with oil heat. "No, you dope," she said, "what I mean is, where do you go when you n**d s**e p***y?" I explained that one of the codicils in my apartment lease forbade the keeping of cats on the premises. "Well, for crying out loud," she said, "ain't you a card?" At this point she made the nature of her reference more nearly clear, and the result was that we retired to my apartment.

Inez   Have taken to "inviting" Inez to my apartment several times a week. Now that we have established a reasonable degree of frankness in our relationship, it is no longer necessary that she employ metaphoric or euphemistic terms to denote certain hitherto-unmentionable objects. She refers, for example, to her th**g (a word I forebear to translate, other than to suggest that it is the English equivalent of the Latin *res*). Asks whether my m*ck*y (using a common Irish diminutive) is st*nd**g (participial form of the Latin word *stare*). A physiological climax is always spoken of in the infinitive form of the English equivalent of the first verb in Caesar's famous summation, *veni, vidi, vici.* And so on. Must say that I had no idea that American vernacular could be used with such richness of reference and yet with such precision.

Ophemia C.   Made the mistake of mentioning my liaison with Inez   **239**
to F. Marion, who in turn was so indiscreet as to allude it to Ophemia. To my embarrassment she declared upon my arrival for dinner last night that she understood that I had decided to surrender my chastity at last. Informed her in no uncertain terms that it was "no affair of hers." "Thank the Lord for that," she said. Poor F. Marion.

Husband   Upon arrival at Bijou Restaurant last night found Inez in highly nervous state. "Don't look directly at me," she said in low voice. "He's outside watching through the window. Act like you're ordering dinner." Noticed that her eyes appeared to have been blackened and her lower lip somewhat swollen. Seems that her husband, who had been incarcerated in Sing Sing until recently, had come by the restaurant last night and had ascertained that she was not working late, as she had told him, and had been waiting for her when she returned home from my place shortly after eleven. Expressed my sympathy, had dinner of liver and potatoes, lingered over lemon meringue pie and coffee, read newspaper, then departed. Out of corner of my eye noted rather sturdily built chap standing near window observing me, but fortunately a taxicab was waiting at the curb. Hastily got in and closed door behind me. Oh, well. Shall have to take meals at another restaurant for awhile. *Sic transit gloria mundi.*

By 1929 Desmond's rising literary prominence was such that his every review and essay was eagerly read and widely discussed. The publication of Eliot's The Waste Land *several years before had revolutionized the poetry world, and it is not surprising, therefore, that when in October Desmond was sent abroad by the Fulton Fish Market* Daily Announcement Bulletin *to report on English marketing techniques in his now-famous "Neptune's Nuggets" column, he was eager to meet and to discuss matters of common interest with Eliot. His journal entries for the period are of especial interest in view of his subsequent writings on the subject.*

London   Odd how British drive their automobiles. Unlike pattern in United States, traffic proceeds along left rather than right side of street. Therefore, much confusion, honking of horns, etc.

Trafalgar Square   Went for walk today, arrived at Trafalgar Square. Noticed rather tall, soberly dressed man, umbrella under arm, standing atop pedestal of Nelson Monument, some thirty feet above pavement. Seemed to be staring into space. Upon drawing closer realized it was the poet Eliot himself. "Hello there, T. S.!" I called up. "What are you doing up there?" Seemed not to notice me, so I called again. "Mr. Eliot! Are you writing a poem up there?" This time he looked down, but said only, "Go away." I was about to explain my presence when a policeman came up (the British appear to refer to them as boobies) and suggested that I move along. Not wishing to cause a disturbance I did so. Curious business.

T. S. Eliot   Another fortuitous meeting with T. S. Eliot. Was in fishmonger's this morning inspecting merchandising techniques, when tall, soberly dressed man, umbrella under arm, came in. Recognized him at once. I reached into nearby tub, grasped large lobster, and held it out, saying, "I should have been a pair of ragged claws, eh, T. S.?" He frowned, turned, and departed the premises.

Traffic   The mystery is solved. Upon taking taxi to boat train this morning I realized that the controls and steering column are placed at the right side of the cab, not on the left as with ours. Surely that must be why traffic in Britain proceeds to the left rather than the right.

When Desmond Goohooligan returned to his native land aboard the S.S. Majestic *in late November of 1929, he found that much had changed. The stock-market crash had touched off the business panic that swiftly became the Great Depression. Though he had not himself invested in the market, his friends had been affected by the new turn of events. The riotous extravagance and waste of the twenties had come to an abrupt and catastrophic end. The F. Marion Crawfishes were in Europe, where Marion was valiantly battling his own addiction to malted milk and the growing signs of serious instability on the part of Ophemia. "Ophemia," Marion wrote to Desmond, "is writing a novel"; to Desmond the news only confirmed what he had long suspected. It was not long before the influential comments that he was making each week in his column "Neptune's Nuggets," which until then had had exclusively to do with literature and the arts, took on a distinctly political and economic cast, which as the business crisis deepened became more and more collectivist in tone. In late 1930 Desmond made the crucial step: he resigned from the staff of the* Fulton Fish Market Daily Announcement Bulletin *and became an associate editor of the* Lower West Side Literary and Socialist Beacon. *The 1920s were over, the 1930s were begun; unlike H. L. Mencken and other influential figures of the twenties Desmond Goohooligan had the sense to realize it. But that is another story, to be told in a future volume of Desmond's journals.* [L. O.]

241

YOUNG MAN IN SEARCH OF A VOCATION

(1991)

I have always envied those who, from earliest years onward, know just what they wish to do with their lives, and proceed to do it. To be able to decide on a future career, and to conduct one's youth and young manhood with the certainty that comes of knowing exactly where one is headed, offers genuine advantages. One is able to avoid much of the discomfort and pain of adolescence and young manhood; for after all, if one is quite sure of one's objectives, there is relatively little occasion for puzzling over who one *is*, a problem which also involves figuring out who one is *not*. And discovering the latter can be a vexatious business.

When I was a youth, I was quite sure what I wanted to be and do. It was very simple. I would be a major league baseball star. To be sure, there was a certain amount of uncertainty involved; it was not entirely clear in my mind whether I would be a first baseman or a pitcher. I could not decide whether it would be more appropriate to replace Carl Hubbell as the New York Giants' premier lefthanded pitcher, or Bill Terry as first baseman and manager. I was open-minded about it; Terry's legs were giving him problems, and he might need help before Hubbell did, but I did rather enjoy the prospect of being a pitcher—there seemed to be a little more finesse involved in it. However, I lost little sleep over the decision I would have to make, because it quickly occurred to me that there was nothing to prevent my being both: I would simply play first base for three days, and pitch on the fourth. It is true that this meant the Giants would have to hire a substitute for me at first base every fourth day, but I felt that they would be willing to do this.

There were, to be sure, certain problems to be solved before I could realize my ambition. As a baseball player on the sandlot teams in Charleston, South Carolina, I was slow afoot, clumsy and erratic afield. I not only couldn't hit a curveball but couldn't see one coming. When I threw a baseball I had only a very general idea of where it was going. But those were unimportant details. Next year, when I finally got my strength and coordination, it would be different. The day would come, I was sure, when my true athletic ability, which thus far had been apparent only to myself, would assert itself. No longer would I be a substitute, non-roster player. I would make a team. I would even be given a uniform. At last I would actually get to play in a game. My name would for the first time appear in the sports pages as a participant *in* a ballgame, instead of as the person writing the article about it. In the meantime I would pursue my other career goal and be a staff writer for the Associated Press, which was my idea of the pinnacle of literary achievement.

The war interrupted my baseball career—interrupted it before it ever got started. In that case, I decided, I would have to switch my career goals, or at least postpone them. I would have to make do as a soldier—I thought the rank of colonel would be about right for me, since I was still not yet twenty. So I went downtown in Richmond, Virginia, where we now lived, and took a physical examination to be admitted into the Marine Corps officer training program.

Unhappily (in retrospect, it was fortunate), I did not pass the examination—I was six feet one inch tall and weighed in at 135 pounds after first eating a sack of bananas—because it seemed that my chest measured exactly the same when expanded as when deflated. Nothing daunted, I began exercising strenuously with a medicine ball, and a few months later went up to Washington on the train for another examination. This time certain other difficulties arose. First they found my ears were too full of wax to examine my hearing. So I located a doctor's office near DuPont Circle and got them cleaned out. Then they found that my eyesight was below standards; they didn't say what the standards were. All they

244

could suggest was that when I got my draft notice I could request the Marine Corps, and apply for an officer's commission later on.

But I was not going to have any of that. It was too indefinite. After all, it might be another year before I got my full strength and my coordination, and the war might be over before they needed any more colonels. So when the Selective Service Board sent its greetings I decided I would settle for the army. (I thought of the navy, but since I couldn't swim, that might not be appropriate.) The army promptly sent me down to Alabama for basic infantry training. There I encountered certain temporary difficulties en route to becoming a general (by then I had expanded my goals; having decided that being a mere colonel would not suffice.) I couldn't shoot straight, I couldn't march straight, I couldn't get through a hike without collapsing from the heat, I couldn't climb up a rope ladder on the obstacle course; I couldn't do *anything* much.

Shortly before the training cycle was over, while we were on bivouac, the lieutenant in charge, a former college football coach, called me over and handed me a stack of cards, one for every soldier in the platoon. Each card had a blank space where the lieutenant was supposed to write an evaluation of the person's overall soldierly abilities. "Fill these out for me, will you?" he said. So for the next two hours I wrote evaluations of everybody in the platoon for him— everybody but myself, because there wasn't one for me. When I was finished he looked through them and signed each one. Then he took a card out of another envelope, with my name and service number typed on it. He wrote on it, signed it, then showed it to me. *Definitely not a field soldier,* he had written.

Oh well, I told myself, I would have to go into military intelligence or something like that, at least for another year, until I got my strength and coordination.

The next thing the army did was to send me to Yale University for an Italian language and area program. I liked that; I was willing to serve my country in any capacity it asked—I would adjust my career ambition, and be a general in military government in Italy. Unfortunately this didn't quite work out the way I had planned, either. Instead of being sent to Italy I was sent down to southwest Georgia. When the war ended I was still several grades away from being a general—to be exact, I was still an enlisted man. However, now that the Germans and Japanese had surrendered, there really wasn't much point in being a general, anyway.

Besides, by then I was twenty-two years old, and I had acquired a somewhat more realistic outlook on what my capabilities were and weren't. When I returned to college in February of 1946 at the University of Richmond, I didn't even go out for the baseball team; the New York Giants would have to get by without me. Instead I decided that I was going to concentrate on becoming a newspaperman, a foreign correspondent for the Associated Press. So I finished my last year of college in the spring and summer of 1946, and began looking for a newspaper job. I was offered a position as a reporter on a newspaper named the *Bergen Evening Record,* in Hackensack, New Jersey. It was only a few miles from New York City, and I decided that I would work there for a little while until either the Associated Press or the New York *Times* invited me to join its staff.

Six months went by, and for some reason neither the Associated Press nor the New York *Times* ever did get around to sending for me. Neither did the United Press, the International News Service, the *Herald Tribune,* the *Sun,* the *World-Telegram,* the *Post,* the *Daily News,* or the *Daily Mirror.* Meanwhile I had gotten myself engaged to be married, and when that broke up, I decided it was time to move on. So I went back home to Richmond, Virginia, and found a job as city editor of a small morning newspaper in Staunton, Virginia.

I felt very proud. Here I was still only twenty-three, and already I was a city editor. It was true that the newspaper that I was city editor of, the Staunton *News-Leader,* was rather small. In addition to myself the staff consisted of one reporter, a half-time society editor, and a part-time sportswriter. There was also a proofreader, an elderly gentleman named Mr. Sheets who had a facial tic; whenever his face gave a twitch he skipped several lines of type. As city editor I also performed the duties of the managing editor, telegraph editor, feature editor, sports editor, state editor, Sunday editor, church editor, and garden club editor. When the reporter was out I answered the telephone. When the editor was away I wrote editorials. When football season came I covered the team of a nearby military academy. I was also the Associated Press stringer, which meant calling the state bureau in Richmond whenever there was a local story that might be of interest elsewhere. So if I was not exactly an AP staff writer, at least I now had a connection with that renowned news service.

The newspaper's composing room personnel consisted of four linotype operators and a makeup man. For the first six months everything was all right, but then the news room, which until then was on the first floor, was moved upstairs, which meant that it was necessary to communicate with the composing room by intercom or by written note via a copy chute. This proved difficult, because the composing room foreman, who also operated one of the linotypes, was a deaf mute, while the makeup man was illiterate. Literally he could not read complete words. He worked by means of individual letters.

I would call him on the intercom. "Simpson?"

"Yes?"

"What have you got on the top left of the front page?"

A lengthy pause, while Simpson located the type. "T . . . R . . . U . . ." he would read the letters out, painfully and slowly.

"Truman. Okay, move that to the bottom of the page and put the Marshall Plan story at the top left."

Another long pause. "Which one did you say?"

"Marshall Plan."

Still another lengthy pause. "I don't see it."

"It's got a two-column headline, twenty-four-point caps."

"P . . . O . . . L . . . ?"

"No."

"B . . . Y . . . R . . . ?"

"No. Keep looking."

Eventually Simpson would find it. "M . . . A . . . R . . ." (a long pause—letters having curves gave him special trouble) ". . . S . . ."

"That's it. Put it on the top left." And often he would—though by no means always.

The newspaper had a non-union mechanical plant, so that I could go into the composing room off hours, set type by hand and proof it, and write feature stories directly into the linotype machine. Another result of the non-union shop was that there was an odd collection of linotype operators. There was one old gentleman, Mr. McGowan, in his late sixties—at the time that seemed very old to me—who claimed to have worked for Horace Greeley. Whenever I would ask Mr. McGowan to reset a headline because of a typographical error, he would demand to know what a young whippersnapper like me thought he was doing, giving orders to someone who had worked for Horace Greeley. One day I looked up Greeley's dates in the *World Almanac*. It turned out that in order to have worked for Horace Greeley, Mr. McGowan would have to have been born about 1855 at the latest, which would have made him ninety-two years old.

The front page was usually proofed about 12:30 a.m. each day, and after editing up the rural correspondents' copy for the next day I waited around until the first and only edition came off the press about 1:30, checked the front page for errors, then after getting a sandwich at the all-night restaurant I went to my room and read for an hour or so until I dropped off to sleep. I woke up about noon, ate breakfast at a restaurant, stopped by the newspaper to get my mail, then I either played golf or else went back to my room and read until about five o'clock, when I reported for the evening's work. First I selected the telegraph news from the AP budget, diagrammed the layout for the front page and the sports page, edited telegraph copy as it arrived on the teletype, then went out for dinner at a restaurant. Upon returning I edited more copy and wrote headlines until it was time for the front page to be made up, whereupon I went into the composing room and oversaw that, making sure that the makeup man placed the headlines on the right stories, and the stories where they were indicated on the layout sheet. This went on for six nights a week, Tuesday through Sunday—for some reason, there was no Monday morning edition.

When I finished putting the Sunday edition to bed, every other weekend I would get into my car, an old 1936 Plymouth coupe that I was able to purchase for $300 with the aid of a bank loan, and drive three hours to my parents' home in Richmond, arriving about 4:30 a.m. Sunday. On Monday afternoon I would drive back to Staunton for another week of it.

For a single man in his early twenties, this was not the most exciting routine in the world. On the other hand, the job did have its attractions. My golf game improved. I got a good deal of reading done. The city library was around the corner from where I lived.

The collection wasn't too good on recent books, but it was loaded with books of history, especially of Civil War military history. With four or five hours a day with nothing to do but to read, as well as Sundays when I did not go home to Richmond, I became a steady patron.

Even so, after a year or so the novelty of being a city editor at the age of twenty-four was beginning to pall on me. I knew almost nobody else in the city of Staunton except for the other newspaper employees, and I was also running out of library books on the Civil War that I had not yet read. It was time to move on.

Several times on my trips to Richmond I had stopped in at the Associated Press offices, and had intimated to the bureau chief that I might like to work there if a position ever came open. Early in 1948 he called me and offered me a job, which I accepted with alacrity. I was thrilled; here I was, not yet twenty-five years old, and I was an AP staffer! I even had a new and very impressive job title: I was now Night State Editor.

249

To be sure, night state editor was low man on the bureau hierarchy, and to take the job I had to accept a $10-a-week pay cut from what I was earning as a city editor. But as always I was willing to make sacrifices for the sake of my career. Besides, the stories I would be writing would go out on the wires to Washington, New York, and throughout the world. Surely it would not be long before I would be transferred to the Washington bureau, and cover the White House, and then be sent overseas to London, Paris, Moscow, and the like.

It turned out that being an AP staffer in the Richmond bureau was the most excruciatingly boring job I had ever held. Even the writing of obituaries was exciting by comparison. Five evenings a week, with Monday and Tuesday nights off, I came in to work at six o'clock. First I rewrote all the afternoon stories, to be sent out over the state wire for use in the next morning's papers. Then I rewrote all my rewrites for the early editions of afternoon newspapers. Meanwhile I took stories from correspondents over the telephone. Not once was I ever sent out of the office to write stories of my own; that was all done by a single staff member, who had been with the bureau for twenty years. And how were the Washington and New

York bureaus ever going to discover what a good writer I was and ask for my transfer there, when the stories that went out over the national wire were unsigned?

During this period the Associated Press was undergoing a program of having its news writing style improved and made more interesting. The complaint was that AP stories were too flat and prosaic. An expert named Rudolf Flesch had been hired to analyze the stories and make suggestions for improvement. His recommendation was that sentences must be short and simple. All complex and most compound grammatical constructions were frowned upon. Language must be basic. Words of more than three syllables must be avoided whenever possible. It was as if the stylistic model for being an AP writer was the Bobbs-Merrill third grade reader.

The desk man on the bureau at night, whose first name was Bob, collected my copy, edited it to remove all traces of individuality, and scheduled it for transmission over the wires. Bob was from Colorado. So far as I could tell, if he had ever read a book of any kind once he finished college, there was no evidence of it. He was also totally devoid of a sense of humor.

He had only one interest, the major league baseball pennant races, and more specifically the doings of the Brooklyn Dodgers. When he was not filing the wire news, which was most of the time, he spent every free moment in front of the sports wire teletype, waiting for the inning-by-inning scores of the Dodger games. He ate his supper each night standing up, in front of the sports teletype. He lived for the Brooklyn Dodgers; it was all he cared about.

For want of something better to do, my friend Paul Duke, who also worked in the bureau at the time, and I used to bait him whenever possible. "The Braves are gaining on Brooklyn," we might remark to him if the Dodgers were losing that day. "By this time next week they'll be in first place." Bob's face would turn red, then white in anger. He would reach for his wallet, extract a ten-dollar bill, and wave it in front of us. "Put your money where your mouth is!" he would declare.

On Sunday nights, one of my assignments was to write a roundup story on the week's Piedmont League activity for Monday sports pages. Trying to think of a new angle on which to hang the story each week could be vexing. One Sunday, knowing that Bob would

not be filing the wire that night, I wrote it in the form of a dialogue
between two fans drinking beer at a tavern, after the style of Ring
Lardner. The wire editor moved it on the wire without comment,
but when Bob read it the next day he was outraged. He took a copy
of the story and marked it up with questions and comments, something which he had no authority whatever to do, and placed it in my
mailbox. When I came for work and found it there, I tossed it on his
desk with a remark to the effect that if I wanted any lessons in writing from him I would let him know. He only glowered; there was
nothing he could do about it.

Preparing weekly Piedmont League baseball roundups was among
the more interesting of my tasks. Usually there was nothing for me
to write except rewrites. Desperate for something interesting to
write about, I took to reading the local stories in the various newspapers throughout the state, searching for material for what the AP
called "brites"—little one- or two-paragraph stories featuring what
were known as "human interest" items. One day I noticed, in I believe the Danville *Bee,* a feature story, with photograph, about a
man who had planted some potatoes in his garden, only to find that
inexplicably the potato vines were producing tomatoes. So I wrote a
brief story about this momentous development, and gave it to Bob,
who was filing the wire that evening, to move on the A-wire, the
national teletype circuit.

The bureau offices were located in the same building as the Richmond newspapers, and it was the custom for a carbon copy of each
story we wrote to go to those papers. About a half-hour after I had
turned in the potato-tomato story, a news editor from the Richmond *Times-Dispatch* came racing into our office, consumed with
excitement. It was botanically impossible, he insisted, for a potato
vine to produce tomatoes, no matter what the Danville *Bee* had
reported.

By then the story had already gone out over the national news
wire, so without further discussion Bob, who was nothing if not
cautious, at once sent out a cancellation notice. It went something
like this: DANVILLE, VA.—KILL STORY TOMATOES GROW-
ING ON POTATO VINE. IMPOSSIBLE. AP RM. Somebody called
the message to the attention of the *New Yorker* magazine, and several months later, to my delight, the kill notice appeared at the bot-

tom of one of that magazine's columns, followed by a comment, "Don't you be so sure, AP. These are wonderful days."

Yet there were evenings when things in the Associated Press news room could be lively. The most exciting event that took place during my tenure there happened at a mountain resort in western Virginia, when one day a loon unexpectedly landed at the lake. Nobody there had ever seen a loon before. The loon stayed for several days, and we wrote nightly news bulletins about its doings. We even gave it a name, Looie (the presumption was that it was a male loon). For more than a week, readers of newspapers far and wide were kept abreast of the progress of Looie the loon. Then Looie the loon died and things settled back to routine in the Richmond AP bureau.

Within a few months of having joined the bureau in Richmond, I had been forced to do some hard thinking. Here I had achieved my longtime goal of working for the Associated Press—and had found it excruciatingly dull. Transfer from the Richmond bureau to a larger bureau was out of the question; the chief of the bureau would have to recommend it, and no one could recall his ever having done so. If this was what being an AP staff writer meant, then clearly I would have to think about doing something else with my life. After all, I was almost twenty-five years old; advancing age was closing in on me.

From time to time I had tried to do a little writing on my own, in particular fiction. It was my intention, while being a newspaper reporter, to write novels on the side, in my spare time. Several times I had begun novels, but had never gotten beyond fifteen pages or so on them. So it occurred to me that the thing to do might be to take time off from newspaper work and go to graduate school in creative writing. I would spend a year learning how to write novels, then return to my journalism career and begin producing novels on the side—say, one new novel each year.

I inquired around, and found that there were two universities then offering graduate programs in creative writing, the State University of Iowa and the Johns Hopkins University. So I wrote to both, explaining what I had in mind, and enclosing a couple of short stories I had published in the college literary magazine as an undergraduate. The director of the Iowa program, Paul Engle, was skeptical. He was willing to take me on a trial basis for a term, he said. The director of the Johns Hopkins program, a man named Elliott Coleman, was considerably more encouraging. (For the life of me I have never since been able to figure out on what evidence he could possibly have been so.) He would not only take me, but offered me a fellowship teaching freshman English which would pay me a small stipend. Along with that there was the $50 a month that as a veteran I was entitled to receive from the GI Bill of Rights. Moreover, by that time I had begun writing occasional feature articles for the *Times-Dispatch* Sunday page, and could count on earning $15 or $20 or so extra each month. Who said that there was no money in the literary life?

So I packed what few possessions I had into the trunk of my car   253
and headed for Baltimore. As I drove across the Potomac River bridge on Route 301, going back to the North again, I felt that I was at last moving toward what I wanted to do and be.

When the Fall, 1948, term began at the Johns Hopkins Writing Seminars, I met my teachers and fellow graduate students. They were a nice enough group. What I discovered, though, was that the authors I was most familiar with and wanted most to emulate were not in favor there. The authors who were studied and talked about were James Joyce, Marcel Proust, André Gide, T. S. Eliot, Wallace Stevens, Allen Tate, John Crowe Ransom, Sartre, Camus, Auden, Kafka, Lorca, and so on. Who were these people? There was also considerable talk about existentialism and the Anglo-Catholic church and Freud and Jung and somebody named Kierkegaard. Nobody seemed to think very much of my favorite writer, Thomas Wolfe. And the magazines they read—unexciting looking things with nothing but print in them, no illustrations on the cover—the *Sewanee Review*, the *Kenyon Review*, the *Hudson Review*, and so on. Didn't anybody read the *Saturday Evening Post* or the *Saturday Review of Literature*?

Of course, like all good working newspapermen I considered myself fully qualified to judge whether any book of any kind, fiction, non-fiction, prose, or poetry, was worth reading or not. What kind of a writer was this Marcel Proust, who took eight pages at the beginning of his novel just to turn over in bed? And James Joyce— his first novel, *A Portrait of the Artist as a Young Man*, was all right, though Thomas Wolfe had done it much better, but what was this *Ulysses* all about? Why couldn't the man write in English that could be understood? And as for the poetry—compared to my favorite poets, Carl Sandburg and Stephen Vincent Benét, this T. S. Eliot that everyone seemed to worship seemed willfully difficult and obtuse.

Yet all in all I rather liked it. However much I resisted all these writers, I began to see, just a little, what they were doing. What I liked best about the Writing Seminars was that everybody around me was writing. Moreover, they didn't think it was strange, or self-indulgent, to try to articulate what one felt in language. And they didn't ask that everything be simplified, made easy to understand; they seemed to believe that the objective of good writing was to get at the complexity of one's experience, not to summarize it as simply as possible.

As for what I had been told was the ideal of good writing with the Associated Press and the Rudolf Flesch report—short sentences, simple language, avoidance of multisyllabic words, reliance upon the muscularity of Anglo-Saxon words, with their ability to convey action vividly, rather than the ponderousness and abstraction of Latinate diction—I remarked something to that effect to Elliott Coleman one day. For answer he picked up a copy of *Life* magazine, which at the time was serializing Winston Churchill's history of the Second World War, and read aloud a sentence from Churchill's account of the cornering of the German pocket-battleship *Graf Spee* off the coast of South America in December of 1939. Churchill was describing the moment when the captain of the *Graf Spee* realized that he would have to fight: "A few moments later, he recognized the quality of his opponents, and knew that a mortal action impended." So much for the superiority of words of Anglo-Saxon derivation.

I was also studying the principles of literary criticism. Why, the very idea! What was the point in reading what others thought about works of literature, or why they thought it? My own response was all that mattered. The notion that literature was something that one ought to have to *think* about, and that one's intellect was not necessarily divorced from one's feelings, was difficult to accept. As part of a course in twentieth-century literary criticism, I undertook to present a report on the critical views of a man named John Crowe

Ransom, about whom I knew only that he was the author of some poems I had read and rather enjoyed. He was discussing the nature of the poetic image. I found it hard going, but since my assignment was to figure it out and present it, I kept at the task until I had worked it out. Having done so, I then concluded my paper with a peroration in which I denounced the whole business, declaring that no matter what Ransom said about the deficiencies of Tennyson's image of the bat in "The Princess," the lines "Come into the garden, Maud, / For the black bat, night, has flown" were Great Poetry. So there!

What I was engaged in doing, of course, was being introduced to the best, and most influential, thinking about literature of my own time—and, as always, actively resisting the process every foot of the way, while at the same time, and without realizing it, learning from it. It would take a while longer before I was willing consciously to accept what I had learned—accept it because it was helping me to understand my own feelings about poems and stories, understand the complex response to human experience that works of literature can offer, instead of reacting to what I read automatically and without thinking about it. Schooled as I was in the Romantic aesthetic, I had been accustomed to place a premium on unmediated emotion, and to suspect the intellect—when if I had anything to offer, surely it lay in the *use* of the intellect rather than its dismissal!

At the same time, however, I did have some reservations about what I was engaged in at the Writing Seminars that were not merely the defensive postures of my own ignorance and inexperience. Much though I enjoyed learning about the writers and ideas that were most studied and discussed by my fellow apprentice writers and teachers, I missed a certain engagement in the hurly-burly, the give-and-take of everyday middle-class experience. I missed any genuine historical grounding, any sense of relationships with American history and society. There was no real consideration given to the literature of American authors *as* American. Yet my country, and the South in particular, was very much an aspect of my own identity.

It was not that I wished literature to be studied *as* literary history—that was what was done in the Johns Hopkins English Department, whose smugly pedantic and narrow approach to literature, and active hostility to contemporary writing and writers, was

255

not what I wanted. Rather, what I was in search of, without realizing it, was the study of works of literature as imaginative artifacts of American life, to be gotten at *through* the literary image, not as so much subject matter. Without that kind of imaginative anchoring in everyday historical and social experience, works of literature tended to seem rootless, thin, exotic.

In the same way, so much of what my fellow apprentice writers produced in the way of fiction and poetry seemed to me to lack body and identity, and to be precious and artificial. It was as if what they were trying to do was to purify their art through removing from it all trace of contamination by mere everyday experience—as if the object of writing was to transcend the details of the life that one lived outside of the classroom, and use language to escape from the demands and occasions of that experience. Yet like myself, my Writing Seminars colleagues were inhabitants of Baltimore, not of Parnassus or even of Canterbury. They might like to think of themselves as Artists, as Priests of the Eternal Imagination, but they were also and simulaneously middle-class American citizens, Democrats and Republicans, reared as Baptists, Methodists, Presbyterians, Episcopalians, Roman Catholics, Jews, and subject to the same regrettable requirements of earning a living in a capitalistic economy as I was. To attempt to isolate and protect what they did and thought about as writers from what they otherwise knew as their daily lives seemed to me to be rather unproductive.

I found myself missing newspaper work and newspapermen. I missed the company of people who were interested in politics, sports, and the like, and who wrote news stories about the doings of the compromised everyday world. Among my fellow apprentice writers there was a talented young man who was a reporter on the Baltimore *Sun,* and who was engaged in writing a novel. He did his newspaper work at night, and was stationed in the press room at the East Baltimore Police Precinct. Occasionally I would drive over there late at night and sit around with him, and afterwards go out for a beer or two. His favorite writer was Ernest Hemingway, and he emulated Hemingway in affecting a sarcastic contempt for the preciosity and aethereality that some of our fellow graduate students affected. "What are you doing for Art these days, Rubin?" he would always ask when he saw me.

In later life he became a distinguished newspaper columnist and memoirist. Yet it seemed to me, although I could share his distrust of the more rarefied and precious aspects of what was done at the writing seminars, that in affecting disdain for anything that smacked of self-preoccupation and the overtly artistic, he was attempting to deny an aspect of his own identity. For however ridiculous and contrived such efforts could be, at least they represented an effort to look beneath the surfaces of one's life and to confront, rather than to evade, the complexity and depth of one's emotions.

What I did not see, and none of us saw, was that the alternative to a too-stylized, too-mannered and affected approach to literature was not to commit the opposite error, either. For if the purpose of writing fiction and poetry was not to escape from everyday experience into a disembodied artistic realm free of the taint of middle-class life, neither was it a matter of adopting an uncritical acceptance of the average, a worship of the least common denominator, with any and all attempts at discrimination, at exercising distinctions, tastes, preferences, viewed automatically as being self-indulgent efforts to escape and avoid reality.

257

What we needed to do as writers, but did not yet know how to do (and few of us would ever learn), was to *use* the insights, techniques, subtleties and discriminations of the literary imagination in order to reveal, interpret and criticize our own experience as it presented itself to us. It was not in the subject matter that the artistry lay, but in its presentation. Good literature—poems, stories, novels—was neither an escape from life nor an uncritical mirroring of its surface aspects, but a way of giving form and meaning to our lives—a way of knowledge. The trouble with so-called photographic realism—"slice of life" writing—was that it was not realistic enough; it portrayed only surfaces. At the same time, the way to perceive and to reveal the universality of depths and undercurrents lay *in* and through those surfaces, not separate from and outside of them. That was the paradox of the literary image. If we wished to write, that was what we had to discover. But we were very young, with so much yet to learn.

At some point during that year I began writing a novel. It was highly, even literally, autobiographical, and drew upon my life as a child in Charleston. So long as I kept to childhood and to the evocation of the local scene, with its harbor and boats and marshland and other aspects of everyday life in an old seaport city, it seemed to be going well, and I soon became highly optimistic about my future as a writer of fiction. Meanwhile I was invited to become editor of the *Hopkins Review,* a literary magazine published by the Writing Seminars. I also found that I enjoyed teaching. And again I was falling in love.

Yet throughout this time, when everything seemed to be unfolding in the way that I had hoped, I felt a secret uneasiness, an apprehension that it could not last: that my novel was not fiction at all but only autobiographical celebration and self-justification, which now that I had moved past childhood was losing conviction and running out of steam; and that the love affair was not going to work out, that I was due for a tumble. Thus it came as no surprise, but a sinking confirmation of what I suspected, that one day the novel came back from the publishing-house editor who had agreed to read it with the statement that it was not a novel but only the raw material for fiction that still remained to be written. Nor was it a surprise when shortly afterward it became quite evident that my incipient love affair was based on equally shaky premises.

In place of my excessive elation and unwarranted optimism, therefore, there was now gloom, depression, and guilt—guilt for being, at the very late age of twenty-five, no more embarked upon a vocation, no further along on the road to being able to use my talents, no closer to emotional, social, financial, or sexual fulfillment than ever. If only I could be someone else other than myself, someone who was free of all the harassing and crippling limitations of personality that afflicted me and made my life so miserable!

One night, therefore, I made up my mind. I packed up my suitcases and my typewriter, taking only a bare minimum of possessions, got into my Plymouth coupe, and drove off into the night. I was going to leave, disappear without trace, go somewhere far away in the Midwest, assume a new identity, get a job on a newspaper, and commence a completely new life. I drove north to Harrisburg, Pennsylvania, checked into a hotel under a false name. In the morning I would resume my journey westward on the Pennsylvania Turnpike.

I lay in bed for two hours thinking about it, and then I checked out of the hotel, drove back to Baltimore, went to bed about 3 a.m., and arose in time to eat breakfast at the Hopkins cafeteria and then play golf with a friend as scheduled.

As the end of the school year neared, I decided that what I wanted to do was to find a position, preferably as a copy editor in order to save my energies for my own writing, on a newspaper near enough to Baltimore so that I could continue to teach a course one evening a week, take part in the Writing Seminars activity, edit the literary magazine, and work on my novel. I located a job on the morning newspaper in Wilmington, Delaware, only an hour away, working Tuesday through Saturday evenings, and leaving me free to be in Baltimore from Sunday through Tuesday afternoons. On the strength of what would be a salary considerably in excess of what I had been living on, I traded in my old coupe for a late-model car.

259

I had forgotten just how tediously dull work on a newspaper copy desk could be. Each night I edited telegraph stories from the Associated Press wire, marking capitalizations and paragraphs, changing abbreviations and references to conform to the newspaper's particular style, then wrote headlines in accordance with the word count assigned by the slot man. The copy editor to my left on the rim was a man whose consuming interest was in playing the horses at Delaware Park. The editor on my right, when not editing copy and writing headlines, would remove several envelopes from his desk drawer containing photographs of scantily clad females, and contemplate them as he shuffled through them, occasionally licking his lips. The sole person on the staff with whom I had anything in common was the city editor, who like myself was a Civil War buff and who painted in oils. At his urging I purchased a supply of tubes of paint, brushes, canvas boards, and an easel and tried my hand at it, with little success. But he was twenty years older than I and was married, with children. I knew no girls, and no one else in town. On weekends I drove to Baltimore, but most of my friends there, male and female, were gone for the summer. I tried to resume writing my novel during the afternoons, but could not; it was lifeless, unconvincing, seemingly a dead end. At night, after work, I would sometimes drive down to the Pennsylvania Railroad station, go out on the platform, find a seat on a baggage cart, and watch the trains arrive and depart until 2 or 3 a.m.

Shortly before the fall term began at Johns Hopkins, I realized I had had enough. Elliott Coleman was able to arrange an additional class of freshman English for me, and between that and what I could earn writing feature stories for the Richmond *Times-Dispatch,* and selling my car, I could get by, at least for a while. I quit my job on the newspaper copy desk and returned to Baltimore. For better or for worse, teaching and writing were what I was intended to do. And while I had no sense of where they might lead me, and was determined not to submit myself to the pedantry and sterility of historical literary study toward a Ph.D. in the Johns Hopkins English Department as then constituted, it was with literature and the literary imagination, not journalism, that I wanted to be engaged.

I found a place to stay, and the term began. I was no longer a graduate student, but a member of the faculty—a very lowly one, to be sure, but a faculty member nonetheless. I had written some poetry the previous year, and I began writing some more, and even had several poems accepted by magazines. I also wrote an essay comparing James Joyce with a writer whose works had long been among my favorites, Laurence Sterne. After it had been rejected by several literary quarterlies, I published it myself in the *Hopkins Review.* I met another girl whom I liked, while also renewing ties with the previous one. This time, however, I was not going to allow myself to be burnt. And this time, too, I was going to stay with my writing and teaching all the way, for however long it might take. There were to be no more evasions and escapes, no more efforts to change myself by changing locales and jobs. Instead I would do my best to look *at* myself in language, both for what I was and was not, as honestly and clearly as possible. That it would not be easy to do, that I was in for a long siege, I recognized now all too clearly. Yet I had no choice.

Sometime during that winter I was sent several novels to review by the Richmond *Times-Dispatch.* At about the same time the *Hopkins Review,* of which I remained editor, received review copies of two more novels, including one by an author named William Faulkner.

I had been hearing about Faulkner from a colleague on the Writing Seminars faculty who was from Mississippi, and who was then engaged in writing a dissertation in the English Department—not on Faulkner, of course, since as a contemporary author Faulkner was not considered a worthy subject of doctoral study, but on Poe. We had occasionally talked about certain writers, including my own favorite author, Thomas Wolfe, *as* Southern authors, but I had never read anything by this William Faulkner.

As I looked at the works of fiction for review, it occurred to me that they were all by Southern writers. What did this mean? Were there any elements in the four books, beyond the authors' geographical identity, that might characterize them as Southern? Did they share anything in the way they were written beyond the fact of that geographical-similar authorship? What might they have in common with works by Southern authors that I had previously read—with Wolfe, with Eudora Welty's *The Golden Apples,* which had enthralled me when I read it the previous summer? And was there any way that the manner in which these novels were told was related to the literary criticism I had read by John Crowe Ransom and Allen Tate, who were also Southern-born?

261

The more I thought about it, the more interesting it seemed. And the more, too, it seemed to have to do with *me*—with my interest in the Civil War and in history; with my feelings for Charleston, and the South, and for *places* in general; with my sense, still largely unarticulated, that the way to approach works of literature was not through isolating the *ideas* implicit in them, but *in* their complexity, as images, artifacts, self-contained entities.

I thought about it a great deal. I went into the Johns Hopkins Library in search of some books that might shed some light on the matter, but except for a couple of essays by Allen Tate I could find nothing to help me. I thought of discussing the matter with the American literature specialist in the English Department, who had edited the complete works of a nineteenth-century Southern poet; but since he had once informed me that Thomas Wolfe's literary imagination and sensibility were essentially Midwestern rather than Southern, I decided there was no point in that.

So if there *were* anything to the matter, I would have to try to figure it out on my own. Therefore, at one point during that winter of 1949–1950, I sat down at my typewriter to write a review essay. I began writing as follows: "The Fall of 1949 saw publication of a number of works of fiction about the South. I wish to discuss five of them both as fiction and as regional literature, with particular emphasis upon the regional approach."

I did not realize it at the time, but at the age of twenty-six I was off and running at last.

INDEX

263

267

271